AN ACCOUNT OF THE KINGDOM OF NEPAUL

BEING THE SUBSTANCE OF OBSERVATIONS MADE DURING A MISSION TO THAT COUNTRY IN THE YEAR 1793

AN
ACCOUNT
OF THE
KINGDOM OF NEPAUL

BEING THE SUBSTANCE OF OBSERVATIONS MADE DURING
A MISSION TO THAT COUNTRY
IN THE YEAR 1793

COLONEL KIRKPATRICK

ILLUSTRATED WITH A MAP AND OTHER ENGRAVINGS

GYAN

Published by

Gyan Publishing House
5, Ansari Road
Daryaganj, New Delhi-110002
Phone: 011-47034999, 9811692060
E-mail: books@gyanbooks.com

Distribution Network
gyanbooks.com
India, USA, Canada, UK, Australia, France

ISBN : 9788121230179 (PB)
First Published, London, 1904

2nd Impression 2020

Printed at: Gyan Press, Delhi.

An Account of the Kingdom of Nepaul
Author: Colonel Krkpatrick

AN

ACCOUNT

OF THE

KINGDOM OF NEPAUL,

BEING THE SUBSTANCE OF OBSERVATIONS MADE DURING

A MISSION TO THAT COUNTRY,

IN THE YEAR 1793.

BY COLONEL KIRKPATRICK.

ILLUSTRATED WITH A MAP, AND OTHER ENGRAVINGS.

LONDON:

PRINTED FOR WILLIAM MILLER, ALBEMARLE-STREET;

BY W. BULMER AND CO. CLEVELAND-ROW, ST. JAMES'S.

1811.

TO

THE HONOURABLE THE

CHAIRMAN, DEPUTY CHAIRMAN,

AND

COURT OF DIRECTORS,

OF

THE EAST INDIA COMPANY,

THIS VOLUME,

DERIVED FROM THEIR RECORDS,

PUBLISHED UNDER THEIR SANCTION,

AND FAVOURED BY

THEIR LIBERAL PATRONAGE,

IS

MOST RESPECTFULLY INSCRIBED.

PREFACE.

No Englishman had hitherto passed beyond the range of lofty mountains which separates the secluded valley of Nepaul from the north-eastern parts of Bengal: and the public curiosity respecting that Terra Incognita* (as it might then be justly called), was still ungratified, except by the vague and unsatisfactory reports of a few missionaries and itinerant traders,† when, towards the close of the year 1792, an opportunity was unexpectedly presented to the British Government in India, of removing the veil which had so long interposed between

* The time will probably be recollected by many persons still living, both in England and in India, when Nepaul was spoken of as another El Dorado.

† Principally Hindoo mendicants of the well known classes called Gusains and Sunafies, who are at once devotees and pilgrims, beggars, soldiers, and merchants.

the two countries, and of establishing a more intimate and beneficial connection with the Hindoo state of Khâtmândû, than had yet been found practicable. Of this opportunity the late Marquis Cornwallis, who then presided over the British Possessions in India, did not neglect to avail himself.

That venerated nobleman had, some time before, formed certain arrangements* with the existing authorities of Nepaul, which, it is to be regretted, were not followed up, as they would have left nothing more to be wished for by the British Government: since, besides being well calculated to promote and protect the commercial intercourse of the two nations, they had a necessary tendency to extend and improve, by degrees, all the other social relations, to which proximity of situation naturally invites.

Such, however, was not yet the case. The habitual jealousy of the Goorkhas,+ fostered, at least, if it was not inflamed by the insidious representations of individuals desirous of preserving the exclusive influence, and profitable monopoly, which that jealousy had

* The arrangements here alluded to were negotiated by Jonathan Duncan, Esq. then Resident at Benares, and now Governor of Bombay.

+ This is the usual designation of the reigning dynasty of Nepaul.

enabled them to acquire, and which they saw endangered by the closer approach of the two governments, either wholly prevented the removal, or soon led to the revival, of many of those impediments to a secure and active trade, which it had been the express purpose of the recent treaty to obviate. Accordingly, little or no progress had been made in effectuating the enlightened views of the framers of that treaty, when the course of events seemed, on a sudden, as already intimated, to furnish a peculiarly favourable occasion for accomplishing their complete realization.

The Court of Pekin, resenting certain encroachments which had been made by the Government of Nepaul upon the rights of the Lama of Tibet, whom the Emperor of China had, for some time past, taken under his protection, or, in other words, had subjected to the Chinese yoke, came to the resolution of chastising the aggressor, or *the Robber*, as the Rajah of Nepaul was contemptuously styled in the Chinese dispatches to Lord Cornwallis on the occasion. For this purpose a considerable army was detached (under the command of a kinsman of the Emperor), which, after traversing the dreary and elevated regions of Tibet, had penetrated, with little other opposition besides what was presented by the nature of the intervening countries, within a short distance of the city of Khâtmândû. It was then that the ruling power of Nepaul, which, in consequence of the minority of the reigning Rajah, was at this period vested in a regency, alarmed at the danger with which it saw the kingdom menaced, earnestly implored the assistance of the Bengal Government.

This Government now beheld for the first time, the extraordinary spectacle of a numerous Chinese force, occupying a position, which probably afforded it a distant view of the valley of the Ganges,* and of the richest of the East India Company's Possessions. It is true, that the military character of that people was not of a stamp to excite, under any circumstances, much fear for the safety of those Possessions from their future enterprizes. Least of all had we any thing to apprehend from this quarter at the period in question, when we had just signally humbled our most formidable enemy, and were at complete peace throughout India. Still,

* The valley of the Ganges being clearly discernible from the summit of Bheem-phede (see p. 52), there is no difficulty in believing that it may also be visible (though not very distinctly) from the heights of Dhyboon. (See Map.)

however, if, subduing Nepaul, the Chinese were to establish themselves permanently in our neighbourhood, the border disputes always incident to such a situation, would be but too liable to disturb, more or less, the commercial relations subsisting between them, and the East India Company in another section of Asia. No event, therefore, was more to be deprecated than the conquest of Nepaul by the Chinese: and yet it would have been a question of considerable difficulty and delicacy how to have frustrated such a design, if it had been actually entertained by the invaders. Military aid, which was what the Regency of Nepaul had solicited of the British Government, could not be afforded without a direct departure from the system of policy laid down for its general guidance by the legislature; or without producing the immediate suspension, if not utter annihilation of our trade with Canton. Such aid was therefore explicitly and steadily refused, but the assistance which could be properly granted was readily offered. This consisted in a tender of the mediation of our Government for the purpose of effecting an amicable accommodation between the belligerents, and in a proposal to dispatch with all practicable expedition to the head quarters of the Chinese army, a British Envoy furnished with suitable powers and instructions for the occasion. This offer, though falling far short of what was desired, and, perhaps, expected by the Nepaul Regency, was, nevertheless, accepted; and Captain (now Colonel) William Kirkpatrick was, in consequence, appointed to conduct the proposed negociation in conjunction with the Court of Khâtmândû.

But although the Envoy lost no time in repairing to Patna, from whence he was to be conducted by a deputation* to be sent thither for the purpose, from Nepaul, he found at his arrival at the former place, that the Regency, either dubious of the efficacy of our interposition with the Chinese, or fearful of the influence which, if successful, it might give us in their future councils, or possibly really intimidated by the menacing attitude of the enemy, had suddenly, and without any reference to the British Government, concluded such a treaty

* This deputation consisted of Bem Sâh (a member of the government), his brother, Rodur Beer (commander of the Rajah's guards), and Deenanâth Opadiah, the Nepaul Vakeel, usually resident at Calcutta. It was joined on its return to Nepaul, by Bajoo Seer, half brother of the Rajah, and a very promising youth, together with one or two others, relations of the Rajah, who had been on a pilgrimage to Ghyah.

with the invaders, as entirely superseded the necessity of the proposed mediation. The treaty alluded to was never formally communicated to the British Government, but there is reason to believe that though it rescued the dominions of the Goorkhali from the more immediate danger with which they appeared to be threatened, it was, in other respects, by no means honourable to the rulers of that country; especially if it be true, as was affirmed at the time by some intelligent persons, that a little more firmness on the part of the Regency would speedily have compelled the Chinese (who had suffered greatly from sickness and scarcity, and were not less impatient to quit Nepaul, than the Nepaulians were to get rid of them), to solicit the accommodation, which they were permitted to make a merit of granting.

Notwithstanding, however, that the original ground of the proposed mission was, by this means, removed, there remained sufficient subject of discussion between the two Governments of Bengal and Nepaul, to make that measure still extremely desirable. Accordingly there was not much difficulty in leading the Nepaul ministers to this point. It would have been, at least, an ungracious return to the friendly disposition recently manifested towards them by the Company's Government, if they had rudely sent back the Envoy of the latter, after he had, as it were, advanced to their door with their own concurrence, and in the prosecution of their immediate interests. He therefore, some time after his arrival at Patna, received a sufficiently pressing invitation to proceed to Noakote, where the Rajah of Nepaul at that time held his court; and having obtained the necessary authority for the purpose, from his own Government, he proceeded thither accordingly.

The gentlemen who accompanied the Envoy on this occasion, were the late Lieutenant Samuel Scott, assistant to the deputation,* Lieutenant (now Major) W. D. Knox,† in command of the military escort; Lieutenant J. Gerard‡ (attached to the escort), and Mr. Adam Freer, as surgeon. The escort consisted of two compa-

* And afterwards Deputy Adjutant General of the Bengal army

† Appointed in 1801, during the government of Marquis Wellesley, resident at Khâtmândû. That part of the accompanying Map which contains the route of the Nepaul army, on its return from its incursion into Tibet, was constructed on the authority of information obtained by Major Knox, from persons holding principal commands in that army.

‡ Afterwards Lieutenant Colonel, and Adjutant General of the Bengal army.

nies of Sepoys, and Moulavee Abdûl Kâdir Khan, an intelligent and zealous native servant of the Company, who had been employed by Mr. Duncan in negociating the treaty of commerce already alluded to, and who had, on that occasion, resided some time at Khâtmândû, was likewise attached to the mission.

It is no more than a bare act of justice to the gentlemen who have been here named, to state, on the present occasion, that it was impossible for any persons to have been more studious than they were during their short stay in Nepaul, to conciliate, by all the means in their power, the good will, and favourable opinion of every class of the inhabitants of that interesting country, and it may be confidently added, that their endeavours for this purpose were as successful, as they were unremitted. It is equally due to the native part of the Deputation, to observe, that their conduct was, on all occasions, correspondent with that of their superiors.

The mission, of which the origin has here been explained, gave rise to the cursory observations composing the present volume. They were thrown together in greater haste than was perhaps entirely compatible either with much accuracy of style, or clearness of arrangement; and more in obedience to the orders of his Government, than from any hope entertained by the Writer of being able to do justice to the subject prescribed to him. They were written, in short, expressly, if not solely, for the information of that Government, and of the Court of Directors; and certainly with no view to future publication. It was not, indeed, till ten years after, on the Writer's return to England, that, after declining to undertake the task himself, he consented, at the instance of some private friends, that the manuscript should, with the permission of the Court of Directors, be put into the hands of a literary gentleman for the purpose of its being properly prepared to meet the public eye. The Court of Directors, always ready to encourage even the humblest attempts to contribute to the stock of useful knowledge on every subject connected with India, not only assented to the proposed publication, but agreed to patronize it with their accustomed liberality. From this time, the fate of the Work rested with the gentleman alluded to; and perhaps its appearance would not have been much longer delayed, if it had not been suggested that, as a second mission to Nepaul had taken place, since the former one in 1793, and under circumstances far more favourable to the prosecution of useful enquiry, it was probable that much new, as well as more correct information, relative to that country, would soon reach England, which, if it did not wholly supersede the necessity of the intended publication, might be advantageously engrafted upon the latter. But the expectation thus excited was not yet fulfilled, when the death of the proposed Editor once more arrested the progress of the Work, which, on that occasion, passed into the hands of the present Publisher, exactly in its original shape.

In the mean while, the latter having incurred considerable expense in preparing the Work for the press, he was naturally unwilling, either entirely to relinquish the publication, or to postpone it to an indefinite period; especially as the additional information, in the expectation of which so much delay had already occurred, did not any longer appear likely to be obtained. On this occasion it was his wish, and he, in consequence, endeavoured, to engage the original Writer of the observations to revise the manuscript, and to give it the form which it was to have received from the literary gentleman before alluded to. Being, however, unsuccessful in this attempt, he was reduced to the necessity of sending the work forth nearly in the same state in which it came to his hands; the only alteration made in it consisting of a few verbal corrections, and in the division of the contents into Chapters.*

The foregoing candid statement of the circumstances which have led to the present appearance of the following sheets, while it is designed, on the one hand, to exonerate the original Writer from any responsibility for the defects of a production, which it was at no time his wish or purpose to obtrude upon the public in its actual state, will, on the other, it is hoped, prove a sufficient apology for the part taken by the Publisher respecting it. Indeed the latter is even willing to flatter himself, that whatever the imperfections of the Work may be, or, however its value may hereafter be diminished by more copious and methodical relations, it will, in the interim, be received with indulgence, as the only attempt hitherto made (with the single excep-

* When the volume was nearly printed off the Publisher was favoured with a copy of Colonel Kirkpatrick's official correspondence with the Governor General of India during his mission to Nepaul, and other Papers relative thereto; these he has given in the Appendix, No. II.

tion, it is believed, noticed below*) to present the public with a general idea of a country and people, particularly interesting to an English reader, on account of their vicinity to the principal settlement of the British Nation in India.

To conclude—if it should have only the effect of stimulating those who are in possession of more just and extensive information on the subject, to communicate their knowledge to the world, the Publisher will think that he has not adventured entirely in vain.

* The publication here referred to is a short Account of Nepaul, which appeared some years ago in the Asiatic Researches, and of which an extract will be found in the Appendix, No. III.

March 1, 1811.

The following Errata, for which the Publisher has to apologize to the Reader, were unfortunately committed in transcribing the Manuscript; and it was not until the volume was nearly printed off that they were detected.

Page line

6 — ult. *for* 43° 8′ *read* 43.8.
20 — 9, *for* George, *read* Georgi.
33 — 4, (note) *for* Surren-dhool, *read* Surren-dhoob.
ib. — ib. — *for* Dhoob-kee *read* Dhoob tree.
41 — 6, *before* Goorkhalies *insert* possession of the
62 — 19, *for* Kurripoot, *read* Kânipoot.
66 — 17, *after* Mooruth *insert* (or idol)
67 — 17, *for* probable, *read* palpable.
70 — 4, *for* 231.75, *read* 23.75 inches.
79 — 21, 22, *for* or bicolor *read* orbicular.
81 — 11, *for* strong *read* deep.
ib. — 13, *for* Tilluh *read* Tilluk.
82 — 19, *for* Ekaro *read* Jhâro.
94 — 3, *after* Kodo *insert* a comma.
ib. — penult. *before* thirds *insert* two-
95 — 12, *for* Chaster *read* cluster.
97 — 6, *for* seven seers *read* eleven seers.
104 — 6, *for* Ghow-hut *read* Gow-bhut.
ib. — 7, *for* Stubhut *read* Stri-bhut.
ib. — 10, *after* Kool, *insert* (or Sorcery).
109 — 22, *for* Koushna, *read* Krishna.
110 — 14, *after* distance *omit* the comma, *and insert it after* side,

Page line

118 — 15, *for* halted *read* hutted.
123 — 2, *for* not so much on account of the rocky channel in which it runs, as owing to the rapidity of its stream; *read*, not so much on account of the rapidity of its stream, as owing to the rocky channel in which it runs.
131 — 14, *for* Arghees, *read* Argus.
138 — ult, *after* in which *insert* direction.
143 — 2, *for* green *read* gum.
148 — 10, *after* Manuscript *insert* (Vide Asiatic Researches, vol. iv. p. 172).
188 — 23, *for* any of her *read* any other.
197 — 8, *for* agreeable *read* equable.
200 — 17, *for* Cuchum *read* Kuchurry.
203 — 1, *for* Tharrehs *read* Thâuehs.
204 — 6, *for* Uluts *read* Uteets.
79 — 19, } 205 — 20, } *for* Teigh *read* Thuj.
207 — 2, *for* raw Sai *read* raw Lac.
208 — 9, *for* Mulmuts *read* Mulmuls.
211 — 19, *for* Mâh *read* Mâl.
217 — 15, } 219 — 6, } *for* Addheeda *read* Uddhaila.
218 penult. *for* Soka *read* Sâka.

CONTENTS.

APPENDIX.

No. I.

No. II.

OFFICIAL PAPERS AND LETTERS, RELATIVE TO COLONEL KIRKPATRICK'S MISSION TO NEPAUL.

No. III.

ACCOUNT OF NEPAUL.

B

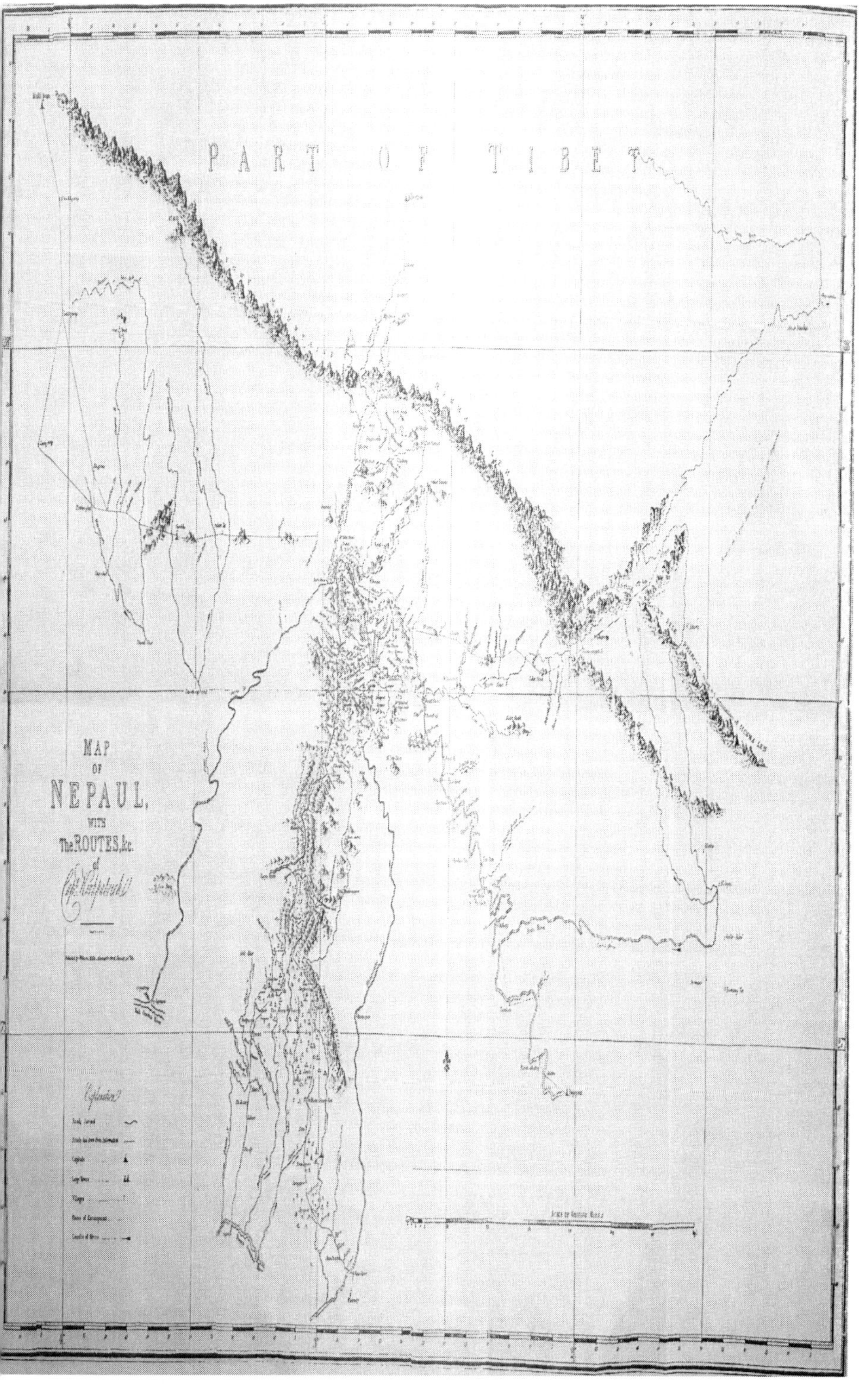
PART OF TIBET
MAP
OF
NEPAUL,
WITH
The ROUTES, &c.
of

ACCOUNT OF NEPAUL.

PRELIMINARY OBSERVATIONS.—CONSTRUCTION OF THE MAP.

When it is considered that my late visit to Nepaul commenced under circumstances peculiarly unfavourable to that free kind of research which alone can lead to accurate information, and that its duration did not, at most, exceed seven weeks, it will hardly be expected that I should be able to add greatly to our former knowledge of that country. It is, nevertheless, but fair to own, that although the extreme jealousy, by which I knew its Government to be actuated, suggested to me the propriety of conducting my enquiries, and of making my observations, with a certain degree of circumspection, yet it was not long before I discovered, in the open and communicative disposition of every description of the inhabitants, that I might safely throw off much of the restraint which I had at first imposed on myself in this respect. Still, however, (had I been even better qualified for the task than I was,) the period of my residence was too short, to allow of my collecting such materials as would be requisite to the furnishing a complete account of Nepaul. The form of the government; its revenue and military establishments; its civil and religious institutions; the customs and manners of the natives, their population, their arts and manufactures, their commerce, their learning and languages; and, finally, the political and natural history of the country, are objects of enquiry to which I certainly was not indifferent; yet it must be obvious, that on some of these points, my information could not but be extremely vague and defective, and that my opinions on others would necessarily be no less liable to error. And although it is true, that both our actual observations, and our researches concerning the Geography of Nepaul and of the adjacent countries, are open to the same objection; yet there is not equal reason for withholding the result of these last, since, with all their imperfections, they will serve to convey a general idea of some considerable tracts, hitherto scarcely heard of, and cannot, if received with no more confidence than what they will be delivered with, materially mislead, while they may possibly contribute, in no small degree, to the advancement of geographical knowledge, by suggesting and assisting future enquiries; an advantage which it is easy to conceive may sometimes be derived from very superficial and erroneous maps.

These considerations have made me determine to confine myself, in the following pages, almost entirely to the illustrating, as well as I may be able, the Geographical Sketch which accompanies them: I shall, accordingly, but rarely stray beyond these limits, and never in the formal manner suited only to a regular dissertation. Indeed, I shall not be studious of much method even in the arrangement of the remarks which constitute the immediate object of this Memoir; but content myself with dividing what I have to offer on the subject, into such notices as may serve, first, to throw light on the topography of our own actual track; and, secondly, to elucidate the geography of those parts which have been laid down altogether on oral authority.

The original of the accompanying Map is the performance of Lieutenant Gerard,* who has also the merit of having taken considerable pains, in the course of our journey, to ascertain with exactness the relative positions of places; a task which was rendered the more laborious, by the circumspection with which he was obliged to employ the compass.

As the use of a perambulator was entirely out of the question; and as, owing, perhaps, to the nature of the country, we did not find the pedometer answer, we had no other means of measuring the distances, but by the watch. No doubt this was a very inaccurate method, but we endeavoured to correct it, in some degree, by comparing notes after each day's journey; and by paying due regard, in our computations, to the varieties of the road with respect to ruggedness or facility. Accordingly, we have allowed, in different situations, from two to four miles per hour, though it was very rarely

* Now Lieutenant-Colonel Gerard, and lately Adjutant-General to the army on the Bengal Establishment.

indeed, after entering the Nepaul territories, that we proceeded at the latter rate, even for ten minutes together.

As I shall occasionally set down the computed road distances, and shall give a table of the whole at the end, it will be seen on a comparison of these with the horizontal distances in the Map, that we have determined the latter by no fixed rule of reduction; we were guided in this particular, as in estimating the road distances, by the nature of the country. Thus it will be found, that in certain situations, we have admitted a reduction of one in three miles: nor, when the great elevation and steepness of some of the mountains which we crossed are considered, will this be deemed, perhaps, too large an allowance.

The points of departure from the Company's Possessions adopted in the Map, are Munniary and Segouly, the former of which is laid down according to Major Rennell; Segouly, the other extremity of our route, is placed agreeably to the result of the observations made on our return; and, although it was not to be expected that the relative bearing and distance of these two primary points should turn out the same in our projection as in the Atlas, yet it will be seen that they do not disagree very widely.

With regard to Hettowra (the Etouda of Rennell), it will be right to notice, that it is laid down in the annexed Map conformably to the observations from Munniary, uncorrected by subsequent results; since all of them being in their principles equally defective, we had no reason to prefer one to another. It stands therefore 43° 8 horizontal miles, N. 16° 40′ W. of Munniary, and thirty-nine miles N. 26° 20′ E. of the situation which we have assigned to Segouly. In the Atlas it is placed sixty-five miles N. 16° 0 W. of the former, and fifty-seven miles N. 18° 40′ E. of the latter.

It is certainly very much to be regretted that we were not able to fix the situation of a few points, at least, of our route by observations of the latitude and longitude; all other means of ascertaining the true positions and distances of places, in so mountainous a country as that of Nepaul, being manifestly very defective. I am obliged to acknowledge on this occasion, that we were not absolutely without the means of accomplishing the former of these interesting objects, but as we did not sufficiently understand the management of the astronomical quadrant, which we happened to have with us, we were too ill-satisfied ourselves with the results of our operations to think them entitled to any confidence.

Having premised thus much concerning the materials employed in the construction of the annexed Map, I shall now proceed to the illustration of its several divisions, beginning with the route from Munniary to Hettowra, after which I purpose passing to that from Segouly to the same place.

CHAPTER I.

THE Bhâgmutty river, which passes between Munniary and the Huttioul of our maps, divides in this place the Company's and the Nepaul territories, in a direction nearly SSW. We found this river, though tolerably wide, not above knee deep. The ford we crossed at led us to the village of Seriva, consisting of a few wretched huts. About one mile to the north-west of Seriva stands Kurrurbunna, a sort of frontier post, which has succeeded Huttioul, the encroachments of the Bhâgmutty having not long since swept away this last place, which was situated a little below Seriva. The fort of Kurrurbunna seems designed to serve no other purpose than that of an occasional retreat for the cattle of its neighbourhood; in a military view it is altogether contemptible. It stands, however, as well as the village adjoining to it, on a high, and, as the Commander of it (who was a native of South Behar) assured me, a very healthy spot. The Bhâgmutty is navigable with great facility, during the rainy season, by boats of all burthens, as high as Seriva, and, no doubt, is practicable also as far as the skirt of the adjacent forest, if not all the way to the foot of the Cheeriaghati ridge;

but the only materials of commerce in this quarter being timber, which is floated, there appears to be no inducement for pushing the regular navigation of this stream beyond Munniary.

For about four road miles beyond Kurrurbunna the country is pretty open, though by no means highly cultivated. Soon after passing Peepra Rajepore, however, a dha'k, or pullâs jungle commences, which continues, with very little interruption, all the way to Patra. This jungle is infested by bears, which, the people of the country pretend, are to be frightened, and prevented from disturbing travellers, by an imitation of the cry of a goat.

Bundâr-pokhrah, laid down in the Map, is a very considerable tank, which, though now useless and neglected on account of its wild situation (as is the case with many others equally large, which, I am assured, this forest contains), indicates that this part of the country was formerly in a more flourishing condition than at present. Indeed the ruins of an ancient and extensive city, called Semroun (and Ghurrsemroure) are still to be seen a few miles to the southward of Bhâreh; and as the Newar princes of the dynasty which was overthrown by the Goorkhalis derived their origin from this city, whence, their historians inform us, they emigrated about four centuries and a half ago, its antiquities are, perhaps, worth enquiring into. These ruins are situated between the Bukkia and Jumne rivers.

The Loll Bukkia, which occurs in this part of our route, is an inconsiderable stream, which has its rise to the southward of the adjacent hills (or Cheeriaghati range), and flows but a little way before it falls into the Bhâgmutty. The Bukkia, which runs under Cachouriva, is, on the other hand, a river of some note, its source being as remote as the Mahabahr mountains, by which name some of the loftiest peaks immediately to the southward and the south-west of Nepaul are distinguished. This last stream, in its progress, passes at no great distance from the fort of Muckwanpore, whence it proceeds across the valley that separates the Muckwany from the Cheerighati hills, and after forcing a passage through the latter, pursues a very serpentine course till it disembogues itself into the Boora-Gunduck, which it does near the village of Jingrye, in Sircar Chemparun. It winds so remarkably at Cachouriva, as to form almost a complete island of the spot on which we encamped at that place.

The Jumne, which is crossed about midway between Cachouriva and Bhârch, and again, very near the latter place, by which it passes, is a dull and turbid rivulet, the springs of which are not far off. Narrow as it is, however, we found it so deep as to be scarcely fordable in palankeens. The cultivation between Cachouriva and Patra is very inconsiderable, being confined to a few specks, at either end of the two or three wretched hamlets which occur on the road.

Bâreh, or Bharra-gharry, although the ordinary residence of the Subah of the Western Turrye, is a mean place, containing from thirty to forty huts: its fort is not more respectable; nor would the

Governor's habitation attract notice any where else; it is built, however, of well-burnt bricks and tiles.

The commerce between Nepaul and Patna passes through Goolpussra, though a much more circuitous route than that of Bhâreh, which is as little frequented by travellers as by merchants. Indeed the former possesses decided advantages over the latter, both with regard to the facility of the roads and the face of the country; as will be further noticed in the proper place. It will be sufficient to mention here, that the company of Nepaul guards, which met me at Bhâreh, came thither from Hettowra by the Goolpussra road, though so much out of their direct way, instead of taking the shorter route, by which we proceeded. The situation of Bhâreh, too, must be unhealthy, surrounded as it is on all sides by a thick wood, and standing so near the foot of the Cheeriaghati ridge, which here rises higher above the level of the Turrye than it does in the Goolpussra quarter. It is not, therefore, to be wondered at, that Captain Kinloch's detachment, which remained here for some time, after the unfortunate attempt, in 1769, to penetrate into Nepaul, should have suffered so much as it did from sickness. The water of the Jumne is, in particular, esteemed very unwholesome.

At Bhâreh it was judged necessary that we should leave our hackeries behind; and although we might certainly have carried them on to the entrance of the Sukti, yet we could not have done so without considerable difficulty. To have transported them up the course of that river would have been utterly impracticable.

Soophye, which is but a mean village, stands very near the skirt of the great forest: we crossed the Jumne twice in our way to it. The only marks of cultivation we met with were limited to a few narrow patches on each side of the road; yet, from the appearance of the corn both here and to the southward of Bhâreh, the soil would seem to be tolerably fertile; and, indeed, I have been frequently assured by intelligent persons, that no land can be better adapted to the culture of rice than that of the Turrye in general. The waste state of the country, therefore, is to be referred to the want of population, and to the defects of the government, which but ill understands the means of promoting it. It is rather extraordinary, perhaps, considering the temptations held out by the vicinity of the Company's dominions, that this dreary tract should have any inhabitants at all; but it will be still more singular, if our late permanent settlement of the revenue, and recognition of proprietory right in the landholder, should not soon have the effect of entirely depopulâting it.

There is a shorter road from Cachouriva to Soophye than that by Bhâreh; it passes to the southward of the latter place; but was described to me as being impracticable except in hammocks.

The Billye or Billarie nullah, a dull stream, which is crossed a few minutes before you enter the great forest, would appear to be a branch of the Bukkia, because its source cannot be traced to the

Cheeriaghati hills, on account of the interposition of the Bukkia; and, on the other hand, cannot be attributed to any springs situated to the southward of the Bukkia's course, on account of the nature of its bottom, which is stony. It probably also reunites with the Bukkia at no great distance from the point where we passed it.

I was three hours in proceeding from what is considered as the proper entrance of the great forest, to the village of Jhurjhoory, which may be said to mark its nothern limit; I therefore judge its breadth by the road to be somewhat under ten miles; for though the ground throughout was very good, yet as we were occasionally not a little impeded by trees that lay felled across our path, and by others under which it was not easy to pass, I cannot allow more than three miles and a quarter per hour. The horizontal depth assigned to this forest in the Map, is eight miles and a half. Our course, for a short time after we entered it, was about north; it was next a good deal easterly; and during the last hour lay considerably to the westward.

This forest skirts the Nepaul territories throughout their whole extent from Serinugur to the Teesta, separating them every where, either from the Company's or the Vizier's possessions. It is not, of course, equally close or deep in every place; some parts having been more or less cleared away, especially those which are situated most favourably for the commerce of timber, or in the vicinity of flourishing towns. To the eastward some considerable tracts are reported to be quite clear. I cannot pretend to enumerate the great varieties of its trees; but the principal for size or utility are, the Saul, the Sissoo, the Setti-saul, the Phullamikhd (or iron-wood), the Kalikâht (a sort of black wood), the Sâjh, the Bhurra, the Summi, and the Mûlta. The ebony is also, I understand, found here. This forest is much over-run in the Jhurjhoory quarter with underwood and long grass. The part most resorted to by the wood-dealers appears to be that which borders on the Boggah district, timber being transported from thence even to the distance of Calcutta. I am inclined to think, however, that, notwithstanding the convenience afforded by the vicinity of the Gunduck, a more advantageous spot might be selected for the operations of the wood-merchants. The Nepaul government levy, I believe, very high, and consequently, in a commercial view at least, impolitic duties on this traffic: whether or not they are influenced, in this respect, by the idea that the vigorous prosecution of it would have the effect of diminishing the strength of the barrier which this forest no doubt constitutes, I had not an opportunity of ascertaining. Upon my remarking on the ill tendency of such restraints, it was thought a sufficient justification of them to declare, that they had not originated with the present government, which did no more than follow the ancient practice in this particular.

Besides valuable timber, this forest affords another source of profit to the Nepaul government in its numerous elephants; but this, like the timber, is not improved so much as it might be. The Governor of the Turrye told me, that in his district, which reaches from Somoisir to the Kousi, there were caught annually between two and three hundred elephants; much the greater part of these, however, are very young, being not above five hauts, or seven feet and a half high; nor can they well be supposed able to catch any of a superior size, as the animals are not driven into a keddah, or inclosure, but are caught by snares or nooses thrown over their necks by a mahoot seated on a decoy elephant. The rope being immediately drawn, the end of it is secured round a tree, from which it is easy to conceive that they often break loose, and are not unfrequently strangled in their struggles. There is, therefore, a double disadvantage attending this imperfect mode of catching these animals, for while it clearly tends to diminish the breed, it renders the elephants so prematurely caught of little value; there are, accordingly, very few of this great number sold for the benefit of the government, who claim an exclusive right to the whole, and dispose of them, for the most part, in presents, or in commutation of occasional services, and pecuniary demands.

A third branch of revenue arising from this forest consists in a duty levied upon the cattle of Chemparun and other districts, bordering on the Nepaul territories, which graze here annually about four months, the pasturage between October and January being deemed excellent; but as this duty is confined to buffaloes (cows being exempted under the present government), and never exceeds two annas per head for the season, its amount cannot be very considerable.

Besides elephants, this forest is said to be greatly infested by rhinoceroses and tigers. The latter appear almost invariably solitary, but two or three elephants, I have been told, will sometimes take possession of the road, and obstruct the progress of travellers a considerable time: a large herd of them assaulted the camp of the Nepaul deputies at Jhurjhoory, when they were on their way to Patna, and were got rid of with difficulty. They sometimes issue from the forest in droves, and over-run the cultivated country on its borders, penetrating even, now and then, a good way into the Company's districts. We did not, however, meet with a single wild beast of any kind in the whole course of our journey.

Travellers cannot make a resting-stage in this part of the forest, it being no where clear, or containing springs. This is not the case in the Goolpussra road.

I took notice occasionally of several trees in the forest, round which wisps of jungle-grass were bound; and in one particular spot they were observable for a hundred yards together. This circumstance was accounted for differently; one person telling me that these marks were designed to indicate the vicinity of wild beasts, and another, that they were propitiatory offerings by passengers to the deities of the forest; it is not probable, however, that any one part of the road leading through it is more dangerous than another, and I am therefore inclined to attribute this practice to a superstitious motive

It appeared to me that the level of the forest, for the last two or three miles, was lower than the preceding part: though, on the whole, Jhurjhoory stands higher, I believe, than Soophye.

Jhurjhoory is a wretched village, consisting of a few herdsmen's huts scattered on the south bank of the Bukkia, the bed of which is here of a considerable breadth, though we found its water confined within a narrow channel. The forest is cleared to the eastward of it to an extent barely sufficient to admit of a few tents.

Father George would appear to have proceeded straight across from this place to Muckwanpore, by which road he travelled to Nepaul; we took a more circuitous, yet certainly an easier route, if we may rely on the Missionary's description of that by Muckwanpore, which is confirmed, indeed, by various accounts I have received of it; by the circumstance of its being distinguished by the expressive name of Khâradahr, or the Sword-edge-road; and lastly, by its almost total disuse.

At Jhurjhoory we met with a tree called Dubdubea, the leaves of which abound in galls, containing from one to six winged insects; its wood was somewhat of the ash kind, and the gall powerfully astringent.

You cannot be said to have quitted the forest on reaching Jhurjhoory; though the continuation of it from thence to the Cheeriaghati hills differs considerably from the former part, the trees, in general, being neither so lofty, nor standing so close together as before.

From Jhurjhoory to the entrance of the Cheeriaghati pass, the road, for a short way, lies along the bank of the Bukkia. At the distance of about six road miles from Jhurjhoory we entered the bed of the Sukkattie or Sukti (called also Suktikhoar), and continued in it till we reached its sources, which are situated near the summit of Cheeriaghati. I was not able to ascertain the course or termination of this stream; I observed, however, that it took a south-east direction from the point at which we entered it; and as it does not occur in the Goolpussra road, I conclude it either empties itself into the Boora Gunduck somewhere below Segouly, or unites with, and yields its name to, one of the nullas of the Turrye which disembogue into that river. There can be no doubt of its passing through the great forest; but whether either its depth, or the nature of its bottom, fits it for the floating of timber, are questions which I had no opportunity of determining.

After ascending for a quarter of an hour the bed of the Sukti (in which there was but little water), we found ourselves enclosed on either side by the high ground of Cheeriaghati, covered thickly with tall trees, chiefly of the Saul and Sissoo kinds. The proper entrance of the pass, however, is a little higher up, where the Sukti runs rapidly between two perpendicular rocks not more than forty feet asunder, and apparently not less than two hundred feet high. At no great distance beyond this gloomy spot is a curious cascade, formed by an impending projection from one of the rocks, resembling the nave of a broad wheel. The water, which trickles, rather than rushes, from this overhanging conductor, is supplied from springs on the summit of the adjoining hill. I placed a thermometer under the falling water, which was so cold as to sink the mercury presently between six and seven degrees. Our progress in the Sukti was very slow, owing to the huge stones with which the bed of it was filled; in one place, in particular, the river was divided into two branches by an immense rock that had been recently detached from one of the enclosing hills, and now occupied the middle of the stream. This obstruction to the free passage of the waters had, I was told, considerably encreased the difficulties of the road.

Ambeah-gauteh is a station in the bed of the Sukti where passengers sometimes rest, and which is so named from two or three mangoe trees growing near it. We, however, did not stop here, but proceeded further up, pitching a few of our tents as well as we could on a small island formed by the river (which in this place passes in a W S W. direction), and near which they sometimes catch a few elephants that are driven from the forest below. The springs of the Sukti, which gush forth in innumerable little rills, that may be multiplied almost at pleasure by slightly pressing the ground, are about two miles and a half beyond this island, from whence the ascent is very perceptible. From the springs to the top of the Cheeriaghati ridge (which is perhaps a mile and a half), it is still more so, being, in fact, of no inconsiderable steepness.

The journey through the Sukti, though fatiguing, was rendered interesting by the wild and picturesque scenery around us. The hills enclosing it were every where well covered with several varieties of wood, among which, however, we saw but few firs. The strata of these hills appeared to be a mixture of sand, gravel, and light clay. We met with no fish of any kind in the river.

From the summit of the Cheeriaghati we had a noble view of the Muckwanpore hills, which rose before us to a considerable elevation. The Cheeriaghati range is no where very high, though I am inclined to think it rises somewhat as it stretches towards the Kousi, which marks its eastern limit, as the Gunduck does its western one. It does not, throughout this extent, every where bear the same name. Its elevation where we crossed it, and where it is properly called Cheeriaghati, would appear, according to the indications of the barometer, to be about 480 yards above the level of Hazipoor.

Descending Cheeriaghati in a direction nearly north-east, and by a very easy declivity, we reached Muckwanpore-mari, or the valley of Muckwanpore, which is formed by the Cheeriaghati and Muckwanpore hills. This valley is of no great extent, not stretching farther eastward than six or seven miles, and terminating near Nagdeo, on the Hettowra side. It is very fertile, yielding abundance and great variety of rice, which is not owing, perhaps, more to its natural situation (though no soil can be finer), than to the peculiar immunities enjoyed by the cultivators of it, who, I was assured, pay no taxes to the government. The reason of this extraordinary exemption may possibly be discovered in the political revolutions of the district. The ancient Rajah of Muckwanpore, who was dispossessed by the

Goorkhalis, and who still resides on the borders of his former territory, under the protection of the Company, has not yet relinquished all hopes of establishing himself in his rights, having recently made a feeble attempt for this purpose; it may therefore be thought necessary, or at least advisable, by the Nepaul government, to give the inhabitants of this district such an interest in the permanence of its own authority, as shall leave them nothing to hope, but much to fear, from the success of an invader, whether it be their former master, or any other power.

During the late war with the Tibetians and Chinese, the peasantry being generally obliged to repair to the army, agriculture suffered a temporary interruption; and when, in addition to this mischief, the scanty crops of Nepaul were destroyed by a hail-storm, very considerable relief was derived from the luxuriant produce of this valley.

The hill fort of Muckwanpore is distinguishable by the naked eye from the banks of the Kurra, on which stands the village of Muckwanpore of the valley, whence the fort bears about E. by N. The ascent to it from the valley is not represented to be difficult, and though we could not well judge of its strength at the distance from which we viewed it, yet it certainly had nothing formidable in its appearance. However, when the Nepaulians were hard pressed by the Chinese, the Regent and some of the principal chiefs dispatched a great part of their most valuable property to this fort.

The Kurra has its rise in one of the hills of the Muckwanpore ridge, whence it descends into the valley, through which it pursues a winding though but short course to the Rapti, falling into that river about two miles below Hettowra.*

In proceeding from Muckwanpore of the valley to Hettowra, you pass through a sort of strait formed by a low ridge or spur of the Muckwany hills that projects into the valley, and the Kurra, which in this particular spot abounds astonishingly with fish. This place is held in great sanctity by the more pious classes of Hindoos, who have dignified it with the name of Nagdeo (or the Divine Serpent), and who, so far from disturbing the fish which swarm here, rarely pass without feeding them.

Hettowra, though a place of much occasional resort on account of its being the centre of all the commerce carried on between Nepaul and the Vizier's as well as the Company's western possessions, is but a miserable village, containing from fifty to sixty houses, the only decent one among which has been lately erected by Zorawar (the Governor of the Western Turrye). It is considered very unhealthy; and indeed, although it stands near four hundred yards above the level of Bauk, and is watered by a pleasant lively stream, yet it is so closely surrounded by high hills covered with

* In an ill-concerted enterprize against Nepaul, which Cossim Ally Khan was encouraged to undertake (on nearly the same grounds which soon after gave birth to Captain Kinloch's expedition), an attempt was made on the fort of Muckwanpore by Goorgun Khan; the issue of which was so disgraceful, that Purthi Nerain had no difficulty in prevailing with the Nabob to abandon the cause of his adversary.

thick forests, that the air cannot fail, during the hot and wet months, of being impregnated with unwholesome vapours.

The Râpute or Rapti (on the bank of which Hettowra stands), issues from a mountain to the eastward of Chusapany, and separated from it only by a narrow bottom or glen. After passing Hettowra, where its bed is of a considerable breadth, it pursues a westerly course till it reaches the Gunduck, into which it discharges itself near Koombia Ghurry, or about fifteen miles to the north of Somaisir. There is another river of the same name, which passes under Goruckpore, and disembogues into the Dewah. The Rapti of Hettowra, though laid down in the map of Hindostan, is not named, and might there be mistaken for the principal branch of the Gunduck.

I will now endeavour to throw some light on that part of the Map which concerns the route from Segouly to Hettowra, by which road I returned from Nepaul.

CHAPTER II.

ROUTE FROM SEGOULY TO HETTOWRA.

Segouly—Boora-Gunduck River—Tellâwa River—Fort of Aloun—Bherra Nulla—Goolpussra—Forest—Nagsote and Bechiacori Rivers—Bechiacori Hills—Purrewa-bheer—Ioona River—Forest of Dumwa—Kurra River—Hettowra—Rapti River—Mode of Fishing—Trade at Hettowra—Hill-porters—Modes of Travelling—Description of the Turryani of Nepaul—its mineral and vegetable Productions—Remarks on Sir Robert Barker's Account of it.

CHAPTER II.

Segouly stands near the south bank of the Boori-Gunduck, which takes its rise in the vicinity of Somaiser. This river is navigable during the greater part of the year, as high as Segouly, by boats of considerable burthen. Its course, which is a very winding one, lies through the districts of Bettia, Chemparun, and Hâjypore. At Segouly and upwards, it is known best by the names of Sekrownah and Kurrah, the appellation of Boori-Gunduck, and Little Gunduck, being chiefly applied to it in the lower part of its course. It passes under both Maisi and Mûzufurpoor, discharging itself into the Bhâgmutty at Roussarah. In the Atlas the Sekrownah and Little Gunduck appear to be laid down as distinct rivers; yet it is nevertheless certain, that they are one and the same. In a commercial view, the Boori-Gunduck is entitled to particular notice; the great extent of its course, its depth, and its communication with various other streams that issue from the adjacent hills or forests, fitting it admirably for the purposes of internal navigation.

North of the Boori-Gunduck, at the distance of about six miles, passes the Tillâwé, a small stream that springs from the foot of the neighbouring hills, and falls into the Boori-Gunduck at Singrowli, a village situated a little to the eastward of Segouly. The common boundary of the Company's and the Nepaul territories, on this side, may be described by a line drawn about midway between Ekdurra and Ullown. The Gurry, or little mud fort of Ullown, which has succeeded the fort of Persa, now in ruins, consists of six round bastions united by a slight wall, and surrounded by a tolerable ditch; it stands close to the Beheera nulla, which we found middle-deep. This stream, which rises at no great distance from Ullown, after receiving the united waters of the Dehar and Gâhd, or Ghadi, empties itself into the Boori-Gunduck near Seemra-butna, about four miles west of Segouly. The springs of the Dehar are situated in a part of the Bechiacori forest, called Koila-bahr, which lies to the westward of Addha-bhâr. You leave this river close on your left in proceeding from Persa to Ullown, and at a point whence it turns short to the westward, emptying itself soon after into the Gâhd near the village of Phoolkoal.

Goorpussra stands very near the skirt of the great forest, which is, however, far from being thick in this quarter. The country all round the village is pretty open, and by no means bare of cultivation; on the west side of it passes a small sluggish stream called the Sunghya, which rises below Cheeriaghati and falls into the Beheera about seven miles to the east of Goorpussra. The Soubah of Turrye has a house here, in which he occasionally dwells; but his most usual residence is at Bâreh, which is, nevertheless, neither so neat nor so large a place as Goolpussra; this last, however, is, after all, but a mean village, though the thoroughfare for most of the merchandize that passes between Nepaul, Benares, Oude, and Patna, over the Chusapany mountains. Besides being watered by the Sunghirja, it has a large square tank on the east side of it, but this is of little advantage to travellers, owing to the shameful manner in which it is neglected.

The road from hence to Bechiacori, through the great forest, is very practicable for wheel-carriages; there are also two or three stations (though no villages) in the way, sufficiently open for the temporary accommodation of passengers. The middle of the forest, which has a clear space of some extent, is usually called Addha-bhâr, which implies its being half way between Goolpussra and Bechiacori. This part of the forest contains the same variety of trees as the Jhurjhoory quarter. We met here with a felled Saul-tree, that measured better than a hundred feet below the branches, and from eight to nine feet in the girth. About three miles to the south of Bechiacori we crossed the Nagsote, a pretty broad stream when at its height; it comes from the north-west, and falls into the Bechiacori nulla, at no great distance from the point at which we passed it.

Two miles and a half beyond the Nagsote you quit the forest, and enter the Bechiacori river, in which you continue up to its source. This stream, which is never considerable except during occasional torrents in the rainy season, takes an easterly direction where we came to it, holding the same course till it falls into the Boora-Gunduck, somewhere below Segouly. Bechiacori is the name by which the Cheeriaghati hills are distinguished in this part of their range. There are a few miserable huts situated on the east bank of the nulla, at no great distance from the entrance of it, which also bear the name of Bechiacori, but which we found abandoned. The bed of this river, through which the road runs, though not obstructed by such huge rocks, or of so perceptible an ascent, as the Sukti, is nevertheless difficult; and must, I think, be impassible for wheel-carriages. From the head of it to the entrance of the great forest is scarcely less than six miles; hence, as well as in allusion to the nature of the bottom, this part of the road is called Lumbabegger, or long stony way. It is enclosed on either side by banks, rising gradually in height till they terminate at the summit of the ridge, which, though probably equally elevated here as at the head of the Sukti, does not appear to be so, on account of the superior level of the forest immediately under it, compared with that of Jhurjhoory; indeed, I am inclined to think that the Cheeriaghati chain preserves nearly the same level throughout the remainder of its course to the Gunduck, though I understand it is there scarcely any longer perceptible, owing, probably, to the gradual ascent of the country which borders it towards the south, and which would at last appear to reach the general elevation of those hills themselves.

The Bechiacori hills seem composed chiefly of light sand and gravel, with scarcely any proportion of indurated or rocky strata; differing herein from Cheeriaghati proper. It is probably owing to this variation of soil, that, while the fir-tree is very scarce along the banks of the Sukti; those of the Bechiacori are thickly clothed with a very fine kind, one of which, that had been felled, and lay across our road, measuring about ninety feet clear of the branches, and not less than eight feet in the girth.*

Proceeding up the course of the river, you pass on the left, at the distance of about two miles from Bechiacori village, a steep lofty bank or hill, of a pyramidal figure, which seemed to be composed of materials so loose, as to be but ill calculated to resist the torrents which sometimes sweep its bottom. This curious peak is called Purrewa-bheer, on account of its swarming with pigeons. Almost opposite to it, the Ioona, a small stream which issues from springs situated in the neighbourhood of those which give rise to the Sukti, falls into the Bechiacori river.

This last stream gushes from two or three small circular fountains, communicating subterraneously, which are met with a few

* This tree is, more properly speaking, a species of pine, having three delicate and spike-shaped leaves issuing from the same foot-stalk, or sheath. I met with no more than a single kind, though I received accounts of others. It is called in Nepaul, Sulla, and Surren-dhool; and emphatically Dhoob-kee, on account of its resinous nature. Its branches are very commonly used as torches; the fragrant turpentine which it yields is employed in sacrifices and in medicated salves, and with its wood they make rafters for their houses.

minutes before you reach the top of the Bechiacori ridge, from the opposite (or Hettowra) side of which, and also near the summit, issues the Kichria; this rivulet we found quite dry, but in the rainy season (the only period it contains any water) it contributes to the encrease of the Kurra, into which its channel leads. The road, in descending the hill to the northward, lies chiefly through the bed of this dry nulla, upon quitting of which you enter a pleasant forest called Dum Dumwa, where you begin to ascend again, though very gently. About midway between this forest and Hettowra you cross the Kurra, the same river that is passed in proceeding from Mukwan-pore-mari. The bottom of the Kurra, though rugged and pebbly, does not oppose any material impediments to the traveller; the more especially as its declivity is scarcely sensible. The stones in it being remarkably white, its channel, I was told, is perfectly distinguishable in fair weather from Chusapany fort. Unfortunately, it was so hazy when we halted on the summit of this mountain, in our return from Nepaul, that though we stopped there expressly for the purpose of viewing, from so commanding a situation, the adjacent country, we were scarcely able to make a single observation of utility.

Hettowra stands at the foot of a hilly ridge, (which appears to be detached from the Muckwanpore mountain,) and just at the point where the Rapti enters the Muckwanpore valley. This ridge, which is by no means regular, extends itself in a direction somewhat to the northward of west, as far as the Gunduck, being the same that is met with immediately to the northward of Boggah. At Hettowra it is composed of a confused heap of hills separated in various directions by narrow bottoms or glens, which is also the appearance exhibited by the greatest part of the mountainous tract known under the general name of Nepaul, nothing corresponding with the idea of a single uninterrupted chain or range being to be met with after passing the Cheeriaghati ridge, if even this can be said to answer correctly to it. The sides of these hills are every where either well covered with tall forests (chiefly of Sissoo, or Saul,) or partially cultivated with grain of different sorts. Those, however, in the vicinity of Hettowra presented few or no marks of husbandry, of which, indeed, there were but scanty traces discernible even in the flats below them.

The Rapti abounds with fish at Hettowra. The upper part of its course is, generally speaking, both too rapid and too shallow to contain any, though there are some depths or pits in which great plenty are occasionally found: the principal kind is the seher, which resembles the roach, and is much esteemed. There are also a few gaoleer, or trout. The manner of fishing here is as follows.

The channel of the river is intersected by seven or eight casting nets, united together by being hooked at their extremities to poles or sticks erected in the water for the purpose. To each net thereis a man or boy, who has a second net fixed to his waist, and hanging behind him, in which he deposits the fish he catches; this he does by diving. They dive head foremost, though in water not deeper than the middle, throwing up their feet nearly quite erect, and seizing the fish sometimes between their teeth, but most commonly with their hands. After remaining as long as they think proper at a spot, all the nets are dragged together further down the stream, when they renew their operations: these being over, they draw casting nets separately, some of which, as well as those round their waists, are often quite full. Both Bem Shah and his brother Roodur Beer * appeared to enjoy this amusement exceedingly, plunging into the river, and going through every part of the process (except that of diving), with the greatest spirit. On this occasion, as well as many others, it was observable that the superior classes of these people admitted of considerable freedom in the carriage and conversation of the lower orders, whom they very rarely affected to keep at any distance. Nor was this sort of easy intercourse confined to particular descriptions of men; it existed equally among the military and the civil ranks; the private soldier being as unembarrassed and forward to deliver his sentiments in the presence of an officer of whatever degree, as the fisherman or porter before a minister of state, or governor. At the same time, this frankness of manner was never seen to degenerate into rudeness or disrespect.

There have been no duties collected on merchandise at Hettowra since the conclusion of the commercial treaty, by which it is fixed

* Bem Shah was a kinsman of the reigning Rajah of Nepaul, and was sent with other deputies to Patna, for the purpose of eventually conducting the British Mission to Nepaul. Roodur Beer was a younger brother of Bem Shah, and commanded a division of the Rajah's guards sent as an honorary escort to the British Envoy.

that they are to be levied by the Nepaul Government only at the stations of Chusapany and Sundooli (or Seedly); at the former on the western, and at the latter on the eastern trade. Previous to this convention, imports were very irregularly and arbitrarily levied.

But notwithstanding that the trade between the two countries has doubtless been freed from many of the restraints which formerly shackled it, yet it is certain that it still labours under difficulties of a very discouraging kind. It is not, perhaps, one of the least of these, that the merchants are liable to be delayed more or less in their journey by the want of porters; and I was sorry to observe, that they appeared but too much exposed to it from the loose or arbitrary form of the government; as no ceremony was used in depriving them, for our accommodation, both at Hettowra and Goolpussra, of the carriers with which they had provided themselves. The evil would have scarcely merited notice, had it been limited to the particular case in question; but I am afraid the instances of it occur too often, when any of the principal men of the country happen to travel (especially on public business) in the route of the merchants.

The general level of the country, in the route from Choprah to Hettowra is considerably higher than in the Bhâreh direction, though the distance between the two roads no where exceeds seventeen horizontal miles. Segouly is much more elevated than Bharragharry, which, indeed would seem to be even lower than Choprah itself. The level of Goolpussra differs little or nothing from that of Segouly; hence, on this side the ascent is so far easy, and in fact scarcely perceptible. One of the consequences of this superior elevation being, that the country is less liable to inundation, we find the roads better, an advantage which, when joined to the circumstance of the Bechiacori forest being so much clearer than the Jhurjhoory, gives a decided preference to the route by Goolpussra, notwithstanding its being more circuitous by a few miles than the other, if Choprah be taken in the way; while, if you proceed to Segouly by the direct road from Patna (which lies to the eastward of the Gunduck), the distance will rather be shortened.

No sort of baggage or merchandize being transportable beyond Hettowra, except on the shoulders of hill-porters, the price of their labour has been regulated by the government. From Goolpussra, the trip to Khatmanda is from $3\frac{1}{4}$ to $3\frac{1}{2}$; from Hettowra $1\frac{1}{4}$ to $1\frac{1}{2}$ Nepaul rupees, each man, who ordinarily carries, either in a Dhoka (or hamper), or otherwise in a bale, a weight equal to eighteen Dharnis, or about forty-five Seers, exclusive of his own provisions. The rates, however, are in some measure governed by the season of the year, being higher in the warm than in the cold weather.* These porters are, for the most part, of the Japoo and Douja tribes

* These rates are also partly regulated by the weight of the burthen agreed to be carried; some porters, especially those of Chitlong, very commonly transporting from 20 to 24 Dharnis.

The Dhoka

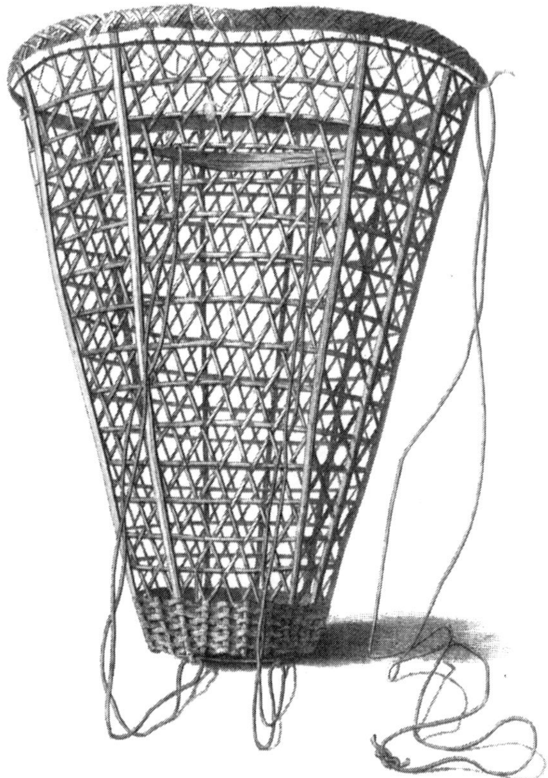

The Hammock

Published January 1810 by W. Miller Albemarle Street

of Newars, though there are not a few Bhautias, or Tibetians, among them; but these latter rarely descend into the Turryani, the climate of which they dread still more than the Newars, whom no offers, nevertheless, can tempt to pass beyond Hettowra after the middle of April. Travellers too, especially women, are very often conveyed over the mountains in Dhol is, which are usually made of bamboos, somewhat of the form of an inverted truncated cone. The carriages employed instead of palanquins are a sort of hammock, nearly resembling those used at Madeira. They consist of a Durwar, or cotton sack, slung upon a pole made for the most part of the juggur-wood, which is a species of palm differing little from the khujhoor of Bengal. From four to eight bearers are assigned to each, two or four (according to the weight of the person in it) being under the pole together. When four are necessary, they usually fix a stick horizontally across each extremity of the main pole, one man supporting each end of the two cross sticks. These bearers receive for the trip, whether from Goolpussra or Hettowra, to Khatmanda, at the same rate as the porters, and are for the most part of the same tribes. Persons of a certain rank have suitable establishments of Durwars, or hammocks, without, however, regularly maintaining bearers for the carriage of them, it being among the obligations of the tenants of jaghires and other landed estates, to perform this service occasionally for the proprietor.*

* The bearers are sometimes engaged by the day, when they receive two annas per man, besides their victuals, which are served out to them three times in the day.

This hammock might easily be rendered a much more commodious vehicle than we found it to be; the addition of a light wooden frame, for the purpose of spreading the sack, and keeping it a convenient breadth, would leave nothing more to be desired by the traveller, than some contrivance for defending him from the occasional inclemencies of the weather, at a less price than the deprivation of the delightful prospects constantly claiming his attention.

Hettowra, though standing very little below the level of Cheeriaghati top, is nevertheless comprehended in the Turry or Turryani of Nepaul, as indeed is the whole of the country situated to the southward of Chusapany, and of the irregular cluster of mountains stretching from thence to the east and west, in a nearly parallel elevation. Turryani properly signifies low or marshy lands, and is sometimes applied to the flats lying below the hills in the interior parts of Nepaul, as well as to the low tract bordering immediately on the Company's northern frontier. The Turryani of Nepaul, confined between the Gunduck and Teesta, is divided into soubahs or governments; that under Zorawar Sing, which stretches from the former of these rivers easterly to the Kousi, and which may be distinguished by the appellation of the Western Turrye or Turryani, consists of five zillahs, or districts, subdivided into twenty-seven pergunnahs. These zillahs are,

1. Subtuni, bounded to the eastward by the Kousi.
2. Mohtuni, west of Subtuni.

Drawn by A W Drew Esq.

Engraved by

Natives of Lahaul

3. Rhohututt, or Rohtut, in which Huttioul is included; it is situated to the westward of Muhtuni.

4. Bhâreh.

5. Persa, which extends to the westward as far as the Turryani of Tannohi. The higher part, as well as the fort of Tannohi, is in the Goorkhalis, but the Turrye still belongs to Hurry Kumar Seen, the ancient or former rightful Rajah of Tannohi.

Extensive as this government is, the Rajah of Nepaul does not draw any considerable revenue from it; this is partly owing to the numerous jaghire and brhemoter lands comprehended in it; but more particularly, perhaps, to the low state of its population, and to mismanagement. It is pretended that the Zemindars of Turrye hold their lands on very easy terms under the present government, which is content to divide the produce of the soil equally with them. It is acknowledged, however, at the same time, that the Buttye is, in most cases, no more than a nominal settlement, as, besides the formal or established cess, the Zemindar or cultivator is obliged to pay occasionally, other irregular and arbitrary taxes in the form of fines, douceurs, and the like.

For lands recently brought into cultivation, the cultivator pays to government eight annas per biggah, the first year, and subsequently, whatever kind of grain he raises in it, three rupees the biggah.

The most that Zorawar (the governor of West Turrye) remits to Khatmanda annually is two lacks of rupees; though his net receipts, after discharging all expenses of collection, are supposed by some intelligent persons, to amount to double this sum; but whatever the surplus may be, he does not enjoy it exclusively, being obliged to divide his profits with the official men at Khatmanda, who would not appear to be a whit less corrupt than their brethren of Hindostan. East Turrye, though it is on the whole a more fertile, or rather more populous, district, does not yield a net revenue of more than from one lack and a quarter to one lack and a half of rupees. It contains, however, more jaghire and brhemoter lands than the other. The Moruny, which is comprehended in the East Turrye (and of which it is indeed the most valuable part) is divided into two soubahs or governments by the Arun, which runs through the middle of it; this river, though it yields its name to the Kousi at Bundharia Ghaut, is, nevertheless, a much more considerable stream than the latter, rising beyond Himma-leh, and winding in a singular manner through a great portion of Tibet, before it descends into the Turryani.

If I might venture to form a judgment from the superficial view I had of West Turrye, I should be inclined to pronounce that it is capable of being rendered highly productive to the Nepaul government; its extensive forests alone contain an almost inexhaustible source of riches, since they might be made to supply with valuable timber, not only the countries washed by the Ganges, but even our other settlements in India. The pines of the Bechiacori, and the Saul-trees, both of that and the Jhurjoory forest, are not perhaps surpassed in any other part of the world, either for straightness or dimensions, or probably for strength or durability.* The Bechiacori pines, nevertheless, seem to have never had an axe applied to them, though they grow in prodigious numbers, are very superior to what we generally met with in Nepaul proper, and, considering the vicinity of the Boora-Gunduck, might be conveyed to us both with little trouble, and at little expense, compared to the channel by which we are at present supplied with this useful article, and the cost at which it is procured. Besides timber for masts and yards, we could draw from hence whatever supplies of pitch, tar, and turpentine we required. Kota, or pure turpentine of the Sulla pine, may be procured, I believe, even in Nepaul, at the rate of ten seers per rupee, and a tree will yield, I have been told, for eight or ten years together, about three maunds annually. Neither the tar of America, nor the pine spars from thence, would appear to be in much estimation in India, though, for want of better, I suppose, we take off, it is said, from the American traders considerable quantities of both at high prices.

It is true that the nearest part of the Boora-Gunduck is not less than thirty miles from the course of the Bechiacori nulla; but

* I had two cut down and floated from Segouly to Calcutta, by way of sample; one of these spars measured 76, the other 73 feet. Mr. Gillet the shipwright has pronounced of them that they promise to prove both strong and lasting, and means to give them a trial in a ship which he is about to launch. They had felled a couple of immense dimensions in girth as well as length, but were afterwards unable to move them. Those examined by Mr. Gillet will work about a foot in diameter.

when we advert to the great number of streams which intersect the intermediate country, some of them springing even from the forest itself, the level of the country from Cheeriaghati southerly, so favourable (on account of its gentle declivity) to the opening of a communication between these several streams and the Boora-Gunduck, by means of canals, and the nature of the soil, so well adapted to the easy execution of such a work, it will be evident that there are no difficulties opposed by nature to the accomplishment of so useful an object, which an active and intelligent government might not speedily remove. Attempts have heretofore been made to transport fir or pine-trees from different parts of the Nepaul, and even of the Rohilcund Turrye, but they have always failed, because a mountainous country, as well as rapid and rocky rivers, opposed their success. In the quarter here pointed out, we meet with every thing calculated to encourage the undertaking, viz. vicinity to a navigable river passing over the borders of Chemparun, a forest by no means much elevated above the subjacent country, and the declivity, such as it is, being gentle; communicating streams, neither rocky nor rapid, and the means of reducing the land-carriage considerably, if not of precluding the necessity of it altogether.

Sir Robert Barker wrote to Lord Clive in 1766, concerning the productions of the tract in question, as follows:

" Bettyah (he meant the northern parts, or Nepaul borders) will, " I think, be of considerable consequence to the Company; its firs " will afford masts for all the ships in India, which must produce

" a new and considerable trade with the other nations in India, as " well as advantage to our own shipping. Gold and cinnamon are " also here (the latter we gather in the jungles); timbers as large " as any I have seen, musk, and elephants' teeth, besides many " other commodities I have not yet got the knowledge of." It must be owned, however, that this is an exaggerated account of the natural riches of the Turrye districts. The quantity of gold dust found in the Gunduck, and other rivers in this quarter (for mines are totally out of the question), is very inconsiderable, though it is pretended that the sanctified stones called Salligrams contain that precious metal. The cinnamon is no other than the Sing Rowla, or Lignea Cassia; and with regard to the musk talked of, it is certain that, if of the true kind, or *Kustoora*, it could not have been the produce of the spot, this animal not being met with to the southward of the Kuchâr, or Lower Tibet.

At Hettowra there is a grove of very fine Saul-trees, in which we pitched our tents: there are but few pines in the environs of this town; nor do they abound greatly on the banks of the Rapti, as you proceed up its course. The mineral contents of the hills through which this river descends appear to be various. We collected many stones, and some ores in the bed of it indicated the presence of iron, copper, and other metals. Among others was a stone which appeared to be an ordinary iron ore, but of which I was told they made a magnet by wrapping it up in a fresh buffaloe hide, and depositing it in this state, for a certain time, in the earth. I transmitted to Mr. Blake specimens of all the metallic ores and fossils we met with, both in this and other situations, but he has not yet had leisure to examine them with attention. The natural productions of the vegetable kingdom most common between Hettowra and Bhimpore, are the Saul, Sissoo, and Simul trees; the nettle, wild worm-wood, raspberries, and mulberries; we also found here a curious shrub called Khaksi, the leaf of which answers the purpose of emery, or sand-paper, giving a fine polish to the harder woods.

CHAPTER III.

ROUTES FROM HETTOWRA TO KHATMANDA.

Rapti River—Dhokha-phede—Bheem-phede—Cheesapany Mountain and Fort—Description of the Military—View of the Mountains of Himma-leh—Tambeh-kan River and Village—Copper-Mines—Markhoo—Ekdunta Hill—Chitlong—Chandraghiri Mountains—Thankote—View of the Valley of Nepaul from the Summit of Chandraghiri—Markhoo River—Khargoo—Seeboodoul River—Pheerphing—Sulti-khul—Bhâgmutty River—Patn—Doona-baisi Mountain—Trees and Shrubs—Pisankeel—Owl, or Plague—Doona Valley—Division of Landed Property.

CHAPTER III.

SOON after our leaving Hettowra, we entered the bed of the Rapti, which we continued to ascend till we reached Dhoka-phede, the road traversing, for the most part, one or other of the irregular and rugged banks that enclose it, but occasionally lying through the midst of its channel, which is uninterruptedly strewed with huge fragments of rocks, rent from the craggy precipices, between which this river must rush with astonishing impetuosity during the autumnal rains. The ascent from Hettowra to Dhoka-phede, though on the whole by no means inconsiderable, is too gradual, except in one or two places, to be much felt; nor are the waters any where deep enough (running off too fast to rise to any great height) to make the passage of them in the least dangerous: the few Ruhas, or pits, which they contain, not occurring in the traveller's route. The chief inconvenience experienced in crossing, or proceeding in the bed of the stream, arises from the slipperiness of the bottom, which is so great as to render it very difficult for the porters or bearers to keep upon their legs. Independent of the danger which would arise from the numerous rocks choaking, as it were, the channel of the river, its navigation in boats would scarcely be practicable, even when its waters were at the highest; for, as Dhoka-phede rises at the least five hundred yards above the level of Hettowra in a distance not exceeding fourteen road miles, it is easy to conceive, what was indeed sufficiently perceptible, that in this space there are several rapids and falls (called by the Nepaulians Chekeera and Chângo) which no loaded boat could pass, while the idea of establishing carrying or portage-places is altogether precluded by the nature of the enclosing banks, which, in general, are inaccessible precipices. The few cataracts which we saw did not, it is true, appear very formidable, the fall of the greatest of them not being more than four or five feet; but it may be presumed, and, indeed, I have been assured, that there are others much grander than these, in some points of the river's course, which were concealed from our view by its windings and the thickness of the surrounding forest, it being probable that the foot-path has been carried along, or across, the most practicable parts of the channel. The perpetual roaring occasioned by the impetuous course of this stream over its rocky bed adds wonderfully to the effect of the wild and picturesque scenery that adorns its lofty banks, the hills which confine it being of an immense, though not uniform height, and abundantly clothed with a great variety of beautiful trees; for the most part, indeed, these are so close, as barely to leave a passage for the waters; at Nimbootân, however, and one or two other spots, they recede so far as to form a plain along the margin of the river sufficient for the admission of a few tents; but even in these situations the ground is over-run with thickets, and covered with stones. The fordable passages of the Rapti are called Junghars, of which there are no less than twenty-four between Hettowra and Dhoka-phede, at the foot of which this river passes, just after rushing from the bosom of the mountain whence it has its rise; it is of course but an inconsiderable stream at this place.

After crossing the Rapti for the last time, we immediately ascended Dhoka-phede, or the Gate-hill, so called from the great straitness of the pass leading over it; this hill is of a moderate height, and, excepting just at the summit, of a pretty easy acclivity. Below it, on the left hand, or to the westward, is the bed of a tolerably wide stream, which flows from certain springs (more particularly noticed hereafter) situated towards the summit of the Cheesapany mountain: we found it quite dry, which is its usual state, though it is sometimes filled by torrents that occasionally rush from the adjoining hills.

After the description which has been given of the road from Hettowra hither, it can scarcely be necessary to add, that it is utterly impassable during the periodical rains, at which time the little intercourse maintained between Nepaul and the Turryani is kept up by the routes of Muckwanpore and Sundooli, which, though abundantly difficult, yet, not lying through the courses or beds of torrents, are in some degree practicable at all seasons of the year.

The space between the farther or north foot of Dhoka-phede and

Bheem-phede is tolerably level and open, and exhibits some traces of cultivation. This last is a mean village occupied by a few Newar families, and standing at the south foot of Cheesapany mountain; it owes its name, according to some etymologists, to the circumstance of the Hindoo divinity Bheem having happened, in a terrestrial excursion, to rest one of his feet here, in making a god-like step: hence it is esteemed a place of sanctity, and the Newars who inhabit here have dedicated to this deity a small spring, or natural well, which stands close to the village.

A little way to the westward of the village, and in the bottom of a close glen formed by a hollow or gorge in the side of the Cheesapany mountain, a small brook was pointed out to me which issues from the springs already mentioned to be situated towards the summit of this mountain. It did not flow, at this time, much below the spot where I saw it quit the mountain, though it occasionally runs, as beforesaid, in a broad stream, till it meet the Rapti. Its water was cold enough to sink the mercury of Fahrenheit's thermometer from 65 to 51 degrees upon being immersed in it about three minutes; it was still colder at its source, the mercury, upon being plunged into it there, falling presently from 67 to 48 degrees. These experiments, it is proper to observe, were made at the hours of nine and eleven in the morning, when the heat of the sun was considerable, even in the shade. I was assured, indeed, that the water of this spring is very often too cold to be drank; and it is in allusion to its frigidity, that the mountain containing it is called Cheesapany, which literally signifies *cold water*.

The ascent from Bheem-phede to Cheesapany fort, is for the most part difficult; the road traverses the side of the mountain, and in many places lies close to the brink of frightful precipices, formed, on one side, by the torrents of the Rapti, and on the other by the Cheesapany stream, which together insulate in a manner the south side of the mountain. Some idea may be formed of the depths of these chasms from the circumstance of our having been actually at a loss, more than once, to determine the genus of the animals which we saw below, the largest cattle often appearing not larger than the size of a bird. As the path does not wind in a wide horizontal range, but stretches abruptly towards the summit, and forms numerous sharp turnings, the ascent is consequently in many places very steep; besides which, the footing is rendered not a little insecure by the loose fragments of rock which are scattered throughout it. Many parts of the road too necessarily over-hanging others, and these stones being easily set in motion by the action of the feet in climbing, those who bring up the rear of a company of travellers are very liable to be annoyed by the tumbling fragments. The perpendicular height of Cheesapany fort above Bheem-phede is about five hundred and thirty yards, which it took me very near an hour and a half to ascend in my hammock. In returning, I descended on foot, in somewhat less than three quarters of an hour.

The south side of this mountain is not so well covered with wood as the north; I speak of the space lying between the two ravines formed by the Rapti and Cheesapany streams, for the hollows, to a considerable way up their steep slopes, are abundantly and beautifully wooded. It is in these situations that the fir is mostly seen in the mountainous tracts, and never near the summits of the more elevated hills. The Saul and Sissoo are produced on the sides of Cheesapany; and after ascending from the springs, and reaching the greatest height of the path which leads over its summit, oaks, and other plants peculiar to the loftier situations, are met with. Indeed, we could always, in the course of our journey, form a tolerably accurate idea of our comparative elevation, by observing the various shades of vegetation which occurred as we ascended.

The fort of Cheesapany possesses no other strength than what it derives from its situation, which though considerably below the summit of the pass, is, nevertheless, as well chosen, perhaps, as it could be, since the space left by the torrents that embrace the mountain on either side being here very narrow, this barrier entirely occupies the whole breadth of the pass, and could not be easily turned on account of the precipices, at the edge of which it stands. It is not capable, however, of containing above an hundred men, and, although the masonry of it appears to be excellent, is altogether unworthy, in a military view, of any further notice.

This fort is not commanded by an Omrah, as almost all the

fortresses in the Nepaul territories are, but, like Muckwanpore, Seedule, and some other places of strength included in Zorawur Singh's government, is in charge of an officer immediately nominated by that Soubah. The Omrahs are every where wholly independent of the civil governors; their garrisons too, are chiefly composed of troops raised and formed by themselves, the regulars, or those of the line, being only occasionally employed under them: they have lands assigned them for the support of themselves and men, and rank very high among the orders of the state. They are distinguished by the simplicity, or what may (in contrast to the refinements elsewhere observable, even in Nepaul) be called the clownishness of their dress, wearing short jâmas, wide drawers, or trowsers, and white turbans carelessly and inelegantly folded. Their arms consist of matchlocks, broad-swords, bows, and arrows, and their class is determined by the number of Kohras,* or swords, which they muster. They are never allowed to remain a long time together in the command of the same place, being relieved for the most part yearly, and not unfrequently in the moment that they are about to reap the harvest of their lands. The same policy, however, is discernible in all the other arrangements of the Nepaul government with regard to its delegated authorities, and the jaghire lands, both of which are constantly passing into new hands. The Omrahs serve very commonly in the armies, but preserve with jealousy their own usages. Their respective forces are generally

* A representation of the Kohra is given in the plate at p. 118.

composed of their own kinsmen; and they affect to despise even the highest situations in the regular troops. They are all, with few exceptions, of the Rajepoot tribe.

Cheesapany is a custom-house station, and the only one, besides Seedli, at which duties are collected on merchandize passing from the Company's and Vizier's territories. The village adjoining to the fort contains about twenty thatched houses. There is a little grain raised here, but by no means sufficient for the consumption even of the few inhabitants of the place, who are therefore obliged to supply themselves occasionally from the neighbouring hamlets. The soil indeed of this mountain (especially of its southern side) would not seem to be favourable to the culture of any species of grain; the scanty fields which appear towards its summit constitute the jaghire of the Jemadar who commands at this station.

From the fort or village it is a tolerably easy ascent of about three quarters of a mile, by the road, to Cheesapany, or Cold-water spring, which lies in a natural hollow of the mountain situated a little below the road, and on the left hand; it is a romantic spot, and being but little exposed to the influence of the sun, owing to the high hills which encircle it, as well as to the trees which shade it, is delightfully cool. Amidst the great variety of plants with which it abounds, our attention was particularly attracted by a tree, some of the leaves of which exhibited, in a striking degree, the phænomenon described by Smellie in his account of the Hedysarum movens. As the people of Nepaul consider it in a great measure necessary both to the copiousness of a stream, and to the coldness of its waters, that its fountains, as well as the superior parts of its course, should be constantly well covered with foliage, they, on this account, make great difficulty in removing the thickets that are occasionally met with in those situations.

After quitting this spring, we continued to mount for very near another mile, before we actually reached the summit of the mountain, or rather of the path which traverses it. This part of the ascent is, on the whole, tolerably easy; though the ground being, as before, loose and stony, the road must be pronounced to be at best very indifferent. Near the top of a peak (but not the loftiest of those which rise from Cheesapany mountain) situated to the noth-west of the highest point of the pass, the mercury in the barometer fell to 23.80 inches, which indicated an elevation of about 780 yards above the level of Bheem-phede. This peak, and, of course, all those around it, most of which are higher, is often covered with snow for a fortnight together during the winter. Indeed the snow lies sometimes a span deep, and for ten days together, even at Cheesapany fort.

On reaching the point of the pass just mentioned, (and which I judge to stand about 120 yards higher than Cheesapany fort), the mountains of Himma-leh suddenly burst upon the view, rearing their numerous and magnificent peaks, eternally covered with snow, to a sublime height; and so arresting the eye as to render it for some time inattentive to the beautiful landscape immediately below it, and in which mount Chandraghiri, and the valley of Chitlong, with its meandering stream, form the most prominent objects. Indeed the snow lay upon them as low down as their sides were visible to us, which in some parts was to a very considerable depth, notwithstanding the interposition of the stupendous mountains which rose immediately to the southward of them, and which, though of a very inferior elevation, were nevertheless streaked with snow. This lower Alps, which would appear to be an inseparable attendant on the Himma-leh chain throughout the whole range of the latter, and which constitutes, to an immense extent, what is called the Kuchâr, or lower Boutan (dividing every where upper Boutan or Tibet from the Nepaul territories), will be more particularly mentioned hereafter. The extreme points of Himma-leh, as discernible from the top of Cheesapany, stretched from east by north to N. N. West, the nearest horizontal distance being about thirty-eight miles. After descending a few yards, we lost sight of these Alpine regions, which were not again visible till we reached the summit of one or other of the hills belonging to the Chandraghiri ridge. The snowy peaks of Himma-leh are distinguished among the Nepaulians by the term of Hima-chooli; Chooli signifying a sharp or pointed peak; a round swelling one, such as generally crown the summits of the Nepaul hills, being called Tumkoo.

The view from the peak of Cheesapany, which I ascended for the purpose of observing the state of the barometer, is said to be, in a clear day, one of the grandest that can well be imagined, the eye reposing from hence alternately on the various sublime objects just enumerated, and on all the subjacent country to the southward, stretching even beyond the Cheeriaghati ridge to the borders of Chemparun. We were unfortunately deprived in a great degree of this noble sight, as, when we were best able, and most at liberty to enjoy it, which was in our return, the mountain was enveloped by one of those thick mists (called here Too-âl) which always hang over this elevated tract, except during the periodical rains, or occasional showers. These vapours, however, did not prevent our observing, in the night, the numerous lights, and extensive conflagrations which illuminating the sides and summits of the surrounding hills, constituted a most picturesque sight, some of the former seeming, from their immense height, like so many stars, and, in fact, not easily distinguished at first from those luminaries; and the latter presenting the image of streams of fire rushing from the eminences into the valleys below. This last appearance was occasioned by the burning of the grass and underwood on the sides of the mountains intended to be cultivated, a practice very common in the low, as well as in the high lands, from an idea that the soil is at once cleared and fertilized by the operation.

The descent from Cheesapany summit to the valley or glen at its north foot, is neither so considerable, nor is the road so bad or dangerous, as the ascent from the Bheem-phede side. The road for the first part winds round the brow of the mountain, by a gently sloping path, which, though carried along the edge of an immense abyss, is too wide to raise any alarm in the traveller for his safety. On reaching the north side, the descent becomes rather more abrupt, but still continues tolerably easy; and during the middle part, is rendered not a little pleasant by the shade afforded by some fine trees which adorn this face of the mountain. Towards the bottom, the declivity is rapid and rocky.

In descending the north side of Cheesapany you meet about mid-way with one of those conical piles of stones, which are frequently raised in similar situations by the superstition of the natives, who in passing these rude temples, never fail to adore the divinity, whose presence they are supposed to manifest. They are called Deoralli, a name which we also find applied both to a very remarkable peak of Himmaleh, situated directly between Dhyboon and Kheroo, and to a mountainous ridge through which the Bhâgmutty rushes, soon after escaping from the valley of Nepaul.

Immediately on reaching the north foot of the Cheesapany, you cross a rapid but not wide stream, which bears different names, according to the villages near which it takes its course. It is here called Tambeh-kan, or Kowli-kan, kola; further up it is known by the appellation of Markhoo-kola, and still higher by that of Chitlong-kola. It has its rise at no great distance from Paloong, a village situated in one of the mountains of the western branch of the Chandraghiri ridge; after descending into the valley of Chitlong, it is there augmented by some other small rivulets issuing from the surrounding hills; it then winds through this valley, and runs to the eastward of Ekdunta hill, washing to the westward, the bottom of the eminence on which the village of Markhoo stands; whence it pursues its course to Tambeh-kan, passing turbulently along the east side of that station. From the foot of Cheesapany, where its bed and banks abound with huge rocks, it rushes with considerable rapidity in a direction nearly east, forcing its way through the intervening mountains till it reachesthe Bhâgmutty, into which it throws itself at Sisniari, at the distance of about seven horizontal miles from Tambeh-kan. Between Tambeh-kan and Sisniari, and rather less than two miles below the ford at which we passed (reckoning according to its course), it is precipitated from a rocky perpendicular height of nearly fifty feet, with a noise that, during the periodical rains, is described to be very grand. Indeed the distant roar of this cataract was by no means inconsiderable, even at the season of our journey.

The glen or hollow of Tambeh-kan (for it is scarcely entitled to the name of valley) stands about two hundred and seventy yards higher than Bheem-phede; on which account, as well as because the soil on the north side of Cheesapany mountain is not altogether so loose as on the opposite face, the descent to it is comparatively easy. I am assured that this spot is extremely subject to violent gusts of wind, which rushing from the intervals of the mountains, and carrying with them innumerable pebbles, render it a very unpleasant stage for travellers, on whom these scattered fragments sometimes descend with the impetuosity of a hail-storm. This glen is also remarkable for the severity of its temperature in winter, at which time it is said that the water of the river that passes through it is almost too cold to be drank.

The village of Tambeh-kan, called also Kowli-kan, is at present a miserable place, though before the copper mines in its vicinity (whence it derives its name) were exhausted, it is said to have been both populous and flourishing. Indeed the sides of the smaller hills, which immediately encircle it, exhibiting every where traces of former forests, is of itself, perhaps, no slight indication of the fact, whether we suppose these forests to have been removed for the purposes of fuel merely, or with a view to the cultivation of the soil.

Though the mines close to this place are now nearly exhausted, yet other veins of copper have been discovered, and are worked at no great distance from hence. It would seem that the miners (who are of the Agrye cast or tribe) move from place to place, according as their discoveries occasionally prompt them; and although I am not exactly informed upon what terms they carry on their operations, yet there is reason to suppose that they find them abundantly profitable, since Kurripoot Ranipoot (or a miner's son and a prince's son) is a proverbial expression in the country, denoting the opulence of these people, who, it is notorious, indeed, throw away their money in the most lavish manner, working only when stimulated by necessity, or by particularly advantageous offers.

Upon quitting Tambeh-kan, we proceeded for some way along the banks, and occasionally through the bed, of the river, which towards Markhoo is of a considerable breadth, and every where confined by hills or rocks of a stupendous height, most of them very steep, and some actually overhanging the channel below: one of the craggiest of these cliffs, of a dark barren aspect, and standing on the right hand in proceeding up the river, presents the striking appearance of a few well grown pines issuing from its perpendicular side, and preserving their erect position in a remarkable manner. Before we reached the village of Markhoo, the road leading to Khatmanda by Pheerphing turned off to the right. I shall take notice of this route, after describing the more direct one by Chitlong.

Leaving Markhoo, which stands near the summit of an eminence on the right, and quitting the bed of the river, we ascended the hill of Ekdunta, over which there lead two paths. Our cattle, and most of our people, proceeded by the safest, but neither the shortest nor easiest. It lies to the left, and partly through the course of a rivulet. That by which I was conducted winds round the right or east face of the hill, at no great distance from its brow, and is the most alarming, if not the most dangerous passage that occurred in our whole journey; the breadth of it no where exceeds two feet, and it is in some places not so much. On one hand is the side of the hill, which, contrary to the general nature of these mountains, is here quite bare, affording neither shrub nor stone capable of sustaining the stumbling traveller, on whose other hand is a perpendicular precipice some hundred feet deep, at the bottom of which the Markhoo-kola rushes impetuously over its rocky bed. When I perceived the situation I was in, I should have been very well pleased to have got on my legs: though probably, so sure-footed are the bearers, I was better in my hammock, where, at all events, I was under the necessity of remaining, as the narrowness of the road did not allow of my quitting it with safety.

After descending from Ekdunta hill, we proceeded for about a mile and a half along an undulating valley intersected with canals and natural rivulets, and swelling sometimes into small eminences, the greater part highly cultivated, and exhibiting several interesting views of scattered cottages and hamlets, some of them standing on the summits, some on the sides, and others in the bottoms of the inclosing hills, the whole constituting a coup-d'œil of the most pleasing and picturesque kind. If, indeed, it had not been for the terraces or steps (resembling an irregular flight of stairs) in which the fields were laid out, both in the low and elevated situations, and which form a striking feature in the landscape of this country, the general scenery might have been compared with the appearance of many a spot in England. As it was, the objects which surrounded us here did not fail to remind us of some of the natural beauties of our native island. The terraces or steps just mentioned are constructed with no small labour (often extending to the tops of the highest hills), for the culture of those kinds of grain which require that the water should remain for some time on the soil. The sides of most, if not of all the mountains in this country, abounding in springs, these terraces are easily overflowed, and the water conducted from one to another, according as circumstances demand. Sometimes two fields or flights of terraces are seen separated from one another by ravines or rivulets several hundred feet deep, watered from the same spring by means of an aqueduct constructed simply of one or more hollowed trees laid across the intervening chasms, and slightly supported at their extremities as far as the nature of the precipice happens to admit.

Chitlong, called also Lohari, or Little Nepaul, stands near the bank of the same stream that passes below Markhoo and Tambeh-kan; it contains a few brick and tiled houses of two and three stories, but is on the whole an inconsiderable place, though certainly the first station having any appearance of a town, that the traveller meets with in the Nepaul territories. It is said to have been formerly more extensive and flourishing than it is at present, and its decline was accounted for to me by observing that its situation on the high road between Nepaul and the Turrye exposing its inhabitants to be pressed as porters by the officers of government and other persons of authority passing through it, had occasioned the greatest part of them to fly from this oppression into the interior parts of the country. There can be little room to doubt this account, when it is considered that the same thing happens under many other governments, which either have not the will or the power to protect the labouring classes of the people from the violence of the superior orders. Whether or not the case was otherwise under the ancient Newar princes, I am unable to determine with exactness, though I suspect that their administration was far from being moderate or just. But be this as it may, it is pretty certain that the Newar tribes (who alone, throughout Nepaul proper, cultivate the ground, and exercise all the other useful arts) enjoy but little security or happiness under their present rulers, who, on most occasions, make but too light both of their civil and natural rights. This observation, however, is by no means meant to convey any peculiar censure on the Goorkhali government, which I believe to be at least as mild and equitable as any other in India, whether Hindoo or Mahomedan.

During the dynasty of Newar princes, Chitlong was for some time a dependency of the Patun Raje, or sovereignty, and had a district annexed to it containing several populous villages, among which were Paloong, Taistoon, Boe-khail, &c. It constitutes, at present, part of the jaghire or fief of one of the four Sirdars, or commanders in chief, of the Goorkhali forces. There is a mooruth of Mahadeo to the eastward of the town, close to which is a spring of excellent water.

We passed about a mile beyond Chitlong, before we met with a spot on which we could pitch our little camp; the situation which we occupied was on the east bank of Chitlong-kola, and at the distance of about half a mile from the south foot of Chandraghiri, or the mountain of the moon, a branch or spur of which, however, stretched close to our encampment, as did another, in the same manner, from the opposite side of the rivulet, hemming us in so closely, that the sun did not rise to us on the 27th February, till half after eight, setting on the same day proportionately early, or between three and four o'clock.

There is no cultivation on the sides of the hills just described as terminating the upper part of the Chitlong valley. They are, however, well wooded, and abound in a vast variety of wild shrubs, forming altogether a very pleasing sight, though not so interesting a one as the fields of corn with which many of the adjacent eminences are enriched.

Although our barometer was not in order for making here our usual meteorological observations, yet both the rapidity of the stream which passes through this valley, and the probable ascent by the road from Tambeh-kan, sufficiently indicate that Chitlong stands considerably higher than the last-mentioned place. The natives, besides asserting the same fact, affirmed it to be still more elevated above the valley of Nepaul; and this opinion we had the means of confirming generally, by observing that the level of Khatmanda was actually below that of Tambeh-kan, though, as to the precise elevation of Chitlong, as well as of some other situations, we could form only a vague estimate. It may serve, however, as a further corroboration of the idea regarding the superior height of this valley, to notice that during the night of the 27th February the mercury in Fahrenheit's thermometer fell to 29 degrees, and that on the following morning we found all the standing water around us frozen to a considerable thickness, the mercury at the same time being at 36.

The Chitlong-kola descends with too much rapidity to be ever frozen, but the Chandraghiri mountain was crowned with snow not many days before our arrival at its foot. We had not an opportunity of judging of the height of this mountain by the barometer; but, from a rough comparison of it with others in its vicinity, which we were enabled to calculate with some degree of exactness, I think it probable that it rises about eight hundred yards above the level of Chitlong valley, which, I conceive, stands within two hundred yards as high as Cheesapany fort itself.

The direct road from our camp to Khatmanda lay over mount Chandraghiri; but as we proceeded to the capital by another route, I can give no satisfactory account of the former: from the report, however, of Lieut. Gerard (who ascended to the top of the mountain for the purpose of taking the bearings of the principal surrounding points), it would appear that the acclivity on the Chitlong side is much easier than that of Cheesapany, the road being on the whole neither so steep, nor of so loose a bottom. The descent to the valley of Nepaul is, on the other hand, described by every one to be very abrupt and rugged.

Thankote is situated near the north foot of the mountain; you pass through it in proceeding to Khatmanda, from which it is distant about six road miles. The horizontal distance between Chitlong and Khatmanda does not exceed nine miles.

From the summit of Chandraghiri there is a most commanding prospect, the eye, from hence, not only expatiating on the waving valley of Nepaul, beautifully and thickly dotted with villages, and abundantly chequered with rich fields fertilized by numerous meandering streams; but also embracing on every side a wide expanse of charmingly diversified country. It is the landscape in front, however, that here most powerfully attracts the attention; the scenery in this direction gradually rising to an amphitheatre, and successively exhibiting to the delighted view the cities and numberless temples of the valley below; the stupendous mountain of Sheoopoori; the still super-towering Jibjibia, clothed to its snow-capped peak with pendulous forests; and finally, the gigantic Himma-leh, forming the majestic back-ground of this wonderful and sublime picture. On the Bhunjan, or flat of Chandraghiri summit, there is a small village and market for the accommodation of travellers; and on one of its peaks, immediately below which the road passes, there formerly stood a small fort, which has lately been allowed to go to decay.

We will now, as proposed above, return to Tambeh-kan, and trace the route from thence to Khatmanda, by what is called the Pheerphing road.

Proceeding for about a mile from Tambeh-kan, partly in the bed of the river, which passes under it, but chiefly along its western bank, you at length cross it, at the foot of a mountain which confines it here on the east side, and which you immediately begin to ascend. This mountain rises to a very great height, and terminates in two or three gently-swelling peaks, on one of which (situated immediately over the road or pass) the mercury in the barometer fell to 231.75 inches, which indicates an elevation almost exactly the same with that of the neighbouring peak of Cheesapany. The road, for nearly the whole way to the top, is exceedingly bad, but the first part is particularly rugged. It winds considerably soon after quitting the river, and therefore is not often very steep; there occur, however, several precipices in it, which are but ill compensated for by the circumstance of this mountain's being remarkably well wooded, and consequently shady. The difficulty of the acclivity is in some degree diminished by a break or step, which, after ascending about midway, stretches forward in a sort of terrace for two or three hundred feet. On approaching the summit, and during some minutes in descending to the north-east, you have a view of Himma-leh, but neither uninterrupted nor extensive. The Markoo-kola, which meanders through the intervals of the hills, appears to the eye of the traveller from above, of a deep dark tinge, nearly as black as ink. I conceive the ascent of this side of the mountain to be little less, by the road, than four miles.

In proceeding to Khargoo, you descend by a very bad path, which winds along the north-east face of the mountain that has just been described, till you reach a small rivulet which separates it from the spur or projecting hill, on the brow of which the village of Khargoo stands. After crossing this stream, which, as well as several others that flow in various directions, has its rise from springs situated, some of them actually within, and some in the skirts of the village, you ascend by a tolerably easy acclivity leading to Khargoo. This is an inconsiderable, and miserable looking place, notwithstanding the few huts it consists of are built of brick, and apparently well tiled. It may be observed, indeed, once for all, of the hamlets scattered over the more mountainous parts of our track, that owing to their favourable situation, which was very commonly highly romantic, they generally constituted most agreeable prospects when seen from a distance; but that, on a nearer view, the delusion vanished, being but too often succeeded by a picture, in which poverty and squalidness formed the most prominent figures.

Instead of ascending to the top of the hill on which Khargoo stands, and passing through that village, the traveller may proceed by a more direct path that lies a little below it to the southward; but this is very unsafe, being as narrow as that of Ekdunta, though not of equal extent, and having a steep precipice on the right hand; the danger of it is not a little augmented by the numerous rills of water which issue from the superincumbent springs, and, by intersecting the road cut out of the side of the hill, must always render it very slippery. I happened to be conducted through Khargoo, and could not view, from the opposite mountain, some of our party passing under that village by the lower way, without strong sensations of alarm.

By advancing, after quitting Tambeh-kan, a little higher up the course of the river than the point at which our route crossed it, and keeping the Chitlong road till you come to the bottom of Ekdunta hill, striking off from thence to the right, I have reason to believe that a great part of the difficulty just described would be avoided. Some of our people proceeded by the way here alluded to, and from their report of it, there can be little doubt of its being considerably easier, than that which we ourselves pursued. Indeed, if the case were otherwise, it would be impossible to account for the preference given by all merchants to the Pheerphing road, since there would not seem to be any thing in the descent from Chandraghiri to the valley of Nepaul nearly so arduous or dangerous as what we experienced between Tambeh-kan and Khargoo, not to insist upon the general ruggedness of the whole of this route, which was, however, far greater than we had been taught to expect.

On leaving Khargoo, you descend till you reach a stream called Khargoo-kola, by a road that, after winding some way round the brow of the hill, strikes rather abruptly down the north face of it. The Khargoo-kola rises from the springs already mentioned, as being situated in and about the village of the same name. I am not able to describe its course; but it is probable that after being joined by the Seeboodoul rivulet, it empties itself, at no great distance, into the Tambeh-kan river. After proceeding for a few minutes along the bank of the Khargoo-kola, you cross it, and presently mount, by a gentle ascent, another hill of no great elevation, the declivity of which, however, towards the north-east, is rather steep. Immediately on descending this hill, you enter the bed of the Seeboodoul rivulet, which is crossed several times in advancing up the valley through which it runs. This stream issues from one of the hills that inclose the valley here mentioned, to the eastward; if that may be called a valley in which we found it difficult to pitch the few tents we had with us. But confined as this glen or bottom was, we nevertheless found it very agreeable, the surrounding eminences being beautifully wooded, and presenting many romantic points of view. Low as this situation appeared to be on account of the lofty hills which in a manner overhung it, the barometer indicated its elevation to be very considerable, the mercury sinking here to 24 inches and a half, or almost exactly to the level of Cheesapany spring. The height of this place is further denoted by the extreme cold which we felt during the night of the 20th March, when on our return from Khatmanda, and the morning following the mercury in Fahrenheit's thermometer stood at 43 degrees and a half. It must not be omitted that we were assured this spot was much infested by tigers; this animal, however, would not appear, from the accounts we received, to be nearly so fierce or dangerous in Nepaul as those of the southern countries.

Proceeding from hence about three-quarters of a mile, you reach the foot of a hill, midway up which there is a small fort, called Gowthân, where some cattle belonging to the Rajah are usually kept. The bottom below it, on the south-side, is known by the name of Phakheil Kurrug, on account of its abounding with wild hogs, which, in the Newar dialect, are called Phâ. This is not a very high hill, yet the ascent in some parts is exceedingly bad, nor is the opposite declivity on the whole much better. You no sooner pass this hill than you begin to mount a second, rather loftier than it, by a road which is at first rugged and steep, but improves as it approaches to the top, where it winds with an easy ascent. Descending again by a tolerably gentle declivity, you cross a third hill, the ascent of which is by no means difficult. On the summit is a level path for about forty or fifty yards, after which you descend once more, passing, at the bottom, the Pheerphing-kola. From this rivulet you ascend to the town of Pheerphing, which stands on the brow of a hill, at the further or north part of which the Bhâgmutty flows over a sandy bed, and through a channel but little obstructed by rocks. Above Pheerphing, whence the hill continues to rise very gradually, and about half a mile to the westward of it, stands the village of Sulti-khul, romantically situated, directly under mount Chempa-daibi. The springs of the Seker are to be seen close to this village, and though it is an inconsiderable rivulet, emptying itself into the Bhâgmutty, very soon after passing to the north-west of Pheerphing, yet its sanctity, and, consequently, its importance, among the natives is very great, giving name to one of the four Arthans of Nerain for which Nepaul is celebrated. The multitudes of small fish which the fountains of this stream contain, cannot fail to attract the notice of the traveller, nor will it sufficiently account for their being so numerous, to observe, that the inhabitants are universally impressed with a conviction, that any attempt to steal them (catching them openly being altogether out of the question) would be followed by immediate death. This rivulet no sooner passes the Arthan of Seker-nerain, at which spot the fish most abound, than it throws itself in a cascade of considerable elevation abruptly into the valley below, whither it would necessarily carry the greater part of the fish along with it, if some means of prevention were not used. The mode adopted has been that of sinking two or three basons in the rock, below the natural bed of the stream, the current of which, however rapid, can only propel the superior part of the water confined in the basons. Accordingly, very few fish are precipitated down the hill by the torrents, even when those are at the highest, the artificial depths affording them a secure retreat from its violence.

Pheerphing, though dignified with the title of a town, possesses but little advantage over Khargoo, either in size or any other respect. The hills and valleys around it, and comprehended in its jurisdiction, and which, in general, appear highly cultivated, are celebrated for the wheat and Karphul which they produce; the latter is a small stone fruit, somewhat resembling the cherry in flavour; we saw also at Pheerphing some very fine-looking peach-trees of unusual height. Whether or not more grain is raised in this district than is required for the consumption of its inhabitants, I had not an opportunity of ascertaining; but it is certain, that neither here, nor at any other town or village in our route (Khatmanda alone excepted) could we easily procure even a single day's provisions for our followers; the authority of the government being almost always necessary for this purpose, notwithstanding our readiness to pay whatever might be demanded; from this circumstance, and the nature of the country, which was every where unfavourable to the transportation of its productions to any distant market, I am inclined to think that for the most part these people are content to obtain from the earth support only for themselves, and that, consequently, we were rarely supplied by them in the course of our journey but at the expense of exposing them more or less to real inconvenience.

From Pheerphing to Patn, the road, though traversing a country broken into irregular and unequal heights, and consisting sometimes of the same narrow sort of path cut out of the side, or carried round the brow or shoulder of a mountain, and impending over immense chasms, which occurs so commonly in this country, may, nevertheless (especially the latter part), be said to be comparatively good. The Bhâgmutty is crossed at the distance of three and a half road miles from Pheerphing. Advancing from this river about a mile, you leave the villages of Sona-koate and Koakna to the left. This last place, as well as Bhâgmutty, which stands close to it, is situated somewhat below the road, which here lies over a hill that separates the Bhâgmutty and Purbâooty rivers, between which the distance is nearly three miles. The Purbâooty issues from one of the mountains to the eastward, passing soon after on the east side of Châpigong; it has but an inconsiderable course before it falls into the Bhâgmutty, which it does a little way below the point at which we forded it. This stream is also called the Nee-khoo, from its abounding with fish; nya, or nee, signifying *fish*, and khoo, a *rivulet*, in the Newar dialect. The city of Patn, which is not above three quarters of a mile beyond the passage of the Nee-khoo, stands on a small, but rather elevated plain, at the distance of about a mile and a half from the south end of Khatmanda. The Bhâgmutty separates these two capitals, being crossed a little above its junction with the Bishnmutty, and at nearly the same distance below the point at which it receives the waters of the Tookeha, a river that will be further noticed elsewhere.

I compute the road-distance from Tambeh-kan to Khatmanda, by Pheerphing, to be twenty-three miles, whereas, by Chitlong and Chandraghiri, it does not, I imagine, exceed nineteen. Of the preference to which this last route appears entitled, in every other respect, I have already offered my opinion; I will here add, that it is invariably used by all natives travelling directly from Hettowra to Khatmanda, which is a journey very commonly performed between sunrise and evening.

I will now return to Chitlong valley, and trace the route we pursued from thence to Khatmanda by Noakote.

Leaving Chandraghiri proper on the right hand, we ascended in a direction nearly north, and by a path neither remarkably steep, nor in any other shape very difficult, to the summit of what may be called Doona-baisi mountain, from the valley of that name lying below it to the northward. It is, however, a continuation of mount Chandraghiri, from which it is only partially divided by a sinking in the top of the ridge, and a separation of the shoulders constituting a deep gorge or chasm, overgrown with trees and shrubs, and formed, perhaps, by the attrition of the waters which spring from above, and meeting in their course down the side of the mountain, with little resistance, from the nature of the strata which compose it, may be readily conceived (especially as these streams are occasionally violent torrents) to have gradually effected this breach. The same description, as well as theory, will apply to the greater part of the mountainous tract over which our route lay; it appearing to consist almost universally of a calcareous rock, and that rarely of a firm or compact kind.

The acclivity of mount Doona-baisi is broken into two steps. The first ascent is, by the road, about a mile and a quarter, the other is a mile; the flat or level separating them is, however, very inconsiderable. The whole of this face of the mountain is delightfully wooded, the lower parts, towards Chitlong valley, excepted, where the principal natural production is a stunted oak of the holly-leafed species. The chasms below the shoulders (along the edge of which the road, as usual, occasionally passes) contain Sissoo, pine, and other trees; among those which adorn the side of the hill, the chief are the Phullaced, the Kâhôlô, the Sing Rowla, the Timmûe, the Chillownia, and the Seidburrooa. The first of these is a species of oak, the wood of which is in high repute in Nepaul for its strength and durability; the acorns are used medicinally, and also serve as food for their hogs. Of the pith of the Kâhôlô, the poorer classes of the people, in times of scarcity, prepare a nutritious bread, which is sometimes eaten by itself, and sometimes mixed with flour. The Sing Rowla is the Lignea Cassia, the leaves of which are very commonly brought into Hindostan, where they are employed in spicery under the name of Taiz-pât (or sharp leaf): the bark of the root does not differ widely from cinnamon, for which it is, indeed, often sold in the upper provinces; but that of the trunk and branches possesses little of the cinnamon flavour. This spice, when not manufactured so as to resemble cinnamon, is vended by the Pussaries or druggists under the name of Thieg. The Timmûe, called also Taizbul (of which there are two species), is a curious plant, yielding a berry somewhat like the black pepper in shape and size; this berry consists of a black or bicolor seed contained in a thin shell or pod, which spontaneously opens when the fruit is ripe. The shell is a strong, pleasant spice, used for various culinary purposes, and is likewise asserted to possess great medicinal virtues.* The Chillownia is also a singular

* This appears to be the Cubeb of Java.

tree; its upper coat is entirely composed of innumerable needle-form fibres laterally united by a kind of glutinous sap. This part of the plant applied to the skin, affects it in the manner of thistles, and is on that account employed as one of the instruments of corporal punishment used in this country. The wood of the Chillownia is very much valued, but whether the estimation in which it is held be founded on experience of its good qualities, or merely on superstitious opinion, I am not quite certain; I have been told it makes good rafters, and have also been assured that it is the god of trees, and that no house can be said to be perfectly secure in which more or less of this timber has not been employed. The bark of the Siedburrooa is manufactured by the people of Nepaul into a strong useful paper; they also make rope and packthread of it, neither of which, however, would appear to resist moisture well. There are two species of this tree, both growing to a considerable size; the one just mentioned is also called Kâghazi-pât, or the paper plant; the other is the Bhootea Siedburrooa, or paper-tree of Tibet, which is deemed the best.

Besides these, there are several other useful or curious trees and shrubs among the natural productions of this and the adjacent mountains, that appear to be very well entitled to investigation, as promising both to reward and gratify an active and intelligent botanist. I shall only notice here, in addition to what has been just enumerated, the Jumne-mundroo, the Gûrras, the Puddiem or Poyeh, the Chootraphul, the Mahail, and the Dhuttola. The first of these bears yellow sweet-smelling flowers, in branches; its leaves resemble those of the holly, and the wood is, both in closeness of texture and colour, very like box. The Gûrras is a tree that affects the highest situations; its flowers are large, and of a deep red; and yield by decoction a purplish colour which ascids convert to a tolerable pink. The Puddiem or Poyeh resembles, in its leaf and wood, the cherry; we did not see it in flower, and as it is not cultivated, could form no accurate idea of its fruit from the account we received of it. The wood is held in great sanctity by the natives. The Chootraphul is not unlike the barberry in appearance; the wood is of a strong yellow colour, but does not afford a permanent dye; the women of Nepaul use it, instead of sandal, for tracing the Tilluh on their foreheads. The Mahail and Dhuttola are both species of plums; the former bears abundance of beautiful flowers. The Okher, or walnut, of Chitlong is reckoned the best of any produced in the Nepaul territories; but those of Tibet are esteemed superior. The shell of the Chitlong, and, indeed, of most of the Nepaul walnuts, is remarkably hard. They have learned to employ the wood in the manufacture of gun-stocks, Behadur Shah having of himself discovered that we put it to that use. Their best charcoal is made of the Bhâng, or holly-leafed oak.

We were just an hour in ascending to the top of Doona-baisi hill, from whence we had a delightful view of the valley below, as well as a broken one of the snowy ranges of mountains before us.

M

The declivity to the northward was in many places extremely steep, the road often lying along the edge of the shoulder by which we descended, and which now and then sunk very abruptly. The distance by the road from the summit of the mountain to the bottom of Doona-baisi, could not, I judge, be less than six miles, as I was two hours and twenty minutes in descending. We passed in our descent two hamlets, situated on small flat projections from the side of the hill; the first of them nearly midway down, the other about half a mile from the bottom. The village of Pisan-keel stands on the face of a detached hill less than a quarter of a mile from the foot of the descent into the valley, and leaning from it about south-west. The north side of Doona-baisi mountain, though of a perpendicular height not less than twelve hundred yards, was cultivated in some parts from its very summit to its base, presenting to the view one of the most interesting and picturesque sights that can be well imagined; many of the fields, indeed, appeared to be so steep as to excite some degree of wonder in us at the husbandman's being able to reach, far less to cultivate them. The grain raised in these situations is principally Towli and Ikâro; they are both species of Ghya, or dry rice, the former of which is reaped in the summer, and the other in the winter solstice.

I am inclined to think that Doona-baisi* lies nearly on the same level with Beem-phede, or perhaps a little lower. The Owl, or low-

* The word Baisi or Biasi, wherever it occurs, signifies a valley.

country plague, prevails in this valley with some force, between the months of April and November, which must be attributed to the great height of the mountains enclosing it, as otherwise it might well be considered an elevated situation, standing as it does more than fifteen hundred feet above the level of Cheeriaghati. During this period, the inhabitants fly to the sides of the surrounding hills, upon which they all have cottages to retire to. They nevertheless, continue, even during the bad season, to visit the valley without fear, while the sun remains above the horizon, never venturing, however, to pass the night below. This endemial disease, of which we have been accustomed to hear such exaggerated accounts, though doubtlessly a very afflicting malady, appears to be nothing more than the jungle fever, so common in the hilly and woody districts of India, and differing in no respect from the Malaria of Switzerland, as described by Coxe.

Our camp in the Doona valley was pitched on a rising ground, which, though not sufficiently elevated above its bottom, to disclose to us the sublime scenery of the Alpine regions in front, was, nevertheless, abundantly favourable to the view of one of the most delightful prospects that occurred in the course of our journey, and the milder beauties of which I should in vain attempt to describe. It must not be omitted, however, that the romantic and rural situations of some of the hamlets with which this pleasing landscape was studded, did not constitute the least striking of its charms; the soil of the nearer hills, as well as of the valley, appeared to be very rich, being, it is probable, mostly composed of decayed vegetables and decomposed lime-stone. On the eminence upon which our tents stood, there was a lofty Champah-tree, which measured in girth eleven feet, though in Bengal this is a shrub of inconsiderable bulk. The Shujh, or milk-tree, also called in this country Sukoor, grew here to a very uncommon size.

The valley of Doona is divided from that of Nepaul by an irregular ridge of hills of no great height, which runs across the eastern head of it, issuing apparently from that part of the Bheerbundy mountain adjoining, towards the elbow formed by the Chandraghiri and Doona-baisi mountains. In passing from Khatmanda to Patn, this ridge presented the appearance of four or five separate ranges, one rising above the other in amphitheatrical order. If they are really distinct ranges, the intervals must be very inconsiderable, the horizontal distance, even from Pisan-keel to Thankote, across these hills, not exceeding five miles. I incline to think, however, that what seemed to be separate ridges were in fact no other than so many steps or risings of the same range, divided severally by gentle sinkings between, a physical disposition which I often observed in this mountainous region, and which always, in a certain point of view, exhibited the appearance of so many distinct hills. With regard to the western extremity of the Doona valley, I can say nothing positive, because though it seemed to be partially bounded very soon in that quarter by some low hills crossing it in a north-west direction, yet the view beyond those was, for this country, uncommonly distinct and extensive. But whatever may be the western limit of this valley, there is no doubt that one may travel hence to Noakote without crossing any hills, and, consequently, turn the west point of Koomhara mountain, by proceeding occasionally through the beds of rivulets. The following sketch of the Rajah's route from Khatmanda to Noakote will both establish the fact, and shew also that the ridge which confines the Doona valley to the eastward, is not actually in contact with mount Chandraghiri.

Proceeded from Khatmanda } in the valley of Nepaul.
to Kertipore
to Thankote

Hence descended into

Doona-baisi; whence proceeded westerly

to Mahadeo-baisi.

to Khaistia-dhoban* (or the junction of the Mahaise and Khaistia, which last stream rises in Ghedia-kan)

to Mahaise-dhoban (or the confluence of the Mahaise and Tirsoolgunga).

to Koolpoo-dhoban (or the junction of the Koolpoo and Tirsoolgunga).

to Bhoodo-sing-baisi

to Daiby Ghaut.

to Noakote.

* Dhoban signifies the confluence of two rivers.

The whole of the way from Thankote to Noakote (excepting, indeed, between the former place and Doona-baisi, where the descent must be rather abrupt) would seem to be a gradual declivity lying entirely through valleys and the beds of rivers, each successively lower than another, the valley of Noakote being deeper still than that of Doona. The first part of this route being westerly, the middle northerly, and the latter easterly, it is evidently so extremely circuitous, as to require several days for its performance, whereas, it is only one good day's journey from Khatmanda to Noakote, by the direct road over Bheerbundy mountain, of which we shall speak in the proper place.

Most of the cultivated grounds in and about Doona-baisi are divided somewhat in the manner of jaghires among the civil and military servants of the Government; a few are in the hands of Brahmins, and some of the least productive, as those situated towards the summits of the mountains, are held under certain stipulations by the peasantry who till them. I do not possess the information necessary to giving a full or satisfactory account of the nature of tenures in this country, but I will here sketch out a general idea of the matter in the best manner my sources of intelligence will admit.

The Sovereign is deemed to be originally the absolute proprietor of all lands, nor is there any tenure under which they can be enjoyed permanently, or considered as hereditary possessions, except the few hereafter particularized. Even the first subject of the state, whether as to birth or office, has, generally speaking, but a temporary and precarious interest in the lands which he holds, being liable, at every Punjunni, or grand council (which is for the most part annual, and assembled during the months of May and June), to be deprived of them altogether; to have them commuted for a pecuniary stipend, or to have them exchanged for others. This council is composed of the principal ministers of Government, and of such other persons as the Prince or Regent thinks proper to invite to it; and its business is to examine into the conduct of all the public officers during the preceding year, to degrade, punish, and reward them, according to their merits, and to bestow governments, military commands, and jaghire lands for the ensuing year, in all which it is the policy of this court to make frequent changes, with the view of preventing local attachments, and the dangerous effects of long confirmed local authority; of accustoming its subjects to serve indifferently in all parts, and of keeping its dependents always in a state fluctuating between hope and fear; imitating herein the practice of the court of Delhi, during the most vigorous period of the Mogul monarchy; I say imitating, because, little as I had an opportunity of observing the political institutions of this government, I saw enough to satisfy me that many of them were directly drawn from that source.

CHAPTER IV.

Division of Lands in Nepaul—Measures and Weights—Cultivation of the Soil—Labourers' Wages—Classes of the Peasantry—Military Service.

CHAPTER IV.

THE lands of Nepaul, under which denomination I comprehend not only those of Nepaul proper, and of Ghoorkha, but of such conquered districts as have been thoroughly settled, may be arranged under the following classes :

First. Those constituting what may be termed crown-lands, or the Rajah's immediate estates. These are situated chiefly in the Ghoorkha territory, but there is hardly any division of the Goorkhali conquests, in which the Prince has not appropriated a greater or smaller share of the lands to himself. Some of these estates are cultivated by husbandmen, with whom he equally divides the produce; others are managed entirely by agents of his own, and tilled by the neighbouring husbandmen, who are obliged to dedicate a certain number of days in the year to this service; and others are farmed out. From those of the two first descriptions he draws almost all the supplies for the consumption of his kitchen and the other departments of his household ; every jaghiredar at Khatmanda furnishing himself in the same manner from his jaghire (unless this happens to be too remotely situated) with so much of its produce in kind, as he may require for domestic expenditure, depending on the markets, whether at Khatmanda or elsewhere, only for such articles as his lands do not yield. This is the reason why the markets of this country appear to be but scantily supplied, when considered relatively to the number of inhabitants; for they may be said to be almost exclusively resorted to by the trading, manufacturing, and other classes of the people not in possession of lands.

Second. The Birtha, or Brhemoter lands, which are of two kinds, viz. the Koos-birtha, and the Soona-birtha. The former are rarely bestowed excepting on Brahmins. The manner of investiture is solemn; the Rajah waters with his own hands a clod brought from the land to be given away, mixing it with some Koos (a species of holy grass,) and Teel (sesame), and, with certain other ceremonies occasionally performed by a priest, presents the whole to the Brahmin, who returns part of the clod to the earth from which it was taken, and carefully preserves the remainder; this gift is sometimes accompanied by a written patent, and sometimes by a Tambeh-putter, or title-deed, engraved on a plate of copper. Lands of this kind are rent-free, saleable, and hereditary; but are also forfeitable for certain crimes. Some titles to estates of this sort are derived from grants confered by former princes, the predecessors of the Goorkhali dynasty, but which the present reigning family have confirmed, by affixing their red seal to the original patents, the proprietors paying in these cases a fine proportioned to the value of the land. It must here be observed, that though, strictly speaking, the sovereign has no claim on the proprietor of such lands for any thing more than his prayers, yet the latter occasionally considers it prudent to propitiate his prince by other more substantial means. This is particularly necessary on the accession of a new Rajah.

The Soona-birtha tenure is that by which certain Newars, and other natives of the different countries subjected by the Goorkhalis, continue to hold their ancient possessions under the government of the conquerors. These lands, though rent-free, saleable, and hereditary, like the others, are not enjoyed altogether on terms equally easy; for besides that a considerable fine was exacted from the proprietors upon the first confirmation of their original titles, these must be renewed on similar terms under every succeeding prince

Third. The Kohrya and Bari lands. The lands which come under this description, are such as are destitute of springs, and have no stream passing through them. Of this kind are the sides and summits of many, perhaps the greater part, of the mountains of this country, though certainly most of those which we passed were very well watered. A Bari is properly an enclosed fruit or kitchen garden, unsupplied with springs or running water, being otherwise deemed of the Kaith kind, and rateable accordingly. Kohrya land is often comprehended in jaghires, but is not productive to the jaghiredar, as it requires considerable labour, and yields, after all, no very profitable grains. The principal are Muckhye (Indian corn), Kodo Murrova, some species of Ghya (a dry coarse rice), and Toori: they also raise in these situations some barley, wheat, cotton, Kagnos, or millet, Suma, and Phaphun. These articles are chiefly consumed by the husbandmen themselves, and others among the lower classes of the people. The cultivator pays the jaghiredar, or government, not according to the produce of his labour (which regularly would be the Buttye, or half), but a cess proportionate to the number of his ploughs or spades: widows are permitted to cultivate as much Kohrya land as they can, without being cessed at all. Considering the difficulty of bringing lands of this nature into cultivation, and the general scarcity of inhabitants throughout these mountainous regions, it is probable the government draws but little revenue from them.

Fourth. The Kaith lands. The Kaith, or plantation lands, are of the first quality, being well watered by springs and rivulets, having a rich soil, and yielding, with moderate labour, all the superior kinds of grain; they are principally situated in the valleys, the lowest of which are, generally speaking, the most fertile; but they are not uncommon even in the higher lands, some of which are abundantly supplied with water. The superficial contents of a Kaith of a hundred Moories are equal to about four Biggahs, and thirds of a Biggah.

The divisions of a Kaith are as follow:

20 Pathies	1 Moorie ($18\frac{3}{4}$ Dhoors of Bengal).
20 Moories	1 Beeswa.
5 Beeswas	1 Kaith.

It is to be observed, however, that this is not properly land measurement, the Pathie and Moori being strictly measures of capacity; nor are Kaiths universally of the same superficial area; but being for the most part equal to about four Biggahs, and two-thirds,* Bengal measurement, and estimated to produce one hundred Moories of grain in the husk, the term is used to convey a fixed idea of superficial quantity, though in a restrained sense it signifies merely a field or plantation.

The proper land-measure of the valley of Nepaul, or of the Newars, is the Roopni, which is equivalent to three Cottahs and three quarters of Bengal. Four Moories make one Roopni, and five Roopnis are equal to a Beeswa, or twenty-five to a hundred Moories, of which last, twenty-one, and rather better than a third, go to one Biggah.

The Biggah is used in the measurement of plantations by the Purbutties only, by which appellation the occupiers of the hilly regions in general surrounding the valley of Nepaul are distinguished from the Newars, or proper inhabitants of the latter, though the term seems most appropriate to those of the western Chaster. The subdivisions of the Biggah are as follows:

2 Hauts or cubits square	1 Renoo.
9 Renoos	1 Dhoor (of Bengal.)

* Or exactly to 4 Biggahs, 13 Cottahs, and 15 Dhoors.

18¾ Dhoors	1 Moori.
4 Moories (or 75 Dhoors)	3¾ Cottahs.
21⅓ Moories nearly (or 20 Cottahs)	1 Biggah.

The Pathie contains eight Manas, and a Mana (which they rate at ten Mooties, or handfuls) is equal in capacity to five Chuttacks three Siccas, Bengal bazar weight; the Pathie may therefore be stated at two Seers, three quarters, and five Siccas, and the Moorie of course at fifty-six Seers, or a Maund and sixteen Seers, Bengal bazar weight, measuring (it is proper to observe) with Dhan or Paddy, by which is meant rice in the husk.

The Dharni is a sort of steelyard, in use not only in Nepaul but in Tibet; it is employed in weighing oil, lumber, ghee, salt, metals, &c. but not grain, and is graduated in a very minute manner; the principal divisions of the scale are the following:

the Dharni, or extreme degree, denoting a weight equal to 2½ Seers, Bengal bazar weight.

the Hummali ¾ of a Dharni (or 3 Seers of Nepaul, each of sixteen Gundahs).

the Bessowli ½ Dharni.

the Barchpul ⅓.

the Authpul ¼.

the Charpul ⅛.

The Seer of Nepaul, it may be right to notice, has lately been raised, in certain transactions, to 17 Gundahs.

The lowest price at which good Kaith Paddy (or rice in the husk) sells, even in the most plentiful times, is a rupee the Moori.

In seasons of calamity (occasioned by hail-storms or blights) it has been known to rise as high as a rupee per quarter Moori; the medium rate would appear to be three-quarters of a Moori, or fifteen Pathies (that is forty-two Seers) the rupee. During our stay in Nepaul, however, middling rice sold at four Pathies, or about seven Seers and a quarter the rupee, which is equivalent to nearly eight Pathies of Paddy the rupee, the ordinary product of a Moori of Paddy being ten Pathies of rice properly so called, or rice separated from the husk. The Mana contains seven Chuttacks, the Pathie, three Seers and a half, and the Moori seventy Seers, or a Maund and three-quarters; thus a Maund of rice, Bengal bazar weight, is equal to eleven Pathies three Manas and a half.

The usual produce of a Kaith is, as has been already said, a hundred Moories, or one hundred and forty Maunds of Paddy; but taking it at 90, and supposing the price of grain in the ear to be at what is considered the medium stage, or three-quarters of a Moori the rupee, a Kaith, one year with another, does not yield in money less than one hundred and thirty-three rupees.

The proprietor of the Kaith divides the produce of it equally with the cultivator, who in return is at all the charges of tillage, unless seed be excepted, of which the proprietor would appear, in some instances, to contribute his share. In the generality of Kaiths seed is reckoned to yield from twenty to thirty fold, "Gherame Mooti," or a handful in a seed, being a proverbial expression in this country, employed to denote the great fruitfulness of the soil.

Besides the Buttye, or half of the produce, it is very common for the jaghiredar, or Tul Singh, as he is called by his renters, to receive from the farmer with whom he engages, a fine or premium of two rupees and a half per Kaith, or one hundred Moories; and unless the soil be of a very inferior quality, this bargain is considered to be extremely favourable to the cultivator.

Though one or two men might, if time allowed, plough a Kaith very well, yet as several hands are required to sow and reap it, there can be but a small proportion of it separately managed by the jaghiredar, or occupier, however numerous his family may be. He generally, therefore, satisfies himself with cultivating a few Moories, in which he usually raises fruit or vegetables, leaving the rest to the Mohi, or undertaker, with whom he engages. Many Kaiths yield three harvests, one of rice, one of wheat, pulse, &c. and one (sometimes two) of Tori, an excellent vegetable so called. There are some grounds which yield two crops of rice successively (one fine, the other coarse), besides affording in the same year a wheat crop. The sugar-cane is cultivated a good deal in the Kaiths about Doona-baisi and Noakote, and is a profitable article; but as the culture is expensive, the jaghiredars rarely raise more of it than they require for their own consumption. The seed is sown invariably by women.

The following detail of the charges attending the culture of a Kaith of one hundred Moories may serve to throw some additional light on the state of agriculture in this country.

	Ploughs.	Rup.	An.
55 ploughs, at 12 ploughs per rupee. (viz.) - - -		4	9¼
For Purthi-joaht, or first turning up the soil -	20		
For Oakhlaouna, or second ploughing -	15		
For Heelo, or Kadokurna, or third ploughing -	10		
For Sehâno, or fourth ploughing - -	10		
	55		
82 labourers at 1 rupee per 24 labourers, (viz). -		3	7
For seeding - - - -	40		
For conducting and distributing the water from the adjacent springs or rivulets, called Ahree Châtna	10		
For mounding or damming the Ahrees -	10		
For plucking and binding the first shoots of rice	12		
For transplanting ditto - -	2		
For levelling and clearing the field - -	5		
For removing the first shoots for transplantation	3		
	82		
For one day's diet to labourers, 24 Pathies of coarse rice at 10 Pathies per rupee - - - - -		2	6½
For seed, viz. 5 Moories, at 15 Pathies per rupee -		6	10½
For Salami, or fine paid by the farmer or undertaker to the jaghiredar, or proprietor - - -		2	8
Total Nepaul Rupees		19	9¼

Some plantations of the more valuable productions of husbandry are conducted at as high an expence as two rupees the Roapni, or fifty rupees the Kaith. Kaiths of this description, however, are cultivated under conditions different from others, the proprietor of them usually receiving from the farmer, instead of Bettye, twenty-five Moories (or a quarter) of the produce, and two Maunds and a half of oil of Sissoo.

With regard to the plough, it is proper to notice, that it is scarcely known among the Newars; it being only very recently that a few of those occupying the lands about Thankote have been prevailed on to employ this instrument of tillage, their prejudice against the use of which would seem to have originated in the extraordinary reverence they entertain for the bullock, since, though they have no scruples with regard to buffaloes, they deem it the highest sacrilege to approach even the image of the former animal, except in a posture of adoration; insomuch, that a malicious person wishing to suspend the agricultural operations of his neighbour, would be sure to effect his purpose by placing a stone or wooden figure of a cow in the midst of his field.

The Newars prepare their ground for the rice-seed by digging it to a certain depth with a sort of spade called Cham Koodali, or Koo; turning up the soil in ridges, as in potatoe plantations, leaving the whole for some time to be well flooded, and finally levelling the field. This mode, though very laborious, is said to be full as productive to the farmer, as that of ploughing.

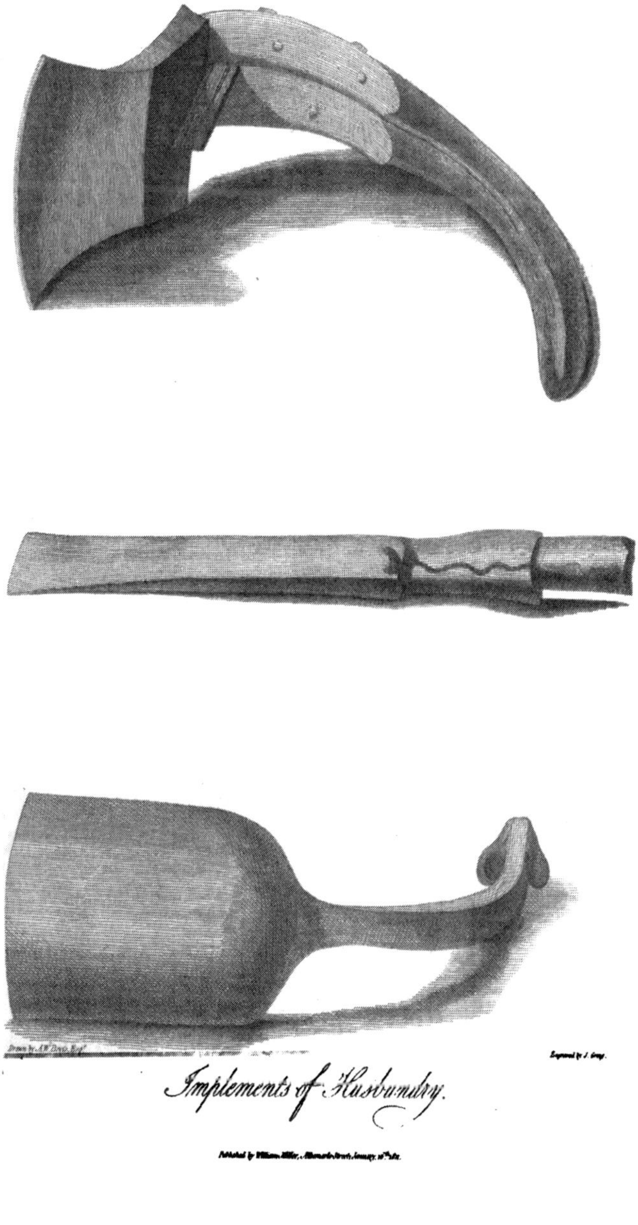

Drawn by A.W. Devis, Esq. Engraved by J. Gray.

Implements of Husbandry.

Published by William Miller, Albemarle Street, January 16th 1812.

It is to be observed, that the foregoing operations are severally performed, or supposed to be performed, in one day; the net profit of the farmer or manager, agreeably to the preceding statement, and taking the produce and price of grain as before, is therefore about forty-seven rupees.

The Purbutties, or the peasantry of the mountainous country, are divided into four classes, denominated Owal, Doem, Seoom, and Chaurem, which are Persian terms, denoting first, second, third, and fourth; this is the more remarkable as no such division of the order of husbandmen would appear to have been made at any time by the Mogul government. The Owals are those peasants who possess five ploughs and upwards; the Doems such as have from one to five; the Seooms are those who, without being proprietors of ploughs, are considered to be at the head of a few or more labourers; the Chaurems are the mere labourers, the price of their labour, whether received in money or grain, being called Nemiak. The lands of Nepaul proper are cultivated almost without exception by Newars, those to the westward, as Noakote, &c. by the Purbutty tribe called Dhenwar.

The Ryots, or peasantry, are distinguished also into Kohrya and Perjah; the former are those settled in Birtha proprietory, or other rent-free lands, and are not liable to be called on by government for any services except the repair of roads, and attendance on the army upon particular occasions. Those Perjahs who occupy lands actually belonging to the Prince, though, perhaps, in the immediate possession of jaghiredars, are, on the contrary, obliged to perform various services, both at the call of the jaghiredar, and of the Prince.

The expenses of the military establishments of this country are for the most part discharged by assignments of land, though in some instances the soldier receives his pay from the treasury, and occasionally from the granary; others are paid partly in money, and partly in land, but the most usual mode, and the one most agreeable to the troops, is that of putting them in possession of Kaiths, on which they very commonly settle their families, whom they can maintain much better in this manner, than by the pecuniary stipend to which they would be otherwise entitled.

There would not appear to be any fixed rate for determining either the quantity or quality of the Kaiths of the several ranks, much depending on the interest of the parties, and other incidental circumstances; and as to the situation of these lands, it is for the most part, as has already been noticed, constantly fluctuating. Subahdars, or commanders of companies of sepoys (of which they have between fifty and sixty of various strength, from 288 to 120 men), receive from fifteen to twenty, and even twenty-four Kaiths, some of which comprehend villages. A jemadar has from seven to twelve Kaiths; what the lower ranks receive in land, I do not exactly know; but in money and land together the pay of the private sepoy amounts to about seventy-six rupees per annum, exclusive of his coat, which is supplied by Government.

One of the jemadars of the Rajah's company of guards informed me that he held three Kaiths, which yielded him (after dividing with the cultivator) about sixty rupees per Kaith, or one hundred and eighty rupees; and that he further received from the treasury two hundred and eighty rupees per annum. He added, that he had been much better off when he belonged to a private company, as he then, instead of receiving any portion of his pay in money, enjoyed sometimes ten, and sometimes twelve tolerably productive Kaiths. It is proper to be observed in this place, that, generally speaking, the Government has so much consideration for its military and other public servants, as to apportion their jaghires to the numbers of their families, being particularly indulgent to the widows, orphans, and other destitute branches of them. Many young men not yet capable of bearing arms hold Kaiths; these indulgences, however, are not so common at present as they were under Purthi Nerain, or even during the reign of his successor.

Some of the villages occasionally bestowed in jaghire, are of considerable value, yielding from three to five thousand rupees annual revenue; they are managed by a Doobaria and a Mizaria, the latter of which terms is evidently from the Arabic, signifying a head husbandman, and being nearly equivalent to the Mukkuddam of Hindostan. The revenues of a village, exclusive of what arises from the produce of such lands as may be annexed to it, consist principally in the rent of houses, and the

Sair, or duties charged on salt, tobacco, pepper, beetle-nut, and similar articles of general consumption. The proprietor or occupant of a village is also entitled to the fines levied on the perpetration of certain crimes, among which the chief are those denominated Punchuk-hut, the number whereof, as the name implies, is five; being, 1. Ghow-hut, or mal-treatment of a Gow; 2. Stub-hut, or ill-usage of a woman; 3. Atma-huttea, or wounding one's self (a violence not unfrequently committed by particular descriptions of Hindoos for sinister purposes); 4. Pur-huttea, or wounding another; and 5. Toona, or Kool. Adultery (termed here, significantly enough, Chak-chukwye, in allusion to the habits of the bird called by Europeans the Brahminy Goose), is likewise fineable in some cases; the injured party, however, is at liberty to put the offenders to death, if he has the power of reaching them immediately on the commission of the crime. The woman often has her nose slit, or cut off, in which case she becomes a slave, the property in her vesting in the proprietor of the village.

CHAPTER V.

ROUTE FROM DOONA TO KHATMANDA.

Mahaise River—Roghalia—Deoralli—Koolpoo River and Valley—Koomhara—Bailkote-kola—Valley of Noakote—Tadi River—Temple and Town of Noakote—Paloong-târ Valley—Daiby Ghaut—Temple of Bhowani.—Gogimara—Brahminical and Chetree Tribes—Mountains of Himma-leh and Jibjibia—Animal and Vegetable Productions of the Valley of Noakote—Bheerbundy Mountain—View from its Summit—Kowhilai-peak—Bishnmutty River—Dherimsilli—Temple of Mahadeo—Sumboonath—Jeea Plant.

P

CHAPTER V.

PROCEEDING across the Doona valley, along the southern border of which, and close by the north foot of the Doona-baisi mountain, flows a small rivulet in a westerly direction, we reached, at the distance of half a mile, a low hill, round the shoulder of which we passed to the Mahaise river; this stream has its rise in Boorhadanga, one of the hills that separate Nepaul from Doona-baisi; it has here a west by south course, and probably preserves nearly the same till it empties itself into the Tirsoolgunga, which it does very soon; its banks are romantic, and its breadth about forty feet. Immediately after fording it, we ascended a tolerably high hill lying before us, the acclivity of which is rendered on the whole pretty easy by being broken into steps, a small flat with a few huts occurring about midway up. This hill and village both bear the name of Roghalia. From hence is a view of the road which leads from Thankote to Doona-baisi, bearing nearly S.E. by S.; from this situation a sort of temples are also seen rising from an eminence bearing E. S. E. called Bheem-doka, of which we had another view from the south end of Khatmanda, whence it bore about north-west.

Directly east of Roghalia, about a mile and a half, is a handsome village called Deoralli; this part of the hill is united to the adjacent one by a kind of natural causeway seventy or eighty yards in extent, on each side of which is a chasm some hundred feet in depth. The breadth of this curious passage being in some places barely sufficient to admit of a hammock, it did not appear totally free from danger. After crossing the causeway we began to descend; the first part of the descent consists of several sharp turnings round the west face of the hill, upon getting to the north side of which the declivity is at first tolerably gentle, but towards the end extremely abrupt. At the bottom passes the Koolpoo river, the bed of which is here of a considerable breadth; its course is nearly the same with that of the Mahaise: its sources are in the summit of a hill called Judpoor, which terminates the head of the Koolpoo valley. Judpoor is a sort of spur issuing from the south-east side of mount Bheerbundy, in descending from which to the valley of Nepaul, you pass very near the springs of the Koolpoo. The river discharges itself into the Tirsoolgunga above, or to the eastward of the confluence of the Mahaise with the same stream; several waters issue from the south side of mount Koomhara, and uniting in their course towards the valley below, rush together at a right angle into the Koolpoo, just at the ford by which we crossed it.

The country between Doona-baisi and Koolpoo-baisi is exceeding pleasant, being, in general, well cultivated, sprinkled with flowering and forest-trees of various sorts, and presenting a considerable diversity of picturesque views. The pine is among the spontaneous productions of this space, and excels in size and straightness any that we met with to the northward of Cheeriaghati. The turpentine adhering to those parts of the trees in which incisions had been made for the purpose of obtaining it, exactly resembled icicles, not only in transparency and colour, but also in its crystallized figure, its fragrance at the same time being uncommonly agreeable. We saw many pines, whose trunks had been set fire to with the view of procuring the turpentine more readily.

This valley, which is called Koolpoo-baisi, stands rather higher than that of Doona-baisi, but affords by no means such delightful views. We encamped very near the south foot of Koomhara, between two of the streams that flow from that mountain. Our prospect was here rather limited, and the pleasant part of it was that which we had left behind. On the west we were enclosed by hills, containing iron mines, the produce whereof is smelted in other hills (better suited, it would seem, for that operation) lying to the eastward of our station, not much further to the westward of which it was pretended that a silver mine had been recently discovered, though not opened. The beds of the streams which spring from the south face of Koomhara mountain are strewed with huge blocks of talc of two or three kinds; the most esteemed is the *Koushno-abruck*, or black talc.

After quitting Koolpoo bottom, or valley, we ascended the south-side of mount Koomhara by a road far the worst of any that occurred in the whole journey, being for the most part exceedingly steep, and lying in many places along the edges of frightful precipices, to say nothing of the great height of the mountain, and the number of rocks necessary to be clambered over in the course of the ascent. The fact is, that this route is scarcely at all in use, being quite out of the way of all but the inhabitants of the valleys of Doona and Koolpoo, whose intercourse with Noakote cannot be very considerable. Rugged, however, as this declivity is, great part of it is laid out in Kaiths, or rice-fields, which are abundantly supplied with water by the numerous springs that issue from this face of the mountain, on the top of which stands the village of Koomhara, consisting of twenty or thirty houses. From this commanding situation is a very noble prospect, comprehending, in front, a continued chain, to a great distance, on each side of the Kuchâr, or lower Tibet, and of all the uneven tract that stretches from thence to the north foot of Koomhara, the whole forming a sublime amphitheatre of hills gradually rising to mountains, and mountains to alps, the latter being terminated by the stupendous Himma-leh, of which, however, we had to lament that the view, though extensive, was too often interrupted by the nature of the interjacent country. This landscape likewise embraces broken views, or occasional glimpses, of the Tirsoolgunga, the Tadi, and various other streams of less note, beautifully serpentining through the subjacent valleys. Below, in the same direction, are also seen the ruined castle of Bailkote, and town of Noakote, which though situated on hills of no contemptible height, scarcely appear, from Koomhara, to be elevated above the level of the valley. To the southward, the perspective, though not so magnificent, is not less interesting.

The ascent of Koomhara mountain, by the road, is about three miles and a half; the acclivity, however, is not continuous, passing partly over a spur, or lower hill, projecting as it were in the manner of a wing or shoulder from the main one, and communicating with it by a path not less than a mile and a quarter in extent, but, however difficult in other respects, of no great steepness. The latter part of the ascent (in which scarcely any other plant is met with than the Bhâng, or holly-leafed oak), is somewhat less than a mile; but the most perpendicular of the whole. The descent, reckoning from the summit, or village of Koomhâra, to the actual termination of the declivity on the Noakote side (which you cannot be said to reach till you have passed beyond Bailkote, a mile and a quarter), is full five miles and a half; this declivity, however, is in the latter part very gradual. For the first mile and a half, during which the road winds but little, it is rather steep, but is pleasantly lined or shaded with wild fruit, and other forest-trees, many of them of a flowering kind; you then come to a small flat at no great horizontal distance from Bailkote; from whence there is another descent of two miles and a half, at the termination of which is a grist-mill, turned by one of the seven or eight torrents that issue from the north side of mount Koomhara and form the Bailkote-kola, which after tumbling for a short space over some huge rocks, mingles very soon with the Tadi at Narain Ghar, a deep bottom or hollow situated near the south skirt of Chundi-baisi hill. The diameter of the mill-stone in this mill did not exceed two feet and a half; and the whole of the machine was on the simplest construction, as they every where are in this country, in which, I understand, they are very common; the stream that turned it, though it descended rapidly, was not above two feet broad; it made in a day and night, during the driest weather, about six Patna Maunds of meal. Close to the mill is a small cultivated level, on which we pitched our tents; but from hence the descent continues better than a mile further, the road, or rather way (for there was no beaten path), lying throughout over ploughed fields constructed one lower than the other in the manner already described, and called Ghoor Ghar, so that we literally descended to the west point of Muddenpoor-hill, or within half a mile of the Tadi, by an irregular flight of steps. After entering the bed of the Tadi (which passes here about west and by south) we proceeded two miles in a N. E. by N. direction, principally along its southern margin, and crossed it just at the south foot of Noakote-hill, which was the quarter assigned for our encampment during the residence of the court in this valley. The town and temple of Noakote, situated on the summit above us, bore from our tents north-west, distance about a mile and a half.

The valley of Noakote is of very inconsiderable extent; its greatest length, which stretches from about north-east to south-west, not exceeding four or five miles, and its breadth being nowhere more than a mile and a half, or two miles. The Tadi, which is here a broad stream, passes through the midst of it, and with such rapidity as would entirely destroy the fields which it fertilizes, if it were not here and there confined within its channel by strong embankments of stone: the dread entertained of its ravages is nevertheless very great, as it sometimes descends in such a body, and with so much violence, as to surmount these artificial barriers, on which occasions the autumnal crop, especially, is liable to be swept away, just as it is ready to be reaped; nor does the mischief stop here, for the land is in such cases cut into deep ravines, the filling up of which the succeeding season is a work of immense labour. To counterbalance these evils, the soil of this valley is exceedingly fruitful, and notwithstanding its great vicinity and exposure to the snowy mountains that enclose it to the northward, is capable of bearing all the vegetable productions of Bahar, in which, indeed, there probably is not a single species of grain raised, that may not be met with here. The rice of Noakote is in particular estimation, the finest kind being called Jeera Serri, and selling, on an average, at the rate of twelve Pathies per rupee, in the husk.

This valley, besides being immediately surrounded by very stupendous mountains (exclusive of the Himma-leh and Kuchâr ranges), on the summits of which snow lies in the winter during several days, is reckoned to be the lowest, if not of any in the Nepaul territories, at least of all those in the vicinity of Nepaul proper; and indeed the barometer denoted it to be but little elevated above Hettowra, the mean height of the mercury, for two or three days in the middle of March, being 28.24 inches, which gives no more than a difference of about sixty yards; whereas, in the valley of Nepaul, separated from Noakote only by Bheerbundy mountain, the mean height of the barometer during nine days towards the end of March was 25.75 inches, indicating a difference in elevation of no less than 2205 feet in favour of Nepaul. This fact will sufficiently account for the great height of the temperature of Noakote valley, the mean of which, from the 3d to the 17th of March, was 70½ degrees, the extreme heat, during this period, having been 98 degrees, and the least 54 degrees: the observations* were made between six in the morning, and nine at night, chiefly in a tent, without a fly, but occasionally in a tent having one, and with two or three thermometers by Dolland, graduated according to Fahrenheit's scale. The sun did not appear in this valley on the 15th March till near half after six o'clock.

The Tadi issues from a lake or bason called Soorey-koondeh, which is embosomed by the lofty mountains lying immediately to the north-east of Dhyboon, and just below Himma-leh. This lake is not more than two or three miles from the springs of the Tirsoolgunga, to the eastward of, and somewhat above which, it is situated. The Tadi, called also the Soorey-mutty (after its parent waters), runs, during the earlier part of its course, at a very inconsiderable distance from the Tirsoolgunga, from which, however, it soon

* The number of which were one hundred and three.

separates, turning off rather abruptly to the eastward. The first place of any note by which it passes is Phalchoak, a Bhootia town about nine miles south-east of Neel-khent, or the sources of the Tirsoolgunga; hence it proceeds winding through the Kuchâr ridge in a south-west direction, to Kerumboo, which is about eleven miles from Phalchoak, and three days' journey from Khatmanda. Continuing nearly the same course for nine or ten miles, it flows through Sindhoo-baisi, after which it strikes off directly west towards Noakote, on the south side of which it passes, while the Tirsoolgunga, separated from it only by the hill on which Noakote stands, runs along the opposite base. Here the Tadi, augmented by the waters of the Sindoora and Bailkote rivulets, winds round the south point of the Chundi-baisi hill (remarkable for its red soil, as is also that of Noakote, of which it is indeed a sort of descending spit,) whence it proceeds for about three miles in a W. S. W. direction, mingling with, and yielding its name to, the Tirsoolgunga at Daiby Ghaut. The eel of the Tadi is of the largest kind I ever met with, and not inferior in taste to the best; it abounds also with a very fine fish called Usla, which differs nothing in flavour, and very little in appearance, from the Helsa, or sable-fish of Bengal. The Phaketa, another species of small fish found in the Tadi, is remarkable both for the swiftness with which it glides through the water, and the singular construction of its superior fins, which resemble a fan both in point of figure and in the manner in which they open and close.

The temple of Noakote is dedicated to Maha Mai, or Bhowani; it stands on the brow of the hill, the ascent to which from our station below was for the greatest part of the way by a flight of steps cut out of the side of it. The building is of brick, and has nothing very striking in its appearance. The accumulated offerings to the goddess suspended from the projecting roofs (which incline to the pent-house form) appeared tolerably numerous, consisting, however, almost entirely of brass vessels, and weapons of various sorts. Among the latter were several trophies acquired during the recent contest with the Chinese. I had been told, previous to my visit, that this temple was also decorated by some arms lost by Captain Kinloch's detachment; but either my information was not correct, or they had been removed in compliment to me. The town of Noakote adjoins the temple, occupying a sort of terrace that stretches northerly towards Maha-mundul, or the highest peak of this mountain, immediately below which the Tirsoolgunga passes. This town is not of any great extent, but it contains some of the largest and best-looking houses to be seen in Nepaul.

Noakote is the favourite residence of the regent Behadur Shah, who was born here. It was also for a long while the station of Purthi Nerain's court, being one of the first places which that prince wrested from the Newar sovereign of Khatmanda, and from whence he prosecuted his invasion of Nepaul:* its situation is of

* See Chapter VIII.

importance, as it commands the only entrance in this quarter from upper as well as lower Tibet, standing immediately opposite, and close to, mount Dhyboon, by which the Chinese army was obliged to descend, when proceeding through the Kheroo pass; this army penetrated almost to the foot of Maha-mundul. The several posts occupied respectively by the Chinese and Nepaul forces during their conflict in the environs of this place, were pointed out to us from the summit of Noakote.

The acclivity of Noakote hill was not so difficult as to prevent my mounting almost to the summit in my palankeen, which I was not obliged to quit till I had reached within a few yards of the foot of the temple, where the ascent is exceeding steep. I was three quarters of an hour in descending, through a road pleasantly shaded by the several varieties of trees which constitute the usual natural growth of these mountains.

The valley of Noakote is not habitable after the middle of April, on account of the excessive heats, which then begin to generate the Owl. If the Regent, therefore, at any time happen to prolong his stay here to that late period, he quits the valley, and repairs to the town of Noakote. His visit, however, does not often exceed the duration of the cold weather, which, though rather severe at Khatmanda, is very mild in this valley. There are no buildings here for the accommodation either of the Regent or his retinue, so that during the residence of the court in the valley, the whole remain under cover of tents or temporary huts, which last are of the simplest construction, and easily and quickly raised in all situations, since they consist of nothing more than a few boughs of trees rudely disposed so as to afford a scanty shelter from the effects of wind and weather. It is in felling small trees or shrubs, and lopping the branches of others for this purpose, that the dagger, or knife worn by every Nepaulian, and called Khookheri, is chiefly employed; it is also of very great use, as I repeatedly experienced, in clearing away the road when obstructed by the low hanging boughs of trees, and other similar impediments. There were not, I believe, more than two small Pauls, or tents, among the whole of the deputation that escorted us from Patna, although the brother of the Rajah, one of his principal ministers, the commander of his guards, and the governor of a province, were of the party; excepting those who lodged in the tents, they all either halted every stage of our journey, in the manner just described, or took up their quarters beneath the tree nearest to them.

In proceeding from Noakote valley to Daiby Ghaut, or the confluence of the Tirsoolgunga and Tadi, we passed over Chundi-baisi hill, which is a kind of narrow spit separating those rivers in this place, and terminating by an easy descent just at the union of the two streams. The top of it is tolerably level, and contains some inclosed fruit gardens. The Tadi is not visible from it, being concealed by a swelling of the hill on the west side: but the Tirsoolgunga is seen meandering on the right, through a beautiful

The Khookeri.

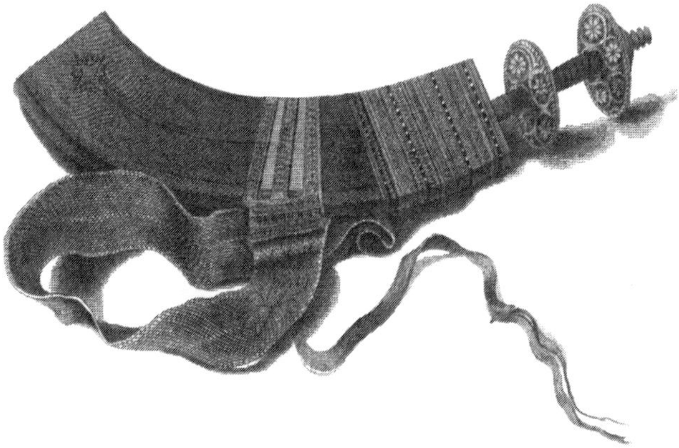

Drawn by A. W. Davis, Esq. — Engraved by J. [illegible]

The Khora.

Published by William Miller, [illegible] Street, January [illegible]

valley called Paloong-târ. Târ properly signifies a wild or uncultivated valley, in contradistinction to Baisi, or Biasi, which is applied only to valleys in a state of improvement. It is necessary, however, to notice here, that the appellation Târ does not suit the present condition of this valley, which has of late been brought into very high cultivation.

Daiby Ghaut bears about W. S. W. of Noakote, from which it is distant between three and four road miles. There is a rude temple at this place, dedicated to Daiby, or the Goddess, as Maha Mai, or Bhowani, is emphatically styled by way of pre-eminence. Here sacrifices are occasionally offered to her in her character of the universal mother, or, in other words, as Nature; the officiating priests at which, are usually Newars, those people considering Bhowani as the tutelar divinity or patroness of their tribe. These oblations consist principally of buffaloes, on the flesh of which the ministers of the goddess unscrupulously regale, a special revelation of her divine will having some years ago rendered it lawful for the Newars to feed at all times upon this animal. The occasion of their obtaining so extraordinary a dispensation is closely connected with their origin as a nation, and will be hereafter mentioned in the sketch which I have given of their history. It is sufficient in this place to notice, that, notwithstanding so revolting a deviation from the Brahminical dogma, the Newars, though certainly holding no high rank among the various Hindoo tribes at present occupying Nepaul, would not by any means appear to be in a state of religious degradation, whatever their civil or political condition may be. There are many doctrinal opinions common to them and the stricter or more respectable sects, who occasionally assist at some of their rites; the Rajah and his court immolating, for instance, during our stay at Noakote, a vast number of buffaloes, and other perfect male animals, at the temple of Daiby Ghaut. Indeed, though the Regent of Nepaul cannot possibly be surpassed by any secular Hindoo, either in devoutness or superstition, yet he would not seem to consider the inviolability even of the type of Mahadeo himself in a very rigid light; since his army, in the late expedition into Tibet, having been reduced to such cruel straits as obliged them to feed upon the flesh of the Chouri bullock, he ingeniously repelled the imputation of sacrilege, by logically observing, that, as the cattle which they had slaughtered and eaten were not of the kind distinguished by long dew-laps, and as this was a necessary generic mark of the sacred bull of the Shaster, it plainly followed, that they had not transgressed against the law. It was somewhat in the same spirit of regulated zeal, that, upon certain missionaries offering to instruct him in the most useful branches of mineralogy and metallurgy (respecting which this Prince is very curious), provided he would embrace the Christian faith, he coolly replied, that his rank in the state made it inconvenient for him to accede to the proposed terms, but that he was ready to substitute two or three men who should make as good proselytes as himself. The missionary rejecting this expedient, and the Regent not comprehending, or affecting not to comprehend, why three souls should be of less estimation than one, very gravely inferred that the holy father could only be prevented from accepting so fair a proposal, by the desire of concealing his ignorance of the arts which he had professed himself qualified to teach.

To return from this digression; the sanctity of Daiby Ghaut is of such high account, that the late Rajah, Singh Pertaub, chose it for his last terrestrial stage; here too he was accompanied in death by one of his wives, the mother of the present Bâjoo Seer, a younger brother of the reigning Prince, and a youth of no inconsiderable promise. The mother of Run Behadur was far from imitating this example of posthumous attachment; for deeming it pleasanter to rule after, than die with her lord, she declined the honour of ascending his funeral pile. She long directed the affairs of this country on behalf of her infant son, with no less ability than success, the present Regent never being able, during her life, to obtain the smallest participation in the government.*

The scenery around Daiby Ghaut is of the wildest and most romantic kind, exhibiting hills of various elevations confusedly heaped together, and for the most part thickly clothed with forests. On one side rolls the Tadi over a stony bed, in the midst, and along either margin of which, are strewed numerous huge rocks, severed at different periods from the mountains which here constitute the stupendous banks of this sacred stream; on the other hand rushes in a broader but rather less precipitous current, the

* See p. 273.

equally holy Tirsoolgunga. The waters of both rivers are perfectly transparent; but their temperature varies at the point of their confluence, that of the Tirsoolgunga being many degrees colder than the other. The fact was familiar to the natives, who accounted for it by observing that the course of the Tadi, especially the lower part of it, lying through a soil comparatively bare and open, while the bed of the Tirsoolgunga was confined, for the most part, between narrow bottoms formed by steep mountains covered to their base with over-hanging forests, the latter river was necessarily colder, because less exposed in its progress to the action of the solar heat.

I shall have occasion to speak elsewhere of the source of the Tirsoolgunga; with respect to its course, after its junction with the Tadi, when it becomes so deep and considerable a stream as to be impassable in the driest season of the year, excepting in canoes (only one of which I saw plying at the Ghauts), my information barely enables me to state generally, that it passes successively through the valleys of Goojoore-târ, Seesa-baisi, and Jogimara, near the last of which places, uniting with the Mursiangdi (a river that rises from one of the snowy ridges of lower Tibet), it pursues a westerly direction till it disembogues into the Gundi at Deo Ghaut.* Throughout the whole of this space, which is described to

* Deo Ghaut is a place of considerable sanctity, the waters of the Tirsoolgunga, the Gundi, the Mursiangdi, and the Saite, mingling at, or near it, with the Kali Gunduck, or Sâlegrâm.

be exceeding wild and mountainous, its navigation is said to be utterly impracticable; not so much, however, on account of the rocky channel in which it runs, as owing to the rapidity of its stream; because, though its descent is probably not a little abrupt in some parts, yet the total declivity between Daiby Ghaut and Deo Ghaut would not appear to be sufficient to authorize the idea of its giving rise any where to considerable cataracts. The road from Daiby Ghaut to Jogimara is carried along the east side of the Tirsoolgunga; the distance being five journies, or about a hundred and twenty miles. Jogimara is usually mentioned with the adjunct of Oopadroong, from a mountain of this name, which rises from the opposite bank of the Tirsoolgunga.

The Tirsoolgunga, previous to the conquest of Nepaul by Purthi Nerain, separated the territories of the Ghoorkhali and Newar Princes, the western limit of Ghoorkha being marked by the Mursiangdi. This tract contains, besides a pretty numerous peasantry of Dhenwars, several Rajepoot families, and some Newars; but the tribes by whom it is chiefly occupied, are of the Brahminical, and Chetree orders; and as these last constituted the principal strength of Purthi Nerain's government, and continue to form the main support of the present one, they rank very high among its subjects, no description of whom possesses such considerable credit and authority as their leaders enjoy. They consist, for the most part, of the Khus and Mangur tribes of the Chetree class; and of the Paure and some other casts of Brahmins; their chieftains are known by the appellation of Thurgur (or one inhabiting a nest) among whom, (with the exception of a few individuals deriving their descent from the same stock as the reigning Prince, and who are consequently Rajepoots), are to be found by far the greatest part of those who conduct the affairs of this state. Their number, strictly speaking, is limited to thirty-six, for though, in loose language, every individual of those clans is sometimes styled a Thurgur, yet the title properly descends only to the heads of certain families. Nor are all these of equal consideration, there being three gradations of this order, of whom the pre-eminent one is denominated Chutter, on account of its consisting of six chiefs. It is from the Chutters that the Kâjees or Dewans are usually selected, which does not, however, prevent the other two inferior classes from being likewise eligible to this office. It is impossible for me, with the slight information which my short visit to Nepaul enabled me to collect, to describe this curious institution with all the accuracy that it would appear to deserve; I can only add to what has been said concerning it, that the leading members of this body, whether actually employed or not, appear to possess such a high authority in the state, as renders it nearly impossible for the executive government, in whatever hands that may be, to pursue any measures of an important nature, in opposition to their advice. I have even been assured, that the throne of the Prince himself would be no longer secure, should the principal Thurgurs concur in thinking that his general conduct tended to endanger the sovereignty, which they profess themselves bound, as far as rests with them, to transmit, unimpaired, to the distant posterity of its founder, and the interests of which they do not allow to be determined by the partial views, or temporary policy of the ruling individual. The great ascendency of this order is the more remarkable, as it would seem to rest almost wholly on the respect they derive from their ancient services, and attachment to the Ghoorkha family, and not to arise in the smallest degree from the ordinary sources of political influence, since I do not understand them to be particularly distinguished among their countrymen, either for their opulence, their extensive possessions, or the number of their adherents. They occasionally hold jaghires on similar terms with the soldiery, and, like them, indifferently in all parts of the Nepaul territories; but their hereditary fiefs, or estates, are situated entirely in the districts of Goorkha and Sumjoong, which constituted the patrimonial inheritance of Purthi Nerain. Besides the produce of these lands, and the emoluments arising from the offices they happen to fill, they receive an annual fine of four annas from every taxable Kaith, or plantation of a hundred Moories, throughout the country, the amount of which they would appear to distribute among their respective clans, according to rules established for the purpose. The only special immunity of a personal kind that they are said to enjoy, consists in their being exempt from the final jurisdiction of the Punjunni, or annual court of inquisition, and liable to be disgraced or punished by a decree of the Rajah alone. They formerly affected, like the Omrahs, a great simplicity of dress, justifying their practice in this point by observing, that it was with their swords, and not with the aid of fine garments, that their ancestors had raised the Goorkhali house to the respectable station which it now occupies; but whatever risk the Thurgurs might have heretofore run of incurring censure or ridicule by appearing in vestments of silk or muslin, it is pretty certain that they have latterly relaxed considerably in this point, and that there are at present some among them who are far from manifesting any solicitude to maintain inviolable this rustic characteristic of their order.

The wind, during our stay in the valley of Noakote, was almost constantly fixed between the west and south-west points; it was usually gentle till about one or two o'clock in the afternoon, when it scarcely ever failed to rise gradually, blowing at intervals in violent gusts, while the sun remained above the horizon. To what distance below Daiby Ghaut this wind is prevalent, is uncertain, but it is observable that its current corresponds exactly with the course assigned to the Tirsoolgunga, which forming a sort of funnel by means of the mountains enclosing it, may possibly contribute in some measure to its transmission. Though certainly not so hot as the westerly monsoon of Bahar, yet it was sufficiently so to render the use of Tatties very agreeable; unfortunately, it terminated but once in a wet squall, and that not till the evening before our departure from Noakote. It was owing to the want of rain that an almost perpetual mist enveloped the superior mountains to the northward of us, while we remained in the valley, from whence, therefore, we never had a single opportunity of contemplating the hither alps which constitute the Kuchâr, or lower Tibet, either with the uninterrupted attention, or in the comprehensive manner, which was so highly desirable. With respect to the further range of Himma-leh proper, the very low situation we were in would, in the finest weather, have but barely admitted of our obtaining a glimpse of a few of its peaks through the occasional opening of the interposing mountains. Notwithstanding, however, all unfavourable circumstances, our view of the Kuchâr was by no means uninteresting; it was at least very extensive, stretching to the eastward especially, to a considerable distance, and though gradually sinking in that direction to such a degree as to appear to subside finally to the level of the subjacent hills, yet exhibiting throughout, both on its shelving summit, and along its sides, abundant streaks and patches of snow, some of which reaching in several places from the top to the bottom of the ridge, presented the image of so many streams of milk rushing into the valleys below. The most striking amidst the points of view which this landscape afforded, was mount Jibjibia, which towering over all the other peaks of the Kuchâr, forms a conspicuous object not only from hence, but from Bheerbundy summit, and the valley of Nepaul. Its form is not perhaps less beautiful than curious, which renders it easy to be distinguished in all its aspects, as well as at a great distance. Hence it conduced admirably towards ascertaining the relative position of several mountains and places laid down in the accompanying map.

Jibjibia, as well as the rest of the range to which it belongs, is by no means scantily provided with wood, though it is constantly strewed with snow throughout the winter and spring, and is so liable to frequent falls during the other half of the year, that it is rarely, if ever, totally free from it.* It was too remote to allow of our discerning clearly the species of trees which covered it, but those which fringed its summit appeared through the telescope to be of the pine kind. Regarding the probable elevation of this remarkable mountain, I shall suspend my opinion till I come to describe the route to Neel-khent, or the sacred source of the Tir-sool-gunga, which is situated at the further or northern foot of Jibjibia.† Its horizontal distance from Noakote does not exceed twenty miles, though it took some country people who brought us a present of frozen snow from its vicinity, two days and a night to perform the journey. These men reported that the snow lay so deep on the road, as to render it nearly impassable; and indeed none but the Tibetians themselves will undertake to traverse the Kuchâr, except in the height of summer; the Nepaulians never venturing to set out on the pilgrimage to Neel-khent before the month of Sauren, or July and August.

Besides rice, a good deal of sugar-cane is raised in the valley of

* The state of the snow on the sides and summit of Jibjibia, and the adjoining mountains of the same range, varied almost daily while we remained at Noakote, and these variations (occasioned by alternate thaws and falls) were usually so evident, that we generally could determine in a morning whether or not it had snowed the preceding night.

† See Chapter IX.

Noakote and its neighbourhood; the Goor or brown sugar brought to market here is in small lumps, and in a much more refined state than that which is usually met with in Bengal. They have the largest garlic here I ever saw, each clove of it being of the size of the ordinary garlic of Bengal. The pine-apple of Noakote is by no means bad, but we did not meet with a single good plantain here, or in any other part of Nepaul. The people of this country plume themselves very much on their guavas, but they are, to say the most of them, no better than those of our own gardens; they have infinitely more reason to be proud of their oranges, which appear to me to be very superior to those of Silket, and, probably, indeed are not surpassed by any in the world. They are here called Santôla, which I take to be a corruption of Singterrah, the name by which a similar species of orange is known in the Upper Provinces of India. Those of Noakote are highly esteemed, but are nevertheless declared to be inferior to the Santôla of Goorkha, Sumjoong, and other more western situations. This fruit is most commonly propagated from the seed, which is sown in earthen vessels filled with a black loam, some time in the month of Assaur (July); if not exposed to the weather, they are watered twice a day; and in Kautic (November) are transplanted, a proper distance being preserved between the young shoots; the third year they bear fruit, which ripens thoroughly by the month of Aughun (November, December). The Santôla continues ordinarily in the highest perfection for three months, and preserves much of its excellence even to the end of six. Many gardens produce them throughout the whole year, but in this case the trees are obliged to be secured against the inclemencies of the weather. There is an orange-tree of a very fine kind in an area before the Rajah's palace at Khatmanda, which was loaded with fruit to the end of March. They pretended that this tree was not merely a perennial, but that if the oranges, which were then mature, were permitted to remain ungathered, they would not only become green once more, but ripen again in proper season; they affirmed the same of another fruit called Kheep. The Santôla may be raised entirely within doors, in which situation I am assured it is often known to yield very good fruit.

The Jeera Serri of Noakote has been already mentioned. To enumerate all the varieties of rice produced in this valley would be endless; the superior kinds are sown in Jait and Assaur (June, July), and reaped in Aughun (November, December). After reaping the Aughun harvest, they sow in some of the fields wheat and barley, which they gather in towards the end of April.

The Kustoora, or musk-deer, is a native of the Kuchâr, or lower Tibet, but is met more commonly in some parts of that extensive tract than in others. They would not appear, however, to be very numerous any where; and though a considerable portion of the Kuchâr is subject to the Goorkhalis, the Nepaulians procure the Kustoora principally from the vicinity of Neyat, Dhyboon, and one or two other places. This animal is most usually caught by means of a snare, made of a particular kind of mountain bamboo, of

J. Tookey sculp.t

Head of the Kustoora or Musk Deer.

Published January 1811 by W. Miller Albemarle Street

which it is reported that the whole species is occasionally blasted at once, not a single tree remaining that does not rapidly decay. The blight, however, never happening till the annual seed has fallen into the ground, the plant is abundantly renewed in due course of production. Very little pure musk is to be obtained at Khatmanda; and there is still less exported from Nepaul; indeed I have been assured, that even the musk contained in the nâfeh, or bag, still attached to the body of the animal, is not always found unadulterated, and that its purity can only be relied on when the Kustoora is received directly as a present from some person on whose lands it has recently been caught.*

The Chuckoar, Moonâl, and Damphia are natives of the same mountainous region; the two last belong to the genus of pheasants, the Damphia being of the golden, and the Moonâl of the argheer or spotted sort; they are both extremely beautiful birds; and though the latter sometimes lays eggs in its captive state, it has never been known, I am told, to hatch them. The Chuckoar is well known to the Europeans in India by the name of the Fire-eater; it is a species of partridge, and derives its latter name from its reputed power of swallowing fire: the fact, according to the people of Nepaul, is, that in the season of love this bird is remarkably fond of red or chean-pepper; after eating two or three capsules of which, it will bite at a red-hot coal if offered to it. The Chuckoar is

* The reader will find some curious particulars respecting this animal, and the musk which is obtained from it, in Captain Turner's Account of an Embassy to the Court of the Teshoo Lama, p. 200.

caught by means of a decoy of its own species surrounded by nets or springes, into which the wild ones, who are very fierce and quarrelsome, are betrayed by their eagerness to attack the captive birds.

The Khâlidge is met with in the thickets which over-run the gorges of the mountains near Noakote; it resembles the common pheasant in its appearance, but I cannot say much in commendation of its flavour. Our party went out once or twice in quest of these pheasants, but without the least success; so that I suspect they are far from abounding in this quarter. In fact, we scarcely ever saw or heard a bird of any kind after entering the mountains. I may add, that this is as bad an angling as fowling country, for though some of the rivers may almost be said to be animated, yet they are at the same time so transparent and so rapid, that the fish with which they swarm can by no means be brought to bite.

The Sârus, ortolan, wild-goose, wild-duck, and several other species of the feathered tribe common to Bengal and the rest of the countries lying to the southward of Nepaul, are occasionally seen in this and the adjacent valleys, where, however, they appear merely as birds of passage, making, as the people of these parts expressed it, only a stage of Nepaul in their flight from Hindostan to Tibet. They begin to migrate from their native plains towards the middle of April, whither they return when the elevated regions in the vicinity of Himma-leh become too inclement for their abode.

The Khalidge.

It may not be improper to notice here the Chowri and Changra of Tibet, as they are both met with in this neighbourhood, though they never descend below the Kuchâr. The Chowri, known best in Hindoostan by the name of Soori-ghâi, is the cow, the beautiful tail of which forms one of the exports from Nepaul and Tibet,* the natives of the latter eating the flesh of it without reserve, while those of Nepaul, though they affect to class it among the deer kind, on account of its having no dew-lap, do not consider it lawful food. The Changra is the shawl-goat, which I suspect to be rather scarce even in Tibet, since it is not without the greatest difficulty that a perfect male of this species can be procured, owing to the jealous vigilance employed by the Tibetians to prevent their being conveyed into foreign countries. This fact, which I derive entirely from the report of the Nepaul people,† agrees in some measure with those accounts which state the Cashmerians to be supplied either with the Changra itself, or its fleece, from Tibet, since we are pretty certain that there are no shawl stuffs of any consequence manufactured by the Tibetians, whose solicitude, therefore, respecting this animal it would not be easy to account for any other way than by supposing it to constitute a material and beneficial article of their

* This animal, called also the Yak of Tartary, is particularly described in the Account of an Embassy to the Court of the Teshoo Lama, p. 186.

† This report appears to have been unfounded; Captain Turner not only saw "multitudes" of these animals, to use his own expression, but also had several of them brought from Tibet to Bengal, from whence he sent a few to England; but they all died soon after their arrival: nor was he more successful with those which remained in Bengal. Vide ut supra, p. 356.

commerce. Both the Chowri and Changra are said to be wonderfully sagacious in discovering the safest track through the deepest snows, and on this account are sometimes employed as guides by persons travelling in the depth of winter. The sheep of Tibet are not less useful as beasts of burthen than the Changra, as guides, the Bhootias transporting on them all the salt with which they supply Nepaul; this animal, the fleece of which seems to be tolerably fine, is about the size of the largest English sheep, and carries with ease over the craggy mountains of the Kuchâr and of Nepaul, a load of twenty Seers, or nearly forty-two pounds avoirdupoise. There are two or three species bred in Nepaul, and its adjacent dependencies, the smallest of which (called Khagia) affords excellent wool: neither the woollen manufactures, however, of Tibet nor of Nepaul would appear to have attained even to mediocrity, and it is certain, that the product of their looms is as inconsiderable in quantity as it is insignificant in quality. The Joos, or flannel, procured from the former, were it really a fabric of Tibet, would, perhaps, be admitted as an exception to the latter part of this observation; but the fact is, that it is made at Siling, a place situated on the western borders of China. With respect to Nepaul, whatever its raw materials may be, still less exception can be made; since, though a kind of coarse warm serge is made here that is in some esteem in Hindostan, yet it is very little superior to the Sooi of Serinugur, which being considerably cheaper is in much more universal use.

The animal known in Bengal by the name of the Nepaul dog,

is, properly speaking, a native of the upper and lower Tibets, from whence they are brought to Nepaul: it is a fierce, surly creature, about the size of an English bull-dog, and covered with thick, long hair. The circumstance of their being good watch-dogs has given rise to the most extravagant stories concerning their vigilance, of which it may suffice, as a sample, to notice, that the Chinese army, in their late progress through Tibet, are affirmed to have employed them as centinels on the picquets which surrounded their camp.

As to the Tanguns or Tanyans, so much esteemed in India for their hardiness, they come entirely from the upper Tibet, and notwithstanding their make, are so sure-footed that the people of Nepaul ride them without fear over very steep mountains, and along the brink of the deepest precipices.

Having thus described as well as I was able whatever appeared to me worthy of notice in the valley of Noakote and its environs, I shall next proceed to the illustration of the remaining part of our actual track, comprehending the route from Noakote to Khatmanda.

After passing the Tadi, over a slight and rudely constructed bridge, consisting of a few layers of hurdles covered with a little soil, and supported by some piles of stones, we entered a gorge or recess formed by certain low hills projecting in the manner of shelving promontories from Bheerbundy. We advanced up this hollow for about half a mile, over a very rugged road, till we came to the Sindoora, a small stream which rises in Than-seen, and after a short course through the valley of Nerjah, turns off rather abruptly to the southward, to meet the Tadi, into which it throws itself a little below the point where we fell in with it; after fording this rivulet, we proceeded by a gentle acclivity about a mile and a quarter along a deep bottom strewed with rocky fragments, when we reached the foot of mount Bheerbundy, the distance of which from our station under Noakote hill, I reckon to be somewhat more than two miles. This stupendous mountain lying in the direct road from Khatmanda to Noakote, Goorkha, and the other western dominions of Nepaul, and being also the passage of a great part of the commerce carried on between Nepaul and Tibet by the way of Kheeroo, it is necessarily much frequented not only by the Court in its occasional excursions, but by various other descriptions of people. These circumstances, however, would not seem to have induced any material exertions for rendering it superior to the rest of the miserable roads in this country; for though it be true that the ascent by the west side of Bheerbundy is, notwithstanding its immense elevation, both easy and safe throughout, yet it owes this advantage almost entirely to nature, as little or no pains appear to have been taken to improve the path which traverses the eastern declivity, or that leading directly into the valley of Nepaul, and which is nearly as bad as any we met with in the course of our journey, being in two or three places carried along the brink of frightful precipices, and considerably obstructed both with loose stones and large immoveable fragments of rock. At the distance of about a mile and a half from the west foot of the mountain we passed a custom-house, where the merchandize proceeding to and from Tibet by the Kheeroo route, as well as the trade with the western territory, pays certain imposts. A little way above the custom-house there stands a Bhootia temple, which had not the appearance, however, of being much resorted to; it is a rude edifice, and in no respect deserving of further description.

The ascent of Bheerbundy from the westward is not only easy, but delightful; being covered with a hanging grove of trees, varying with the climate, to the very summit, and furnishing from certain points some highly interesting views. On the right appeared mount Koombara, united towards its summit with Bheerbundy, and therefore belonging in fact to the same ridge, but separated below by a deep narrow gorge or vale, the bottom and sides of which afforded the most pleasing proofs of population and fertility, in the hamlets scattered over them, and the corn-fields with which they were chequered. To the westward the eye looked down upon the valley of Noakote and its lively stream; nor required to be raised in order to contemplate the most elevated point interposing between the temple of Maha Mai and Daiby Ghaut. Turning next a little to the northward, the lofty Dhyboon, recently sprinkled with snow, engaged the attention, which, however, by an attraction wholly irresistible, was presently drawn off from any other object to the magnificent sight exhibited on the left, where "Ossa seemed heaped upon Pelion, and Olympus upon Ossa."

I am conscious, though, I confess, not ashamed, that I never have occasion to mention the stupendous mountains which constitute this most interesting picture, that I do not indulge in an enthusiasm of expression, as well as of imagination, that may appear either very affected, or very extravagant, both to those who have never beheld, or those who are familiar with such alpine scenes. Possibly much of the sensibility of myself and fellow travellers on this point might be owing to the circumstance of our not being at any time fortunate enough to enjoy so long or favourable a view of this sublime scenery as could sufficiently gratify even the coldest curiosity; this was the case in the present instance, for although we remained a whole day on the summit of Bheerbundy, and purposely protracted our departure till late the ensuing morning, yet the clouds hung so heavily over the northern horizon, and the intervening space was, besides, so much pervaded by a thick mist, that it was only occasionally that we obtained even an imperfect glimpse of either of the snowy ranges before us; such, nevertheless, as our prospect was, it could not prevent our observing with astonishment, that, notwithstanding the immense height to which we had ascended since quitting the valley of Noakote, the elevation of Jibjibia was not, in the smallest degree, sensibly diminished. The picturesque effect of this remarkable mountain was greatly encreased from our present point of view by the striking circumstance of one of the pyramidal peaks of Himma-leh just peeping over its towering summit. I could discern also from the same situation, and immediately to the eastward of Jibjibia (in which this mountain has already been said to subside very rapidly), what seemed to be two distinct ridges of enormous alps, the remoter rising considerably above the nearer; but it is not difficult to conceive that such an appearance might very well be produced by an irregular cluster of mountains confusedly piled one upon another. This, however, is a matter that must for the present remain undetermined, my information on the subject by no means enabling me to clear it up.

The spot occupied by our little encampment on mount Bheerbundy is distinguished by the name of Rani Powah, which may be rendered Rani Serâi, or inn, the term being in this country applied to a single building erected on a convenient situation for the accommodation of travellers. This Powah, though standing on the highest point of the pass, is much beneath the actual summit of the mountain, which rose greatly above us to the southward in a rotund peak, the sides of which were covered with brushwood, and low trees. The nature of the ground obliging us to disperse, some of the party spread themselves along a gentle acclivity that stretched from the pass towards the bottom of the superior peak, while others took possession of a small eminence on the opposite side of the road over-hanging an immense deep valley to the northward, through which the Lykhoo, after issuing from Sindoobunjan, describes a meandering course in its way to join the Sindoora. Upon this eminence the barometer stood at 24.30 in. denoting a perpendicular elevation of nearly twelve hundred yards above the valley of Noakote. The air, however, was not so sharp as might have been expected at such a great height, for though during the night the cold was pretty severe, yet on the following morning the mercury in the thermometer was not found to be lower than fifty-three degrees. I reckon the ascent of Bheerbundy by the road to be very little short of five miles, as I was about two hours and a half in mounting from the west foot of it to the top of the pass. The sun continued visible to us from this elevated station on the 16th March till thirteen minutes after six, when it did not actually set, but disappeared in a thick haze that enveloped one of the western hills.

The descent from Rani Powah to Kowhilai-peak is for the most part very gentle, the road being at the same time tolerably good, and delightfully shady for very near two miles. Kowhilai-peak overhangs from the right an angle of the declivity, on which stood formerly a castle, which was the first post occupied by Purthi Nerain, when he advanced from Noakote towards Khatmanda. From hence the road winds considerably, successively sinking and rising; occasionally passing along the brink of tremendous gulfs; and generally traversing the sides of steep and scantily wooded hills of limestone, whence several transparent brooks rush into the Koolpoobaisi, where they probably mingle with the stream already represented as flowing through that valley, into which the traveller looks down just as he is on the point of descending to the banks of the Bishnmutty. The distance from Kowhilai to this river, on reaching which you may be said to have entered the valley of Nepaul, is not less than five miles by the circuitous path we described, of which the four last are certainly in no respect deserving of the encomiums passed by our Nepaul friends on the whole of the road from Noakote to Khatmanda, which they affected to consider in the light of a royal highway, assuring me that I might proceed by it in my palankeen with perfect ease and safety.

After fording the Bishnmutty, which passes here in a westerly direction over a sandy but not very broad bed, and proceeding about a mile and a half along the slopes of some waving lands, exhibiting plentiful traces of cultivation, we reached Dherimsilli, a small town containing a few tolerable looking houses, but on the whole of a mean appearance. Continuing our way a mile further, over the same kind of swelling grounds, we again crossed the Bishnmutty, at the distance of a mile from whence stands the Arthan of Bâlâ Neel-khent embosomed in a pleasant grove, and enclosed to the westward by a hill of moderate height, which being well covered with trees, contributed both to the shadiness of the temple and its precinct, and to the picturesque effect of the general scenery.

Bâlâ (or little) Neel-khent, is a place of great sanctity, boasting a colossal image of Mahadeo, which appears in a supine position, in the midst of an oblong bason of water, constructed of stone, and supplied from springs rising in the overhanging hills. Part of the waters issuing from the latter pass off through a conduit consisting of one and twenty projecting stone pipes, fantastically carved, at the fall of which pilgrims are obliged to perform certain ablutions previous to their being admitted to worship at the shrine of the incumbent deity. Bâlâ Neel-khent is so called to distinguish it from Boora (or great) Neel-khent, which is situated a few miles to the northward of Khatmanda, and exhibits an image of the god similar in all respects to the other, excepting that its magnitude is said to be four times greater. They are both representations, on a small scale, of the Himma-leh Neel-khent, or source of the Tirsoolgunga, described in another place.

As we proceeded to the place marked out for our encampment in the valley of Nepaul, we observed some of the cultivated fields to be skirted with the Jeea, or plant that yields the drug called Cherris, for which Nepaul is so famous, though the truth is, that the best kind is brought from Mullebum, a dependency of Nepaul lying far to the north-west. This plant would appear to differ in no respect from the hemp, excepting it be in the odour of its leaves, which is of a most overpowering strength. I could not ascertain to my satisfaction in what manner the Cherris was procured from the shrub, all the accounts I received of the matter varying more or less. It is nevertheless certain, that the operation is a manual one, requiring considerable nicety and attention both as to the period and the mode of compressing the leaves. With respect to the former, the proper season would seem to be when the plant is in flower, and its seeds on the point of maturity, it being material to the purity of the extract, that the leaf should not be parched or dry, as in this state it would not only yield less green, but a portion of its grosser parts would be apt to enter into the product. In regard to the manual management, it consists principally in rubbing the leaves gently between the two hands till these become sufficiently charged with the juice, which adheres to the palms in the form of a dark, viscid, and tolerably consistent substance; this being removed with a spatula, or knife, is made up into balls or lumps, which, while unrefined, are sold under the name of Cherris. The clarified Cherris is called Mômea (from its resemblance to wax), and burns with a flame as bright as that of the purest resin. This gum is a most potent narcotic, possessing, it is said, very valuable medical qualities. The grosser products of this plant are called Ganjâ and Bhang, or Subje, the former being a preparation of flowers, and the latter of the leaves. Both of these are obtained in the southern parts of Hindostan from the shrub called Ganjâ, which, however, though entirely corresponding in appearance with the Jeea of Nepaul, does not yield any Cherris. From the hemp the Newars of Nepaul fabricate some coarse linens, and also a very strong kind of sack-cloth.

CHAPTER VI.

VALLEY OF NEPAUL—Temple of Sumbhoo-nath—Extent of the Valley of Nepaul—Surrounding Mountains—Bhâgmutty and Bishnmutty Rivers—Khatmanda—Patn—Bhatgong—Kirtepoor—Chobbar.

CHAPTER VI.

Our camp, during the single week we resided in Nepaul, was pitched on a rising but broken spot of ground, close to the east foot of Sumbhoo-nath, and not quite a mile distance from Khatmanda. This situation would have been sufficiently favourable to our viewing the whole extent of the valley, had the weather happened to be less adverse than usual to our wishes. Not only, however, all the mountains which encircle it, but almost every one of the numerous villages with which it is dotted, were so perpetually shrowded either by clouds, or a thick mist, that even the opportunities which offered of using the compass were very few. But before I describe the valley of Nepaul, I will here notice the curious temple of Sumbhoo-nath.

This temple stands on the summit of an insulated hill, which rises rather abruptly from the level of the subjacent plain to the height of about three hundred feet; the ascent to it is by a broad flight of steps cut out of the rock, the sides of which are pleasantly clothed with trees. At the foot of the steps is a colossal image in stone of the god Boudh, who is considered by some to be the law-giver of the Bhootias or Tibetians, and to be the same as the Fo of the Chinese. The doctrines, however, usually attributed to Boudh, would appear to be so much at variance with many of the usages of the Bhootias, that this opinion is by no means to be hastily admitted; a reference alone to the Boudh Pouran itself can satisfactorily clear up this point, and happily such a reference is now no longer impracticable to the learned, as I have been fortunate enough to obtain from Nepaul a copy of that rare and valuable manuscript.

Sumbhoo-nath is a very ancient edifice, having, it would seem, been erected at a period when Nepaul was ruled by a race of Tibetians who being subsequently expelled by the Newars, obtained the name of Khat Bhootias (or Bhootias of Khatmanda), which they preserve to this day, occupying at present the mountains of the Kuchâr, but principally that part of the range situated in the Koote quarter. The possession of this temple has been always claimed by the Dalai Lâmâ (or sovereign pontiff of Lehassa), on the ground of its having been a dependency of his spirituality from the earliest times, and this pretension appears to have been usually yielded to by the existing government of Nepaul. Upon the rupture, however, which some years ago took place between the Tibetians and people of Nepaul, the Lama's vicar was obliged to evacuate this sanctuary, which is now held by a legate on the part of the Dewa Dhurma, whom we call the Deb Rajah, and whom, in

Sumbhoo-nath.

such a conjuncture, the government of Nepaul was naturally desirous of conciliating by every means in its power. It is scarcely necessary to add, that this prince is among the followers of the Tibetian idolatry.

The annexed sketch of Sumbhoo-nath will convey a much better idea of its exterior figure and perspective, than any description I am able to furnish. It is proper to notice, however, that this view comprehends little more than that part of the sanctuary which appears to be more particularly appropriated to the rites of the Bhootia worship, and which is encompassed by a sort of quadrangular edifice, containing a variety of small shrines and images. The whole building rises from a terrace that occupies completely the summit of the hill, but though it is pretty evident that the several divisions of it have been erected at different periods, yet its history being involved in the greatest obscurity, there is no possibility of ascertaining any thing satisfactory concerning the origin, either of the middle and superior temple, or of those which encircle it. Sumbhoo is one of the appellations of Mahadeo, and the word, signifying self-existing, or self-created, is applied to a stone image of the god, supposed to be the spontaneous production of nature. But whatever may be the fact with regard to the antiquity of Sumbhoo-nath, it is certain that this temple is at present resorted to only by the Bhootias, and the Bahaurâs, the latter of whom are a tribe of Newars who seem to have apostatized in a certain degree from the religious creed of their countrymen at some period subsequent to their conquest of Nepaul, or at least to have grafted upon it a considerable portion of the idolatry of Tibet. After all, however, it is highly probable that the sanctity of this spot might be safely referred to a period very anterior both to the Newar and Khat Bhootia dynasties of Nepaul, since the sacred books of the Hindoos scarcely leave any room to doubt that the religion of Bramha has been established from the most remote antiquity in this secluded valley, where, in truth, there are nearly as many temples as houses, and as many idols as inhabitants, there not being a fountain, a river, or a hill within its limits, that is not consecrated to one or other of the Hindoo deities.

The first object that engages the attention on reaching the summit of Sumbhoo, is a cylindrical structure of masonry, about breast-high, and from two to three feet in diameter; over this work is placed a circular plate of brass, called Dhurmadhat Munsera, and also Kinkoor, which is covered with various engraved figures and characters, and serves to sustain a gilt Bejjerbân, or thunder-bolt of Indra, of immense size, but better corresponding to the figure of a double sceptre.* This structure is not solid, being raised, it is said, round a well; but whether now dry or containing water, was more than any person I saw, pretended to know, as it had never been examined since the time of Puttâr Mull, a Newar Rajah of Khatmanda, who flourished about a hundred and fifteen years ago, and by whom this singular fabric was erected to the Hindoo Jupiter.

* A representation of this is given in the title-page.

The temple principally visited by the Bhootias and Bahaurâs rises from the middle of the flat or terrace of the hill, and is distinguished at a great distance by its spires or turrets, which are covered with plates of copper very highly gilt. It is indebted for this decoration to the Dalai Lama, by whose order the work had been but recently finished, when his vicar was under the necessity of relinquishing the charge to the Dewa Dhurma. I ascended by a steep ladder to the entrance of this edifice, the interior of which consisted of a single apartment, so filled with smoke, and strewed with various utensils, that it actually had infinitely more the appearance of a miserable kitchen, than of the temple of a divinity. But though my curiosity was far from being damped on this account, yet it did not avail me much, as my ignorance of the Tibet language made it impossible for me to hold any conversation with the officiating priests, one of whom was seated on the floor between two round deep vessels filled with Ghee, that served to feed a considerable number of lamps, in trimming of which he seemed earnestly employed. Sumbhoo-nath, indeed, is chiefly celebrated for its perpetual fire, and I was assured that the flame of the two largest wicks I saw, had been constantly preserved from time immemorial. But though this altar is in a situation pretty well defended from the external air, yet it is sufficiently exposed to it to incline me to suspect that no small share of the great reputation which the two superior lamps have acquired, ought, in fairness, to be assigned to the lesser.

In a corner to the right of the everlasting lights, stood a cylindrical machine placed vertically on a stand; round this machine was curiously wrapped either some leaves, or a complete copy, I could not ascertain which, of the Bhootia scriptures. The attending priest was obliged to tear off part of its covering to shew me this singularly disposed volume, the writing of which I could just distinguish to be in the Tibet character. Upon my signifying a desire to be informed of the title of the book, I repeatedly received for answer, Mani; but whether this is the proper name of its author, or no more than a general denomination by which they discriminate sacred from prophane writings, I am unable to determine. I observed that as often as those who entered the temple approached and touched the holy volume (which action was always accompanied by certain gestures denoting profound respect), either the priest who attended, or the worshipper himself, put the machine in motion, every revolution of which occasioned a bell to strike, that was suspended over it. If it were not that this ringing, which, it must be confessed, was by no means of a musical kind, doubtlessly appeared to us in the valley to be much more unceasing than it really was, I should have been disposed to conclude the Bhootias and Bahaurâs, to be the devoutest people on earth; but in whatever degree of reverence these nations hold Sumbhoo-nath, it is certain that the Hindoos of Nepaul have no opinion of its sanctity, for upon my putting a question to a Rajepoot of some distinction, which implied that I entertained a contrary idea, he manifested no

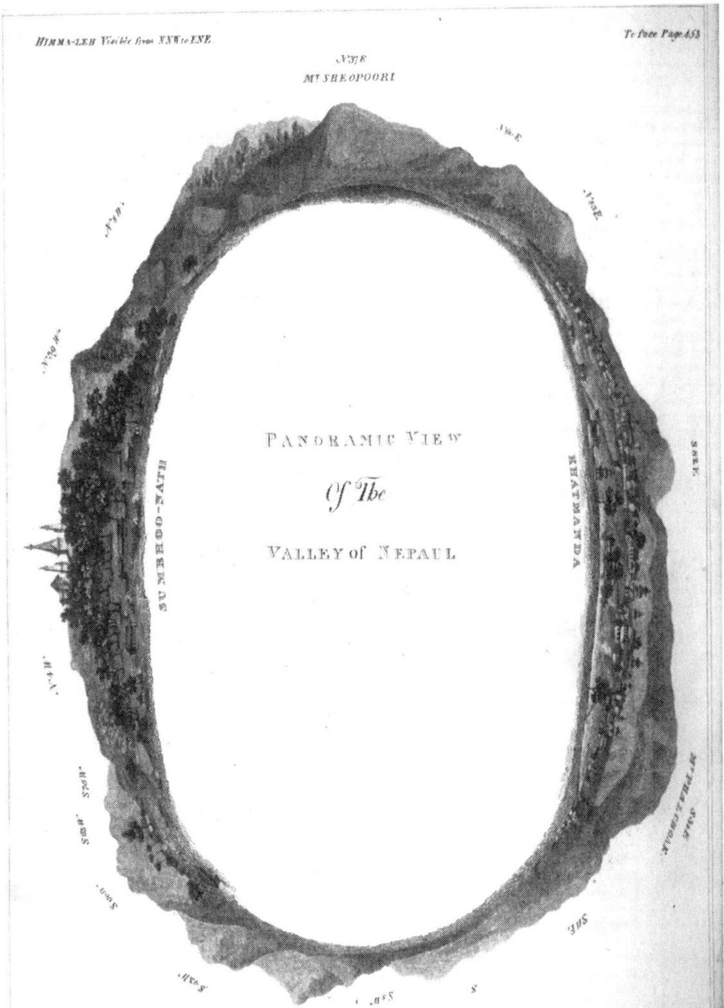
HIMMA-LEH Visible from NNW to ENE.
To face Page 153
Mt. SHEOPOORI
SUMBHOO-NATH
KHATMANDA
PANORAMIC VIEW
Of The
VALLEY of NEPAUL

small solicitude to undeceive me, and a good deal of eagerness to convince me that those of his tribe never visited this temple.

The valley of Nepaul is nearly of an oval figure; its greatest extent is from north to south, in which direction it may be computed at twelve horizontal miles. It stretches from east to west about nine miles, and its circuit is roughly estimated by the inhabitants at twenty-five coss, or from forty to fifty miles. It is bounded on the north and south by very stupendous mountains, near the foot of which rise several of those humbler eminences called Collines in Switzerland: indeed the bottom of the valley, besides being in general extremely uneven, and intersected by deep ravines, occasioned by autumnal inundations, is speckled throughout at various distances with similar little hills. To the east and west the enclosing mountains are much less lofty, the immediate head of the valley to the westward being defined principally by a low steep ridge covered with brush-wood, and anciently called Maroor, but at present, most commonly, Nagâ-Arjoon, from the name of an idol for which it is famous. This ridge passes close behind Sumbhoo-nath, and is itself backed by a more considerable one, named Dhôchoak, of which some mention has already been made in describing the valley of Doona, and regarding which, I have nothing further to add, than that it is said to contain a lake strongly impregnated with mineral salt, and celebrated under the name of Indra-pokhra. To the eastward, the most remarkable hills are those of Ranichoak and Mahabut or Mahadeo-pokhra; but they by no means reach the elevation either of Phalchoak (which is the most towering of the summits that illustrate the southern confine of the valley) or of Sheopoori, which constitutes its principal barrier to the northward, and is unquestionably by far the highest of all the mountains that encircle it. The other chief links of this superb chain are mount Kukunni, which stretches westerly from Sheopoori, being united to Nagâ-Arjoon by mount Bheerbundy, and Chumpa-daibi, which, with one or two more inferior peaks, complete the girdle by joining Chandraghiri to Phalchoak.

As it was not in our power to ascend to the top, either of Sheopoori or of Phalchoak, and as the nature of the ground, no less than considerations of prudence, opposed any attempt at the actual measurement of a base, we had not the means of ascertaining either by the barometer, or geometrically, the altitudes of those mountains. I am inclined to think, however, on a comparison of the result of a rough calculation, built upon their computed horizontal distance, and the angles of their summits with the heights of some adjacent peaks, as denoted by the barometer, that mount Sheopoori is not much less than fourteen hundred, and that Phalchoak is nearly twelve hundred, yards above the level of Sumbhoo-nath. Mount Jibjibia erects its aspiring head about a point to the westward of Sheopoori, which, notwithstanding its respectable elevation, sinks before its super-towering neighbour to the rank of a moderate colline. But though Jibjibia rises probably more than two thousand yards above the loftiest part of Sheopoori, yet it yields in its turn to the amazing rampart of snow which shoots up on its right, and, in spite of its vicinity and the immense height of the interposing mountains, is easily descried from the foot of Sumbhoo-nath. Indeed this magnificent object is said to be visible at Khatmanda, in clear weather, from between the points of N. N. W. and E. N. E. It will hardly be supposed, however, that such a spacious prospect can be unbroken throughout. To enjoy so august a sight, one must ascend, perhaps, to the top of Chandraghiri, though I am inclined to think that the landscape is not less entire from the inferior height of Cheesapany, whence the sides and summits of this stupendous chain stand, to a very great extent, completely revealed to the eye. The eastern extremity of this interesting view is marked by a pile of snowy mountains, which I imagine to be that part of Himma-leh lying just above Koote, the horizontal distance of which from Khatmanda, is forty-eight miles.

Sheopoori gives rise to the Bhâgmutty and Bishnmutty rivers; the sources of the former, (which also bears the name of the Bremha-serassutti,) are situated on the north side of the mountain, round the east foot of which, this river winds, and soon enters the valley of Nepaul, traversing it in a meandering course, the general direction of which is southerly. It is a very inconsiderable brook at Pussputty-nath, close under which it flows, but receiving in its progress from thence, several tributary currents, its channel gradually widens, till it assumes, in passing between Patn and Khatmanda, the appearance of a respectable stream. Upon the Bishnmutty's yielding its waters and name to it a little way below the south end of Khatmanda, it hastens towards Gunnaish-than, and some other low hills standing at the foot of mount Chandraghiri, along the bottom of which it rushes precipitately, as if impatient to force a passage through the superior ridge, and at length escapes from the valley by an opening that presents itself between Phalchoak and Chumpa-daibi, after which I know nothing certain concerning it, till it re-appears at Hurrihurpoor, from whence its continuation to Munniary has been probably laid down with sufficient accuracy by Major Rennell. I have been generally informed, however, that its course between the valley of Nepaul and Hurrihurpoor lies through an immensely wild and rugged country, that its channel is choaked with huge rocks, and overhung by impenetrable woods, and that it falls, in two or three points, in very considerable cataracts, the most remarkable of which is said to occur at a place called Bysia. Its descent also immediately from Hurrihurpoor is represented as exceeding rapid; but it would appear to resume a tolerably gentle current almost immediately after precipitating itself from thence into the valley below, as boats from the Turrye occasionally ascend to within an easy distance of that town.

The Bishnmutty, called likewise the Dhurma-nuddi and Bremhabode, issues from the south side of Sheopoori, entering the valley of Nepaul not far to the northward of Bâlâ Neel-khent; and, after washing the west face of Khatmanda, empties itself into the Bhâgmutty. The water of this river is not in equal estimation with that of the Bhâgmutty, which is said to be much lighter and wholesomer; indeed the people of this country pretend, that all the streams which descend along the north faces of mountains, are preferable to such as spring from a southern aspect; but perhaps the inferiority of the Bishnmutty in this respect may partly be owing to the circumstance of its receiving no accession of water throughout its course, and of its being every where a very shallow, and, comparatively with the other, rather a sluggish stream. With regard to the nature of the soil over which it passes, it would not appear to differ from that which constitutes the bed of the Bhâgmutty.

Besides the rivers just described, there are several other streams which flow through the valley of Nepaul, and contribute greatly to its fertilization. The principal of these are Dhobee-kola, the Munnokra, the Hunnumunta, and the Kushen-kooshen, the Bhâgmutty finally receiving the waters of the whole. Dhobee-kola (or Roodurmutty of antiquity) rises, as well as the Bishnmutty, from the south side of mount Sheopoori, and passing at the distance of about a mile and a half to the eastward of Khatmanda, pursues a course nearly south till it falls into the Bhâgmutty, which it does a little way above the junction of that stream with the Bishnmutty. The Munnokra, called also the Munmutty, issues from a small lake near Bujjur-joogni, a place of considerable sanctity in the vicinity of Sânkû. It runs, like the generality of the streams which intersect this valley, in a southerly direction, passing, at the distance of about a mile, to the eastward of the Bhâgmutty, into which it discharges itself, after a very short course, near Patn. The Hunnumunta, or Bhuddermutty of the sacred writings, springs from Mahadeo-pokhra, and after winding round the south-west angle of Bhatgong, hastens to meet the Kushen-kooshen (or Kausabutti), which it does about half a mile to the westward of that city. This last rivulet has its rise from Chângoo-nerain; and after passing along the north-east side of Bhatgong, soon yields its waters and its name to the Hunnumunta, which proceeds but a short way before it disembogues itself into the Bhâgmutty.

It will not be expected that I should be able to describe, or even to enumerate, all the towns and villages of this valley, nor are there, indeed, many of them that merit any particular notice. I shall content myself, therefore, with a slight review of the most remarkable among them.

Of these Khatmanda is entitled to the first rank, not so much, indeed, on account of its superior size or population, as because it is at present reckoned the capital of Nepaul, from being the residence of the Rajah. It stands on the east bank of the Bishnmutty, along which it stretches in length about a mile; its breadth is inconsiderable, no where exceeding half, and seldom extending beyond a quarter of a mile, its figure being said by the natives to resemble the Kohra or scimetar of Daiby. The entrance to it from the

Khatmanda the Capital of Nepaul

westward, near which extremity of the valley it is situated, is by two slight bridges thrown over the Bishnmutty, one of them at the north, the other near the south end of the town. The name by which it is distinguished in ancient books is Gongool-putten: the Newars call it Yindaise, whilst among the Purbutties, or mountaineers, it is styled Kathipoor, an appellation which seems to proceed from the same source with Khâtmândû, the present popular appellation of this city, and derived, as it is said, from its numerous wooden temples, which are, indeed, among the most striking objects it offers to the eye. These edifices are not confined to the body of the town, but are scattered over its environs, and particularly along the sides of a quadrangular tank or reservoir of water, situated a short way beyond the north-east quarter of the town, and called Rani-pokhra. They appear to differ nothing in their figure or construction from the wooden Mundubs occasionally met with in other parts of India, and are principally remarkable for their number and size, some of them being of considerable elevation and proportionate bulk. Besides these, Khâtmândû contains several other temples on a large scale, and constructed of brick, with two, three, and four sloping roofs, diminishing gradually as they ascend, and terminating pretty generally in pinnacles, which, as well as some of the superior roofs, are splendidly gilt, and produce a very picturesque and agreeable effect.

The houses are of brick and tile, with pitched or pent-roofs; towards the street, they have frequently enclosed wooden balconies of open carved work, and of a singular fashion, the front piece, instead of rising perpendicularly, projecting in a sloping direction towards the eaves of the roof. They are of two, three, and four stories, and almost without a single exception, of a mean appearance; even the Rajah's house being but a sorry building, and claiming no particular notice. The streets are excessively narrow, and nearly as filthy as those of Benares.

Khâtmândû was reckoned, during the time of Jye Purkaush, to contain about twenty-two thousand houses; but this amount is affirmed to have been very much augmented since that period, though not without some consequent decrease in the numbers of Patn and Bhatgong. This statement, however, must of necessity be understood as comprehending not only the population of the town itself, but of its dependent villages, it being manifest that there cannot stand, at the most, above five thousand houses on the ground occupied by this city; and, indeed, though all those I discoursed with on this point, appeared desirous of magnifying the number of its inhabitants, yet some of them pretty clearly admitted that the specified statement was meant to include most of its subordinate towns or hamlets, which are not less than from twenty to thirty, of which Sânkû, Chângoo-nerain, Ghokurna, Deopâtun, Hânrigong, Pâpigong, Chuprigong, and some others, rank as considerable places. Allowing then ten persons to a house or family, which is probably rather a low standard for the houses of Khâtmândû, its population will amount to about fifty thousand

A Nepaul House.

souls, which I should take to be its full complement.* At the same rate the numbers occupying the remaining seventeen thousand houses formerly included within the jurisdiction of Khatmanda, would be one hundred and seventy thousand; but as the buildings of the inferior towns are, generally speaking, on a much smaller scale than those of the metropolis, I should judge eight to a house, on an average, to be an ample allowance, which would reduce the population of the subordinates to one hundred and thirty-six thousand, giving one hundred and eighty-six thousand for the total population of the capital and its districts, in which last, however, it is not intended to include Doona-baise, Noakote, Nerjah, or any other of the dependencies of the Khatmanda sovereignty lying beyond the valley. I confess that this calculation is exceeding vague, and that, with respect to the canton or principality at large, I think it likely to be under the truth, though, perhaps, not in any considerable degree. It is proper, however, to notice here, that the most reasonable of my informants would not admit Sânkû to have ever been comprehended in the population attributed to Khatmanda. Sânkû was formerly a place of great magnitude, but does not contain at present above a thousand families.

The city of next importance in the valley of Nepaul is Patn, which occupies a rising spot of ground situated about two miles to the south-east of Khatmanda, and close to the confluence of the Munnokra, Fookacha, and Bhâgmutty rivers. While an independent

* Perhaps 4000 houses, at twelve inhabitants each, would be nearer the mark.

capital, it would seem to have been of much greater extent than the present metropolis, being said to have contained, during that period, twenty-four thousand houses; which number, however, as in the case of Khatmanda, must be understood to comprize also most of its dependencies within the valley; and though my information does not enable me to describe the exact limits of each of the three states, into which the valley of Nepaul was divided at the time of Purthi Nerain's conquest, yet there is good reason to believe that the sovereign of Patn possessed the greatest portion of it, since, among the various towns enumerated as belonging to that canton, we meet with the names of Kirthipoor, Chobbar, Thankote, Pheerphing, and a few others, which, besides continuing to be still of principal note, include a wider tract of territory than the dependencies either of Khatmanda or Bhatgong. The dominions of Patn beyond the valley stretched southerly, comprehending, Chitlong, Tambeh-kan, Cheesapany, and some other places in the same direction.

Patn is called Yulloo-daisi by the Newars, and it is likewise occasionally distinguished from Deopâtun (celebrated for its temple of Pussputnath), by the appellations of Luttit-Patn and Loll-Patn, both of which, it is supposed to have derived from the name of its founder, who was a favourite, and Purdhân, or minister, of one of the ancient princes of this country. It is a neater town than Khatmanda, and boasts also of containing some very handsome edifices.

Bhatgong is, perhaps, still more superior to Khatmanda; for though doubtlessly the least considerable of the three, in point of size, being rated only at twelve thousand houses, yet its palace and buildings, in general, are of more striking appearance, and its streets, if not much wider, are at all events much cleaner than those of the metropolis. It owes this last advantage to its admirable brick pavement, which has not received, or indeed required, the least repair for thirty years past. Nepaul in general is remarkable for the excellence of its bricks and tiles, but those of Bhatgong are commonly allowed to be very far preferable to the rest. Certain it is, they surpass any I ever met with in India, but it is not equally certain from whence their excellence proceeds. Some of those whom I questioned on the subject, referred it to the nature of the earth used in making them, and some to the water employed in tempering them; while others affirmed it to arise purely from a particular mode of burning them. I had no opportunity of seeing this operation, the success of which, I was told, depended materially on the manner of laying the bricks and fuel, at the time of forming the clump or kiln.

Bhatgong lies about east and by south of Khatmanda, from whence it is distant nearly eight road miles. Its ancient name was Dhurmaputten, and it is called by the Newars Khôpôdaise, by whom it is also described to resemble in its figure the Dumbroo, or guitar, of Mahadeo. It appears to be the favourite residence of the Brahmans of Nepaul, containing many more families of that order than

Khatmanda and Patn together, all those of the Chetree tribe (to which the reigning prince belongs) flocking on the other hand to the capital, while Patn is principally inhabited by Newars.

With respect to what may be termed the ultramontane dominions of Bhatgong, there is reason to believe, that though the sovereigns of this state seem to have possessed the smallest of the three divisions of the valley, they nevertheless established their authority to a greater distance beyond it, than either of their neighbours. I am not acquainted with the exact limits of the Bhâtgong principality to the eastward, in which direction it chiefly extended itself; but I fancy they no where fell short of the banks of the Kousi, near which, and at the distance of five journies from Khatmanda, there still stands an ancient Newar town of considerable eminence, called Dhoalka.

Kirthipoor occupies the summit of a low hill, about three miles west of Patn; it was at one time the seat of an independent prince, though at the period of Purthi Nerain's invasion, it was included in the territory of Patn. The reduction of this place cost the Ghoorkhali so much trouble, that in resentment of the resistance made by the inhabitants, he barbarously caused all the males he captured in it, to be deprived of their noses. We came to the knowledge of this fact in consequence of observing among the porters who transported our baggage over the hills, a remarkable number of noseless men, the singularity of the circumstance leading us to inquire into the cause of it.

Chobbar is also situated on an eminence, which, with that of Kirthipoor, forms a kind of saddle hill. The latter is said to represent the body, and the former the head of Mahadeo. Kirthipoor is said to have reckoned, at one period, no less than six thousand houses or families within its jurisdiction. It is at present a place of no great extent or consideration.

Having in the preceding pages illustrated, as well as I could, the particular topography of the tract actually traversed by us in our route, I shall now proceed to offer a few brief observations on the country of Nepaul in general, which will necessarily, however, be principally confined to that part of it properly so called, and strictly comprehending no more than the valley just described. I shall afterwards finally close the present Memoir, with as accurate an account of the boundaries, extent, and subdivisions of the Goorkhali territories collectively, as the scanty information I have been able to obtain on the subject will admit of.

CHAPTER VII.

Name, Climate, Season, Soil, and general face of the Country of Nepaul—Metals and Minerals—Animal and Vegetable Productions—Population and Classes of Inhabitants—Customs and Manners—Religion, Temples, and religious Festivals—Government—Laws—Administration of Justice—Commerce, Arts, and Manufactures—Revenues, and Military Force—Coins—Learning—Languages.

CHAPTER VII.

NEPAUL, or more correctly, Nypaul, is said to have been distinguished during the Sutheo-joog, when the dynasty of Bhujjer-joogni are reported to have ruled over it, by the name of Siddoo-buttipoor. It is also called in some ancient books Decarie Tapoo, or the Southern Isle, in reference to its situation with respect to Himma-leh. It derives its present appellation, it is pretended, from the founder of the Nymuni dynasty, in whose possession this country is supposed to have remained during the Treta and Dwaper. The fables on which this etymology is built merit no attention; but it may be worth noticing that all the records of Hindoo antiquity concerning the Himma-leh mountains, and the northern regions adjacent thereto, are affirmed to represent the present valley of Nepaul as having been originally an immense lake, which, in the progress of ages, gradually retired between the banks of the Bhâgmutty. Other accounts state, that the Bhâgmutty remained without any outlet from the valley during three centuries, when Sree-kima, the last of the Nymunians, opened its present passage through the southern ridge of mountains. Major Rennell informs us, on occasion of a similar tradition regarding Cashmere, " that appearances have im-" pressed a conviction of its truth on the minds of all those who " have visited the scene, and contemplated the different parts of " it;" and he afterwards reasons at some length, and with much ingenuity, in its support; nor is there a single argument advanced by our illustrious geographer on the subject, that does not apply with conclusive force to the valley of Nepaul. The waving or broken nature of the ground, which resembles, in a striking degree, the bed of a large body of water, and the soil consisting to a considerable depth of a black, fat earth, manifestly the product of deposited mud, are particularly circumstances of the most demonstrative kind. In short, if any difficulty be here opposed to the theory in question, it presents itself solely in the character of the strata that form the base of the mountains through which the Bhâgmutty has forced a passage, it being perhaps doubtful whether these be of a hardness capable of resisting the attrition of the waters for any great length of time.

The northernmost part of Nepaul scarcely lies in a higher parallel of latitude than twenty-seven degrees and a half; yet this valley enjoys, in certain respects, the climate of some of the southern countries of Europe. My knowledge on this point is, of course, almost entirely confined to the narrow limits of oral enquiry, our residence here having been too short to admit of our acquiring more satisfactory information. It is not to be doubted, however, that not only the tops of the surrounding mountains are sprinkled with snow for several days together during winter, but that it even sometimes falls in the valley below: a hoar frost, too, at this season, very commonly covers the ground; but though the cold is occasionally, for three or four months, severe enough to freeze the tanks and pools of standing water, yet the rivers are never frozen. Nepaul would seem to be indebted for its favourable climate entirely to its great elevation; for though lying in the vicinity of a region eternally buried in snow, yet its temperature is probably little or nothing affected by this local circumstance, since, besides the shelter it derives from the interjacent mountains, it is affirmed that a north, or Himma-lehan wind never blows in this valley, except now and then in transient gusts. The height of Nepaul above the level of the sea, if we may rely on the indication of the barometer, cannot be much under four thousand feet; but this elevation did not prevent the thermometer from rising once during our stay in this valley to eighty-seven degrees. Its usual height about noon varied from eighty-one to eighty-four degrees; a little after sunrise it commonly stood between fifty and fifty-four, but was once so low as forty-seven, and at nine in the evening generally fluctuated from sixty-two to sixty-six degrees, the mean temperature, from the 17th to the 25th of March inclusive, on an average of fifty-one observations, was sixty-seven degrees.

The seasons of Nepaul are pretty nearly the same with those of Upper Hindostan; the rains commence a little earlier, and set in from the south-east quarter: they are usually very copious, and break up towards the middle of October. The torrents from the mountains being often extremely violent during this period, while the descent of the rivers through the valley is not so precipitate as to carry off the waters with much rapidity, the consequence is, that their banks, wherever they happen to be low, are very liable to be overflowed. The effect of these occasional inundations is sometimes very injurious to the husbandman; and is exhibited also, in the great number of ravines into which the plain is cut.

In describing the climate of Nepaul, we ought not to confine ourselves to the valley, since a few hours journey enable its inhabitants to pass at pleasure, by ascending the sides and summits of the enclosing mountains, through a considerable variety of temperatures, and in three or four days one may actually exchange a heat equal to that of Bengal for the cold of Russia, by barely moving from Noakote to Kheroo, or even to Ramika; nor are, perhaps, the numerous gradations and quick succession of climates attainable from hence the least of the advantages to be derived from an unrestrained intercourse with this charming country, a short residence in which would, in most disorders arising from relaxation, probably answer every purpose of a voyage to Europe, by enabling a patient to remove, as circumstances might demand, from one temperature to another, though I am inlined to think that there are few cases of the nature in question that would require his seeking a higher one in winter than that of the valley of Chitlong, or, in summer, a more elastic and sharper air than he might breathe on the summit of Chandraghiri. Here, too, if we may judge by the spontaneous productions of the spot, among which are the peach, the raspberry, the walnut, the mulberry, and others, all the fruits and esculent vegetables of England might, with proper attention, be successfully raised. With respect to the salubrity of the more elevated valleys and situations, it would seem to be abundantly proved in the general looks of the inhabitants, among whom, if the Newar peasantry take the lead in point of robustness, it is to be attributed to their laborious, but invigorating occupations. The fever called the Owl has already been said to be confined to the very lowest vallies, and to the Turrye; but this is not the case with regard to the guttural tumours known in Hindostan by the name of Ghaigha, and in Nepaul by that of Gânoo; this malady appearing both at Deopâtun and Kaurigong, within a few miles of Khatmanda, and being very prevalent, indeed, at a place called Mungultai, which is about three journies eastward from thence. The natives have no clear ideas concerning the cause of this distemper, though they attempt to treat it medically; some of them conceive that it is produced by a certain insect generated in the water usually drank by the inhabitants of goitrous places; others suppose that it is owing to some mineral impregnation, but without suspecting particularly the influence of the calcareous matter called *Tuf* in Switzerland, and supposed by Mr. Coxe to be the cause of this malady. The water, however, commonly drank by the people of Kaurigong and Deopâtun, being that of the Bhâgmutty, which is equally used in several other places unaffected with this endemial deformity, the goitres of those two towns are gravely believed by many of the inhabitants to be an effect of imagination in their pregnant women, who, it seems, are constantly exposed to the disgusting sight presented in the protuberant pouches of the innumerable monkies with which the adjacent sacred grove of Gorja-sirre swarms; sallying thence, these animals take possession at pleasure of the neighbouring houses, from which it would be an act of the greatest impiety to dislodge them forcibly.

It was formerly a very prevalent idea among the people of Hindostan, from whom it would appear to have passed to the Europeans, that Nepaùl contained gold mines, and it was probably this notion (corroborated from time to time by the exaggerated reports of obscure travellers concerning the opulence and splendour of its cities) that stimulated Cossim Ali Khan to his unsuccessful attempt against this country. As to the enterprise embarked in by the English during Mr. Verelst's administration, whether undertaken on better grounds or not, it was equally unfortunate. It may appear difficult to conceive how the neighbouring nations could so long abide by a persuasion originating in no stronger a circumstance than the gold of Tibet passing into Bengal and Bahar through Nepaul, for it would not seem that much stress has been laid on the occasional separation of a few gold grains either from the sand, or from those consecrated pebbles of the Gunduck, known by the name of Salegrams. Our surprize, however, on this occasion, will be diminished, if it does not entirely vanish, on considering, that while the unremitted jealousy with which the administration of the country had at all times discouraged the free ingress of strangers deprived us of the means of acquiring accurate information, it was also calculated in some degree to confirm the impression which had been received of its natural riches, and which the government of Nepaul itself has, though most probably not intentionally, contributed to keep up by occasionally sending specimens of gold ore to the Governor General of India, by way of presents, or curiosities. It is now pretty clear, however, that, except the small quantity sifted out of the sands of certain rivulets, which pass through, without rising in the Nepaul territories, these latter produce not a grain of gold. It is true I have heard of a gold mine in the neighbourhood of Listie, but if any thing more be meant by the account than the scanty particles of gold dust sometimes discovered in the beds of the torrents which rush through the Kuchâr in that quarter, I am inclined to believe it is not situated within the Nepaul limits. It it also true that Summerpâ (the fugitive Lama of Teeshoo Loomboo, or Diggercheh), who, by taking refuge with the Goorkhali, occasioned the late war between Nepaul and China, and who appears to have been a person of considerable science, gave the government of Khatmanda reason to hope that the precious metals might be discovered in its dominions. It is equally certain, however, that his researches proved fruitless, as I have been assured that the produce of his various experiments did not defray the expenses attending them.

But though Nepaul can boast of no gold mines, yet it doubtlessly contains most of the other metals. Its copper and iron mines have already been noticed; excepting those in the vicinity of Tambeh-kan and Koomhara valley, I am not acquainted either with the precise situation, or history of any of them. The iron of Nepaul is not, perhaps, surpassed by that of any other country, and among its copper ores, of which there would seem to be several varieties, some are said to be rich, and of an excellent kind. Oude was formerly supplied with this metal from Nepaul, but of late years the European copper, without appearing to be in any respect of a superior quality, has, by actually underselling, driven that of Nepaul out of the western markets, a phænomenon in commerce which ought not, probably, to be attributed entirely to the difficulty and expense of transportation through a mountainous tract, having no navigable rivers, since it is likely to arise in a great degree from the backwardness of the natives in the arts of mineralogy and metallurgy. In short, copper, the produce of Nepaul, has been known to bear so high a price as a rupee and a half the Seer, at the same time that European copper was procurable in Calcutta for a rupee the Seer.

With regard to silver, I have been informed that some veins of it have been discovered to the westward of Noakote; but I doubt the truth of the account, and suspect it to have no other foundation than the fact of certain ores of lead, supposed to contain a considerable proportion of the precious metal, having been recently met with. I have seen several specimens of these ores, some of which were very rich in lead, while others appeared to be a species of galena well worth the working for the sake of its silver; and indeed, I found some attempts, with this view, had been made previous to our arrival in Nepaul; but as in all their endeavours to obtain the nobler metal, they had, owing to their ignorance of the proper process, lost most part of the baser one, the result of their experiments had been very discouraging. In fine, they have hitherto so little known how to avail themselves of their natural treasures, that they are still obliged to supply themselves with lead from Patna.

There is no better authority at present than vague information for believing that the Nepaul territories contain either the ores of antimony or mercury. It is pretty certain, however, that the western parts in particular abound both in arsenic and pyrites, though it is also true that the government has been obliged to desist from working the sulphurous ores on account of the deleterious effects produced by the operation. With regard to volcanoes, although I met with no traces of any in our route, yet it is certain that there are some eruptions to the westward; but whether these arise merely from bituminous or other inflammable substances, or are actually volcanic, I am unable to determine.

The houses in Nepaul are universally built of brick, because the use of stone, though every where procurable within an easy distance, would be intolerably expensive in a country not admitting either of wheel carriages, or of water transportation; hence, notwithstanding the great plenty and variety of stones adapted to the purposes of building, which are to be met with in this country, among which are some kinds both of marble and of jasper, the sight of a stone edifice or structure of any sort, if we except their idols, and some of the ornamental parts of their temples, is more uncommon in Nepaul, than even in Bengal. There is said to be a very considerable mass of rock crystal near Goorkha, and lime-stone, as well as slate, seems to abound every where. There are, however, no lime-kilns in this country, the cement commonly employed being mud, which, the natives pretend, answers in their humid climate better than lime mortar. The small quantity of the latter which they use, is procured from the incrustations and crystals of lime that are found in some of the natural grottos or caves scattered over this romantic region. I lament exceedingly that none of these happened to lie in our route, as the description I have received of them appears to render them very well worth the attention of all who receive any delight in contemplating the beauties or wonders of nature.

The foregoing, it must be owned, is a very superficial account of the mineral or fossil productions of Nepaul; but I trust it will be indulgently received, as the best that I am enabled to furnish either by my sources of information, or my acquaintance with such subjects. It is to be hoped, indeed, that the period is not very remote when every chasm in our knowledge concerning this country will be completely filled up; for as it is not to be doubted that it presents a noble field for the most interesting researches, both of the mineralogist and botanist, so it may safely be presumed that no favourable opportunity which may hereafter offer for prosecuting useful enquiry in departments of science so intimately connected with the improvement of commerce and manufactures, will be suffered to escape.

I have already occasionally enumerated some of the animal and vegetable productions of this country, and have therefore but little to add here under these heads, which indeed can only be satisfactorily treated of by a professed naturalist.

The cattle of Nepaul, generally speaking, do not seem much superior to those ordinarily met with in Bengal, and the upper provinces; but it is otherwise with regard to the herds which enjoy the double advantage of browsing amidst the delicious herbage of the less cultivated valleys, and of watering at the pure, wholesome brooks which every where intersect them. It is true that even these are but little distinguished in respect to size; yet they appear sleek and plump, and exhibit a greater variety in point of colour than is usually seen in the lower parts of India. I was particularly struck with the good appearance of some cows which we fell in with in passing from Bailkote; but, after all, it must be confessed that the best of them would suffer considerably in a comparison with English cattle. Their milk, however, is not surpassed, perhaps, for sweetness or richness, by any in the world, though I am obliged to acknowledge that the inhabitants did not seem to have any to spare.

It will be readily conceived that a country so over-run as this is with aromatic and sweet flowering shrubs, must necessarily produce honey of the finest quality: but though its excellence is accordingly very well known and acknowledged, yet it is a fact that I had some difficulty in procuring a single comb; this scarcity is owing to there being no more made or stored than is requisite for domestic consumption, bees being reared here principally with a view to the preparation of wax, which forms one of the exports of Nepaul.

I had heard, before my visit to Nepaul, that our most esteemed kitchen vegetables did not only grow there in much higher perfection than in Bengal, but that the propagation of them was annually continued from their own seed, whereas the short duration of our cold season admits but of a scanty and degenerate produce not to be depended upon. My disappointment, therefore, was very great on finding the fact otherwise, and on being assured that they could not raise even potatoes, without procuring every year from Patna fresh roots for sowing; I think it extremely probable, however, that their failure in this respect has been occasioned solely by want of attention or skill, having no doubt, for my own part, that with proper management, there are few of our hortulan productions, whether fruit, flower, or herb, which might not be successfully reared, and abundantly multiplied, either in the valley of Nepaul itself, or in one or other of the numerous situations adjacent to it. The only kitchen vegetables we met with here were cabbages and peas, both of which were of the worst kind. They have the Tibet turnip, but cannot raise it, any more than the potatoe, without renewing the seed annually.

I have elsewhere, in the course of this Memoir, given as full an account of the several species of grain cultivated in this country, as my limited opportunities of obtaining any knowledge of them would allow; there doubtlessly remains much information to be supplied on this, and other interesting subjects of Nepaul agriculture; and in particular it seems highly desirable that we should thoroughly ascertain the nature and history of the various dry rices cultivated by these people under the general name of Ghya, because some of them being actually raised in situations very much exposed to falls of snow, it is extremely probable that they would succeed in England, while others which do not require being flooded, but flourish in the loftiest and driest spots, would be no less likely to answer in the Rajemahl hills.* There are also among the spontaneous

* An experiment has since been successfully made here with four or five species of Ghya.

productions of this luxurious soil, several edible roots and herbs, as the Tooral, a species of yam, the Kurraila, a kind of wild asparagus, and others, well deserving of examination and description, as forming a considerable part of the sustenance of the poorer inhabitants. The medicinal plants, as well as the dying drugs which rank among the natural growth of this country, are likewise very numerous, and some of them very valuable; of the former the Teetea-pât, Juttha, or Jaitamâsi, the Kootka, the Bikmah, the Cheraita, and the Roopmenger (all of them bitter or aromatic woods) are in the most estimation.* Of the colouring plants, I should decline, for the present, even a partial enumeration, as well on account of the subject being too important, in a commercial view, to be slightly discussed, as because measures have been taken by Government for obtaining the fullest information regarding them. I need only observe in this place, that, besides the well-known creeper called Munjheet, some shoots of which I left in a thriving condition at Boglepore, on my return to Bengal, there is good reason to suppose, that the Nepaul territories produce a rich variety of dying materials, and among the rest, two or three sorts of vegetable black. The Kuchâr is known to contain many, and probably, indeed, yields most of the alpine plants.

Adverting to the very wild and rugged nature of the country, we shall see no great room for imagining its population to be

† The Teetea-pât is a species of worm-wood; the Jaitamâsi is supposed to be the spikenard of the ancients, and the Bickmah is a kind of gentian

considerable; the valleys only are of any account in estimating the numbers of the inhabitants, and they are, with the exception of Nepaul itself, and perhaps two or three others, little better than so many mountainous cavities. Even the Turrye, or Turryani, generally speaking, would seem to be but indifferently peopled, the villages throughout it being, as far as I can learn, very thinly scattered, and in most places of a mean rank in point of magnitude, as well as appearance. But whatever the fact in this respect may be, it is certain that we are altogether unfurnished with any documents that would warrant our hazarding even a conjecture on the subject, the materials we possess for judging of the population of the valley of Nepaul itself being at the best extremely vague, and enabling us only to state it loosely at about half a million.

The inhabitants consist principally of the two superior classes of Hindoos (or Brahmins and Chetrees with their various subdivisions), of Newars, of Dhenwars, of Mhanjees, of Bhootias, and of Bhanrâs. The former of these, who compose the army of the state, and engross all situations of trust, whether civil or military, are found dispersed promiscuously throughout the country; the Newars are confined almost to the valley of Nepaul, the Dhenwars and Mhanjees are the husbandmen and fishers of the western districts; and the Bhootias, though some families of them are planted in the lower lands, occupy, generally speaking, such parts of the Kuchâr as are included in the Nepaul territories. With respect to the Bhanrâs, they have already been mentioned, as being a sort of separatists from the

Newars; they are supposed to amount to about five thousand; they shave their heads like the Bhootias, observe many of the religious rites, as well as civil customs, of these idolaters, in a dialect of whose language they are also said to preserve their sacred writings. To the eastward again, some districts of the Nepaul dominions are inhabited by tribes, such as the Limbooas, Nuggerkootees, and others, of whom we know at this time little more than the names.

The Newars are divided into several casts or orders, most of which derive their origin, like those among the more ancient Hindoos, from a primitive classification according to trades and occupations: I reserve an enumeration of these, as well as a full account of the history, religion, government, customs, and manners of the Newars, for a future period, when my information on these points shall be more complete and satisfactory than it is at present: in the mean time, although I have not thought it necessary to refrain altogether from noticing occasionally some particulars concerning this interesting people, yet these sketches are to be considered as a mere outline arising incidentally, and, as it were, unavoidably, out of the nature of our immediate enquiry, and by no means as proceeding from a puerile desire of anticipating a subject, which I am of opinion is well entitled to a very full and deliberate discussion.

Nepaul having been ruled for many centuries past by Rajepoot princes, and the various classes of Hindoos appearing, in all periods, to have composed a great proportion of its population,

Drawn by A.W. Devis Esq.

Engraved by P. Condé

A Male of Nepaul.

we are naturally prepared to find a general resemblance in manners and customs between this part of its inhabitants, and the kindred sects established in the adjacent countries; accordingly, the characteristics which separate them, whether in point of manners, usages, or dress, are so faint as to be scarcely discernable in a single instance, insomuch that I own the agreement greatly exceeded what I could have expected upon adverting to the peculiarity, in many respects, of the local circumstances in which the Hindoos of this valley are placed, to the little fraternity they have ever entertained with the neighbouring nations, to their political union or intermixture, during several centuries, with the Newars, and above all, to the very important consideration presented in the remarkable, and indeed (if I am not mistaken) solitary fact, of Nepaul being the only Hindoo country that has never been disturbed, far less subdued, by any Mussulman power. In one essential particular, nevertheless, these mountaineers appear to me to be very prominently discriminated, and that is by a simplicity of character universally observable amongst them. I am aware that this is a feature, which, with a few exceptions, more or less strikingly marks the Hindoo character throughout India, but whether it be owing to the secluded situation of Nepaul, or to some cause still more operative, the simplicity which distinguishes the inhabitants of this rugged region is manifested no less in the superior than the lower ranks of people, appears in all their modes of life, whether public or domestic, little of ostentation or parade ever entering into either, and is very generally accompanied by an innocency and suavity of deportment, by an ease and frankness in conversation, and I am disposed to think too, by an integrity of conduct not so commonly to be met with among their more polished or opulent brethren.

Between the Newars, however, and the other Hindoo inhabitants of Nepaul, there subsist, as well in character, customs, manners, and features, as in religious rites and language, very essential differences, all of them abundantly proving that they are an insulated race of men, whose origin is not to be traced to any of the nations immediately surrounding them. They are a peaceable, industrious, and even ingenious people, very much attached to the superstition they profess, and tolerably reconciled to the chains imposed on them by their Goorkhali conquerors, although these have not hitherto condescended to conciliate them by the means which their former sovereigns, who were Rajepoots of the Soorej-bunsi race, adopted, and who, among other compliances with the usages of the Newars, made no scruple, it seems, of feeding on the flesh of buffaloes.

I doubt whether this nation have been at any period of a warlike disposition; be this as it may, it is certain that their courage is at present spoken of very slightingly by the Purbutties, or Hindoo mountaineers, and that the instances of their being employed in the armies of the state are exceeding rare. Their occupations are chiefly those of agriculture, besides which they almost exclusively execute all the arts and manufactures known in this country.

Drawn by A.W. Devis Esq.r

Engraved by P. Condé

Female of Nepaul.

Published January 1811 by W. Miller Albemarle Street

Their modes of husbandry prove them to be capable of immense labour, no less than the burthens which they carry shew that they possess great corporal strength, while many of their mechanical operations equally evince that they are tolerably well skilled in some of the most useful arts. They are in general of a middle size, with broad shoulders and chest, very stout limbs, round and rather flat faces, small eyes, low and somewhat spreading noses, and, finally, open and cheerful countenances; yet I cannot agree with those who affirm that there is in the general physiognomy of these people, any striking resemblance to the Chinese features. Many of the women we saw, especially at Bhatgong, had a remarkable florid tint about their cheeks; for the most part, however, their complexion, like that of the men, is somewhat between a sallow and copper colour; the ordinary cast of their features corresponds with that of the males, notwithstanding which, there are said to be many handsome women among them. The illicit progeny of a Newar female and a Chetree, or other Purbutti (for they cannot intermarry) might almost be taken for Malays, at least, that is the physiognomy by which it appears to me the features of this mixed race may, on the whole, be best illustrated; though, perhaps, the faces both of Bajoo Sheer and Rodur Beer (who are the issue of Rajepoots, by Newar women) approach still nearer to the Tartar or Chinese. It is remarkable enough that the Newar women, like those among the Nairs, may, in fact, have as many husbands as they please, being at liberty to divorce them continually on the slighest pretences.

As I am not without hopes of being able, at no very remote period, not only to explain at large the superstitious dogmas, rites, and ceremonies of the Newars, but also to be instrumental, at least, in throwing some light on the Boudhite system of theology, at present so little understood, I shall not touch in this place on either of those subjects. With regard to the popular religion of Nepaul, in general, seeing that it differs nothing from the Hinduism established in Bengal and other parts of India, excepting so far as the secluded nature of the country may have conduced to preserve it in a state of superior orthodoxy and purity, it would be altogether superfluous to enter into any details concerning it; I shall therefore content myself with naming here the temples of most consideration in the valley of Nepaul, and with subjoining an account of the most remarkable festivals annually celebrated by its inhabitants.

1. Pusput-nath, situated on the west bank of the Bhâgmutty, and contiguous to the eastern extremity of the town of Deopâtun. This edifice is said to have been erected by the fourth prince of the Soorej-bunsi dynasty, named Pussoopûsh Deo, and to have been dedicated by him to Pusputty Mahadeo. It is esteemed the holiest temple of Nepaul, and is of such great sanctity, that a pilgrimage to it is deemed here an act of purer devotion than the observance of any of her similar rites prescribed by the Hindoo law. Pusput-nath consists of several courts or squares filled with numerous images and shrines consecrated at different periods, and by various princes. In the centre of the interior court stands the principal

sanctuary, before the gate or entrance of which, is a figure of a kneeling bull, well executed in copper, and superbly gilt; this was an offering of Dhurrum Deo, the twentieth successor of Pussoo-pûsh Deo, and the reputed founder also (according to some accounts) of Sumbhoo-nath. It was this last prince (a very considerable personage in the annals of Nepaul) who is said to have first divided the general mass of his people into the four grand and well known Hindoo tribes of the present day.

2. Changoo-nerain. This is a temple dedicated to Nerain Bishen, or Vishnou; it is situated at Changoo, a small town lying about eight miles to the eastward of Khatmanda, and not uncommonly called (after the temple, for which it is celebrated) Changoo-nerain. The interior of this temple is only accessible by means of an offering of a tolah of gold to the god, though the individual thus propitiating his priests, is at liberty to introduce to the interior, along with himself, as many other persons as he pleases. Poorer, or less profuse zealots, are obliged to content themselves with a distant adoration of the deity, by making the circuit of the exterior enclosure.

3. Bhuddur-joogni, or Bhujjur-joogni. This temple stands in the town of Sânkû, which lies about twelve miles north-east of Khatmanda. It is dedicated to Bhowani.

4. Tillijejoo, or Tullijoo-mâi. No one but the reigning Rajah is permitted to enter the interior of this temple, which is dedicated to Bhowani, and stands in the middle of the city of Bhatgong. The

image of the goddess now erected here was removed from Semroun Ghur to Bhatgong by Hur Singh Deo.

5. Dukhen Kâli. This temple, which is also consecrated to Bhowani in her destructive character, is situated in the hollow of the Pheerphing mountains.

6. Jagaisher. This is a temple dedicated to Mahadeo, and standing in the town of Tannohi, which lies near twenty miles by the road to the eastward of Khatmanda.

7. Seker-nerain. This temple has already been noticed in the account of Pheerphing, near which town it stands. It was erected by Hurry Dutt Burmah, who ruled over Nepaul a few generations before Bukh Deo.

8. Mutchendernath. This temple is situated in the city of Patn, and is called by the Newars Bhoogadeo, written in Father Giuseppe's account of Nepaul (as published in the second volume of the Asiatic Researches) Baghero. It is pretended to have been erected by Nurrender Deo of the Soorej-bunsi dynasty, on the following occasion: Goorkhnath, a disciple of Mutchendernath (who was himself a votary of the sun), visiting Nepaul, and not receiving from its inhabitants those marks of reverence to which he considered his sacred character entitled, resented this treatment by fixing himself in a particular spot, where he remained immoveable during a period of twelve years. The consequence of this holy person's stationary posture appeared in Nepaul being visited by a dreadful drought, which could only be terminated by obliging the offended minister

of the sun to quit his fatal position. To effect so essential a point, Mutchendernath, by means of a certain form of incantation, was prevailed upon to proceed from Kamroof* to Nepaul, where, upon presenting himself before Goorkhnath, the latter was necessarily compelled, through respect for his Gooroo (or ghostly father), to rise; this movement happily restored the country to its wonted prosperity, by occasioning an abundant and immediate fall of rain; and it was in requital and commemoration of the services thus derived from the beneficent interposition of Mutchendernath, that the grateful prince erected the present temple to him, and established the festival in his honour, still annually celebrated in the month of Bysack, or latter end of April.

9. Toolaja Bhowani. This temple stands close to the palace of the present Rajah, in the city of Khatmanda. The interior part of it is accessible to none but the reigning prince; the people at large, however, have an opportunity, annually, of worshipping the goddess, her image being carried in procession every year in the month of Aughun.

10. Bishen-nath. This is a temple erected by Bishn Gupt, an Asheer of the race of the first sovereigns of Nepaul, who deprived the successors of Dhurrum Deo of their kingdom, which, however, was soon recovered by them. It is dedicated to Bishen, or Vishnou, and is situated about eight miles to the northward of Khatmanda, and near the west bank of the Bhâgmutty.

11. Gooshja Kâli. This is a temple dedicated to Kâli, or

* Part of modern Assam.

Bhowani, and is situated about half a mile to the eastward of Pusputty-nath.

12. Goorukh-nath. This temple stands at the distance of a musket-shot to the eastward of Pusput. It is consecrated to Goorukhnath, whom the Goorkhalis consider as their patriarch, and from whom they derive their national appellation.

13. Chundais-sere, is a temple near Bunnipa, or Punnipâ, a town situated about eight miles to the eastward of Bhatgong. It is dedicated to Bhowani.

14. Bhugowty. This is a temple at Phallanchoak (a day's journey to the north-east of Bhatgong), dedicated also to Bhowani.

15. Unnunt-ling. This is a temple consecrated to Mahadeo in his generative character, and situated about four miles south-west of Bhatgong.

16. Sheebâ-dhol is a temple of Mahadeo standing four miles south of Bhatgong.

17. Bheem Seen. This is a very famous temple at Dhoalka, a considerable Newar town, already mentioned. Bheem Seen is one of the demi-gods celebrated in the Mahabharat.

18. Khânda. This is a temple dedicated to Bhowani. It stands on mount Kalia-choak, where the Soona Kousi has its rise.

19. Doomja Koossaiseer. This is a temple of Mahadeo erected at Doomja, which is three journies east of Khatmanda.

20. Goorkha Munkâmânâ. This temple, consecrated to Bhowani, is situated five journies to the westward of Khatmanda.

The following are the principal festivals celebrated in Nepaul,

1. Chownsuthi-jâtra. This is preparatory to the Pusputty-pooja, or worship of Pusputtynath: it is performed in the month of Aughun (November, December), and consists in visiting all the shrines and temples situated on the borders of the valley, some of which are at the distance of two journies from Khâtmândû. They are sixty-four in number, whence this jâtra has obtained the name of Chownsuthi.

2. Koond-jâtra. This occurs in Bysack (April, May), when such devout persons as purpose celebrating the festival of Goojesseri (the consort of Pusputtynath) are previously obliged to perform their ablutions at the eighty-four sacred reservoirs, situated in the environs of Pusputtynath.

3. Bhâgmutty-jâtra. This is a sort of religious progress, or procession, commencing at Chucker-teerut (which is a ghaut or ford of the Bhâgmutty, about a musket-shot to the southward of Pusput), and terminating at Bhâgdwâr, where the Bhâgmutty, quitting mount Sheopoori, enters the valley of Nepaul. Bhâgdwâr is from nine to ten miles to the northward of Pussputtynath. This jâtra occurs in the month of Chyte (or March, April).

4. Bishnmutty-jatra. It is celebrated in Bysack, and consists in a progress similar to the former, commencing at Puchli Bhyroo (a temple consecrated to one of the votaries of Mahadeo, and situated about a mile to the southward of Khâtmândû, and ending at Bishen-nath, near which (I believe) the Bishnmutty enters the valley.

5. Munmutty-jâtra. This festival is also observed in Bysack. It consists in proceeding from Sunkhmool (which is a ford of the Bhâgmutty about a musket-shot to the northward of Patn) to Buddur-joogni.

6. Roodermutty-jâtra. This is another holy progress, beginning at Sheooka Bhal, or the Car of Sheoo, or Siva, whence the pilgrims, passing by Boora Neel-khent (where they bathe), and Hunnamunt-teerut in Bhatgong, proceed to Mahadeo-pokhra, which is about six miles east of Bhatgong. This jâtra occurs in Jait (or May, June.)

7. Gunnaish-jâtra. This procession takes place in Kaurtic (October, November), beginning at Chowbhal (a mile to the south-west of Patn), and ending at Soorej-bunâik, a temple dedicated to Gunnaish, and standing a mile to the southward of Bhatgong.

8. Bhugowty-jâtra. This is a similar ceremony, which occurs also in Kaurtic, commencing at Chowbhal, and continuing as far as Phallanchoak, a place situated about a day's journey to the north-west of Bhatgong, and celebrated for its eighteen Daibies.

9. Pokhra-jâtra. This festival is observed as well as the two last, in the month of Kaurtic, when the pilgrims proceed from Kherkotuck to Munnichoor, a sacred mountain that defines the north-east extremity of the valley of Nepaul. This jâtra obtains its name from the numerous reservoirs at Munnichoor, which are said to be not less than three hundred. Here the pilgrims perform the prescribed ablutions, worshipping at the same time the Deotas, or deities of the environs.

10. Indra-jâtra, takes place in Srawren (July, August); it is a holy progress from Deh-choak (one of the mountains forming the western limits of the valley) to the temple consecrated to Bhowani by the name of Bâlkoomâri, and situated in Tumi; in the course of the procession, the shrines of many Deotas occur, at some of which the pilgrims stop to worship. Tumi is a town of considerable note lying between Khatmanda and Bhatgong, and at present annexed to the fief of Behadur Shah.

11. Seesutty-jâtra. This festival is observed in Bysack. It consists in a progress from Munjessury (which lies about a bow-shot to the westward of Sumbhoo-nath) to Buddur-joogni. Several Deotas are visited in the way.

12. Mutchender-jâtra. The origin of this festival has been mentioned above. It takes place in Bysack, when the idol is transported in an immense car, or moveable shrine, from Patn to the village of Bhâgmutty, where there is another temple consecrated to Bhoogadeo, or Mutchendernath. This appears to be the ceremony alluded to by Père Giuseppe, under the name of Yatra.

13. Bhoagnath-jâtra. This festival is observed in Chyte, consisting in a procession from Jummal (a temple in the suburbs of Khatmanda) to Sugguntoal, within the city.

14. Bhyroo-jâtra; a procession, in the month of Chyte, from Sogal-dhoka in Bhâtgong to Chopingal (about a bow-shot to the south of that city), where Bhyroo is more particularly worshipped.

15. Pustair-mookh. This jâtra occurs also in Chyte; it consists in a progress from Deopâtun to Toondikheel. At Toondikheel (by which name they call the plain immediately beyond the south-east extremity of Khatmanda), the pilgrims worship the Loomri Bhowani, surnamed Mehenkâl.

16. Besides the foregoing, and some others not particularized, there is a grand festival occasionally observed, which lasts four months, commencing in Bysack, and ending in Srawren. It consists in visiting the shrines of all the gods in Nepaul, which are said to be two thousand seven hundred and thirty-three.

The genius of a government unacquainted alike with the positive and implied restraints imposed by a precise, not to say immutable law or constitution, and taking its colour, for the most part, from the character and temporary views of the ruling individual, must necessarily be of too fugitive a nature to admit of any delineation equally applicable to all periods and circumstances. Of this unsettled kind is the government not only of Nepaul, but perhaps of all the Asiatic countries. It is formally, and in a great degree essentially despotic; but its despotism is, on the one hand, modified and in some measure meliorated by certain observances enjoined by immemorial usage, and not to be disregarded with impunity even by the most powerful prince; while, on the other, it is controlled by the active influence enjoyed and occasionally exerted by the aristocratic order already mentioned, under the appellation of Thurgurs. But at the same time that it may reasonably be doubted whether the body of the people ever derive the least advantage from the political struggles of these chieftains, it is also obvious that the extent of the authority possessed by the latter, must always materially depend on a variety of contingencies liable to constant fluctuation: hence it would not be safe to deduce the general spirit of the government from its present condition, especially since it is certain that although the administration of Behadur Shah, during the minority of his nephew, has on the whole been tolerably agreeable, yet considerations of expediency, suggested by a solicitude to maintain himself in his situation, have often compelled him to conciliate his colleagues, by compliances, which, according to the declaration of an intelligent person who communicated with me very freely on this subject, have reduced the strength and energy of the Goorkhali dominion to the mere shadow of what it was under the more vigorous, or, properly speaking, the more arbitrary sway of Purthi Nerain. Without attempting, therefore, to determine the actual force of the machine of government, we must be content to illustrate its construction as well as we are able, by adding to an enumeration of the principal officers of state, a brief account of the ostensible nature of their respective employments.

These officers are, in order of importance, as follows:

1. The Choutra.
2. The Kâjees.
3. The Sirdars.
4. The Khurdars.

5. The Kupperdars.
6. The Khuzânchee.
7. The Ticksâli.
8. The Dhurma-Udhikar.
9. The Bichâries.
10. The Dittha.
11. The Jaithha-Boora.
12. The Soubahs.
13. The Omrahs.

1. The Choutra is considered as the prime-minister of the Rajah, to whom he is invariably akin. The office has sometimes been executed jointly by two commissioners, but is usually, as at present, administered by a single person. Behadur Shah once filled this station, and I believe still enjoys some of the emoluments annexed to it. Srikishen Shah, however, is at this time nominally sole Choutra, the Regent being distinguished simply by the appellation of Saheb, which I understand to be a title appropriated to the nearest legitimate relation of the reigning prince, in the manner that Monsieur, applied absolutely, is restrained to the second son of France.

The business of the Choutra consists chiefly in receiving and examining all written and verbal communications regarding, in any way, the conduct of those filling public employments, whether civil or military. He appears to be a sort of comptroller general over the various inferior departments of administration; submitting his statements, in the first instance, to the Rajah, or Regent, who, if he sees reason, refers the further investigation of such reports to the Punjunni, or court of inspection, already cursorily described, or otherwise decides upon them immediately. The Choutra is annually liable to be removed from his station, as well as all the other principal officers of government. The predecessor of the present Choutra was his elder brother, Bulbhudder Shah, whom the Regent found it expedient to supersede on account of his intractable spirit. At the late Punjunni, (which was held in July,) the partisans of Bulbhudder attempted to obtain his restoration to his place in the administration, but he was again obliged to yield to the less embarrassing pretensions of Srikishen Shah, who, after all, however, is not quite so pliant a minister as is necessary to the views of the Regent. The Choutra, besides the fiefs or jaghires he possesses, in virtue of his office, appears to be entitled to a commission, or fine of eight annas on every Kaith, or rice plantation, throughout the kingdom, those of the Thurgurs and military excepted.

2. The Kâjees resemble the superior Dewan of the Mogul government. The term imports a performer of service, or a man of business: there are generally four of them in commission; such as are actually in employ being called Pugruwâllas, in contradistinction to the Dakhra, by which appellation those out of office are known. The Kâjees superintend, generally, all civil and military affairs. On particular occasions, indeed, a Kâjee is placed at the head of the army, but for the most part these officers are employed

in the management of the revenue, and the direction of the jaghire lands, in the latter of which functions they exercise considerable military authority. The red seal of the Rajah is usually deposited with one of the Kâjees, who, by virtue of this trust (to which also the office of public treasurer is commonly annexed), is considered as the first efficient officer next to the Choutra. The four Kâjees divide equally among them a commission of one rupee per Kaith, on all taxable lands.

3. The Sirdars resemble in some degree the Bukshies of the Mogul empire. They generally command the armies of the state, in the management of the civil affairs of which, however, they likewise participate; there are four of them, each of whom receives two annas from every Kaith of a taxable description.

4. The Khurdars. There are two of these, who act as secretaries, preparing all the Hindoo dispatches from the Rajah, whether to foreign states and princes, or to the officers of government: they also attend the Cuchum, or council, in the deliberations of which, they commonly take part. They each receive a commission of two annas, or four annas jointly, on every taxable Kaith in the country.

5. The Khupperdar. This officer has the charge of the Rajah's particular or private wardrobe, jewels, and kitchen.

6. The Khuzânchee. This officer, besides making all disbursements as treasurer, superintends what may be called the public wardrobe, whence honorary dresses, &c. are issued.

The foregoing six officers being esteemed the principal administrators of the government, are, on that account, denominated Bhardârs, a term denoting " bearers of burthens."

7. The Ticksâli, or superintendant of the mint; his profits consist in a commission on the duties levied on imports from Tibet, and in a certain share of a tax payable by all merchants, natives of Nepaul, on returning thither after a residence for any time at Lehassa, Diggercheh, or other parts of Tibet. This tax or fine is said to be fixed at seven tolahs of gold, and to be usually exacted with a good deal of rigour.

8. The Dhurma-Udhikar is the chief criminal judge, whose business it is to pronounce sentence in all cases cognizable by the tribunal, in which he presides on the part of the Rajah, by whom, however, such sentence must be approved before it can be carried into execution. The under judges, in every part of the kingdom excepting the farmed districts, hold their appointments from him, and in most cases they require the seal of his confirmation to render the judgments they pass valid. The Dhurma-dhun, or fees of this department, are said to be very great, and I have reason to think, that it is principally on this account, that the farming governors usually stipulate for the privilege of commissioning their own officers of justice. Most offences, according to the Dhurma Shaster (which is the foundation of the civil code of Nepaul), being punishable by amercement, and the catalogue of crimes of this description being extremely long, it is easy to conceive that such penalties constitute a considerable source of emolument.

9. The Bichâries, of whom there are four, compose the tribunal which investigates and reports on (as the term implies) all civil questions, and the members of which are usually Brahmins. Two of them are commonly appointed to take cognizance of such disputes as relate to personal property, cases concerning real or landed possessions being referred to two others. The Dhurma-Udhikar occasionally presides in this tribunal, the decrees of which must receive the sanction of the Rajah before they can operate. Intricate cases are sometimes decided by the water ordeal, which is conducted here much in the same manner as in other countries of India.

10. The Dittha. This officer, as the name implies, is an overseer, or superintendant, whose business it is to regulate the police; he answers to the Cutwal of Hindostan. He participates, as well as the Ticksâli, in the produce of the duties and tax mentioned in the article describing that officer.

11. The Jaithha-Boora. This word signifies senior, or ancient. The minister who bears this title is occasionally employed in embassies of a temporary or complimentary kind; is sometimes charged with the delivery of orders of a particular nature to the governors of districts and other public officers, and in certain cases is deputed into the country for the purposes of local investigation. His ordinary station, however, is about the person of the Rajah.

12. The Soubahs are governors of districts, and the appellation is indifferently bestowed on farmers and government collectors.

13. The Omrahs are commanders of Tharrehs, or military posts, and have already been spoken of.

Having said above that the Dhurma Shaster forms the basis of the civil and criminal jurisprudence of Nepaul (as it does of most other Hindoo states), it would not be necessary, were I able, to enter, in this place, into any detail concerning its laws. Of their general spirit and defects, a reference to the publication of Mr. Halhed will enable us to judge with sufficient accuracy, while, with regard to their execution, it will be fair to conclude that the criminal branch, at least, is administered with as much energy and probity, as in other eastern countries; the more especially as there is good reason to believe that theft, in particular, is an offence very little known in Nepaul. Whether, however, on the other hand, we consider the general scope, in a judicial light, of the Dhurma Shaster itself, or the suspicious nature of the courts established for giving effect to its institutes, there is not perhaps the same ground for drawing so favourable an inference with respect to the civil department of their law; and it was probably, indeed, a consciousness of some glaring imperfection in the latter, that suggested at one time to Behadur Shah the design of applying to our Government for a code of laws, with a view to the better regulation of his country.

The trade of Nepaul is by no means so extensive nor, consequently, so beneficial to its government and inhabitants as it might soon be, under proper regulations. Some of the restraints by which it was formerly shackled have, it is true, been removed by the treaty concluded with the Company in 1792, but it still languishes under several impolitic restrictions, originating partly in the jealousy, and partly in the ignorance of the Nepaul administration, but attributable also, in a great degree, to the monopolies which certain Uluts or mercantile Gosains, and a few other merchants, have been long in possession of, and which they labour to preserve by every insidious and corrupt means in their power. If it were not for these obstacles, there is reason to believe that an extensive trade might be carried on between Tibet and the Company's dominions, by the channel of Nepaul, highly beneficial both to the government of the latter, and to the commercial interests of the English nation. A full discussion of this subject, however, must be reserved for a fitter occasion and place than the present. It is proper nevertheless to observe here, that notwithstanding the narrow spirit which directs the commercial concerns of this people, the government affords, on the whole, considerable protection to foreign merchants, rendering them in all cases, it would appear, as strict and as prompt justice as the imperfect nature of its general polity will admit.

The following are the principal imports and exports of Nepaul, the duties on which, as far as relate to the British trade, are regulated by the treaty before referred to. The case, however, is unfortunately different with regard to the commerce carried on directly between the Tibetians and Nepaulians, the imposts on which are ordinarily very enormous, and at all times arbitrary.

Exports from Nepaul to the Company's and Vizier's dominions.

Elephants.

Elephants' teeth.

Rice of kinds.

Timber of sorts.

Hides of sorts.

Ginger.

Kuth, or Terra japonica, white or black.

Turmeric.

Wax.

Honey.

Behroza (or pure resin of the pine).

Walnuts.

Oranges.

Long pepper.

Long pepper root.

Ghee

Teigh (or aromatic bark of the root of the bastard cinnamon).

Taiz-pât (dried leaf of ditto).

Large cardamums.

Roal or Dammer.

Lamp-oil.

Cotton (of the Simul-tree).

The above articles are the produce of the Moruny and other parts of the Turryani, and of Nepaul.

The following articles are the produce either of Tibet proper or of the Kuchâr.

Tanyans, and small Turki horses of Luddakh, and other northern parts of Tibet.

Sheep.

Shawl goats.

Chowri bullocks.

Musk-deer.

Dogs.

Falcons.

Pheasants.

Chuckoars, or fire-eaters.

Gold in dust, grains, and small lumps.

Borax.

Salt.

Sulphur.

Antimony.

Arsenic.

Orpiment.

Musk.

Chowris, or cow-tails.

Rugs, or coarse blankets.

Munjheet.

Raw Sai.

Cherris.

Bikmah.

Jaithamâsi, and various other medicinal drugs.

With respect to the Munjheet, which is chiefly produced in the lower parts of the Kuchâr, it would appear to be in great demand among the Tibetians, who use it in dying their coarse cloths and stuffs. The Nepaulians most commonly barter it for the rock salt and borax of Tibet, which, I was assured by several intelligent persons, were invariably found in the same situations, in proof of which, it may be observed, that there is scarcely ever a bag of salt imported into Nepaul in which numerous lumps of crude borax are not met with. There are small quantities of both salt and salt-petre made in the eastern parts of the valley of Nepaul, but the former is not so much esteemed by the natives as that of Tibet.

The following are the principal commodities exported from the Company's dominions to Nepaul, either for the consumption of that country, or for the Tibet market.

Doputtahs.

Saries (worn by women).

Dhoties.

Kenkhabs.

Goolbudduns.

Bhoolams.

Mushroos.

Oornies (or veils), and various other stuffs the manufacture of Benares.

Taffetas.

Baftas.

Cossahs.

Dooreas.

Chintz.

Mulmuls.

Broad cloth.

Shawls.

Jamawar pieces of shawl.

Shawl Reejais.

Raw silk.

Gold and silver laces.

Carpets.

English cutlery of sorts.

Saffron.

Cloves.

Mace.

Nutmegs.

Guzerat cardamums.

Black pepper.

Betle-nut.

Red sandal wood.

White sandal wood.

Allum.

Vermilion.

Quicksilver.

Shell Lack.

Red wood.

Cotton in the pod (Kuppas).

Tin.

Zinc.

Lead.

Soap.

Camphire.

Red pepper Chilly.

Conch shells.

Oud Billa.

Tobacco.

Coral.

With respect to the state of arts and manufactures in Nepaul, interesting as the subject doubtlessly is, it will scarcely be expected that I should be able to say much. The Newars, who, as I have elsewhere observed, are almost the sole artizans, appear to be acquainted with and exercise most of the handicraft occupations of their Behar neighbours. Of cloths, however, they fabricate only a very coarse kind, partly for home use and partly for exportation to the Tibets; the cotton employed in which, is the produce either of Noakote or of the Muddaise, by which last name they commonly distinguish the Company's territories. They work very well in iron, copper, brass, &c. and are particularly ingenious in carpentry, though it is remarkable that they never use a saw, dividing their wood, of whatever size, by chissel and mallet. They export to the southward some of their brazen utensils; and their cutlery (as swords, daggers, &c.) is by no means contemptible. They have latterly manufactured some fire-arms, but not successfully. They gild exceedingly well, and among the bells they construct for the use of their temples and other religious purposes, some are of a considerable size; one at Bhatgong in particular being five feet in diameter. The paper which they make from the bark of the Seid-burrooa, or Kâghazi-pât, has already been noticed. They distil spirits from rice, and other grains, and also prepare a fermented liquor from wheat, Munooa, rice, &c. which they call Jhâur; it is made somewhat in the manner of our malt-liquors, which it would appear to resemble, though I fancy, from the accounts I have received of it, it is rather more intoxicating; the Newar peasants consider it as much in the light of a necessary of life, as our hard-labouring people do porter.

The Nepaul territories being for the most part parcelled out in jaghires, the proportion of their produce received into the treasury of Khatmanda is by no means considerable. It was not possible, however, during the short stay I made in this country, to ascertain with much exactness or minuteness the amount of the annual revenue realized by the government; I have notwithstanding tolerable good grounds for believing that it never exceeds thirty lacks of rupees, fluctuating at all times, between that sum, and twenty-five lacks. It arises from the following sources:

	Lacks.
Sâir, including profits on elephants and duties on the export trade, from - -	3 to 4
Mint, including imports levied on the import trade from Tibet. (The reason of these duties being received at the mint, is that the returns from that country consist chiefly in gold and silver bullion,) from - -	7 to 8
Formerly the profits on the silver coinage alone yielded a lack of rupees annually; but since the war with Tibet, this branch of the revenue has been much less productive. Should the Tibetians, conformably to ancient custom and treaties, continue to supply themselves with a silver currency from Nepaul, it is probable that the mint revenue will soon be restored to the standard it was usually at anterior to the war.	
Mâh, including duties on salt, profits on salt-petre (which appears to be a monopoly), profits on copper and iron mines, and land-tax, from - -	15 to 18
Lacks of rupees	25 to 30

It is to be observed, that all the silver brought into Nepaul from Tibet, in the way of commerce, must be carried to the mint at

Khatmanda, no silver bullion being allowed to pass into Hindostan. In exchange for his bullion, the merchant receives Nepaul rupees, the government deriving a profit of twelve per cent. from the transaction; four per cent. being charged on account of coinage, and eight arising from the alloy of the rupee.

With respect to gold, it has usually been a monopoly in the hands of government, who oblige the traders from Tibet to sell it at the mint, at the rate of eight rupees per tolah, whence the Ticksâli retails it sometimes at the advanced price of fourteen rupees the tolah.

The copper mines of Nepaul formerly yielded an annual revenue of from three to four lacks of rupees; but owing to the causes noticed at page 176, this profit does not now exceed eighty thousand, or, at the most, a lack, of rupees. The lead mines have not yet produced any advantage to the government, that article still continuing to be exported from Patna to Khatmanda.

Considering how generally the charges of the government, civil as well as military, are defrayed by jaghires, or assignments of land, that the personal estates both of the Rajah and Regent are numerous and productive, and that this court affects on no occasion either splendor or munificence, it is easy to conceive that the receipts of the treasury are fully adequate to the discharge of all demands not provided for in the ordinary manner; and which consist chiefly in the provision of fire-arms and military stores; of broad cloth for the clothing of the regular troops; of jewels; and of silk and cotton stuffs, the manufacture of Benares and Bengal. I have no notion what these several items amount to; but there is reason to believe from the economical, not to say parsimonious habits of the Regent (who, by the bye, is far from being liberal in his pecuniary grants to the Rajah), that the idea pretty generally entertained of his having accumulated considerable treasures, is not altogether without foundation.

Regarding the military force of this kingdom, I have very little to add here to what has been elsewhere occasionally stated on the subject. It was a point, indeed, on which it would not have been prudent to have appeared inquisitive, and perhaps not easy, at any rate, to have obtained accurate information. I confess, therefore, in the first place, my total ignorance of the number and state of their ordnance, which, however, I suspect to be rather contemptible in both respects, although the solicitude of the Regent to augment and improve it, has induced him once or twice to entertain some European adventurers in his service, who would seem to have promised much, but to have performed nothing. After all, I do not see how artillery could be advantageously employed in such a rugged country as that in which the military operations of the Goorkhali, with the exception of the late inroad into Tibet, have hitherto been confined, for even in a defensive view, they would appear to be totally useless, where nature presents almost at every step, impregnable positions; hence, should this government persevere in its endeavours to increase its ordnance, it will be fair to conclude that it has not relinquished its views upon Tibet, notwithstanding the engagements it has recently entered into with the Chinese court, to which that country, before virtually, is now actually and completely subject.

I can form no precise judgment of the amount of the irregular militia enrolled under the Omrahs; but considering the immense tract of country over which these officers are distributed, the great number of Kotes, or castles, that they occupy, and the very recent subjugation of the ancient proprietors of these posts, it is reasonable to suppose that they must be pretty numerous. Besides matchlocks, they are generally armed with bows and arrows; and Kohras, or hatchet swords; of the two last weapons, drawings are annexed.

The regular troops, as they may be called, for the sake of distinction, rather than on account of their superior discipline, are clothed somewhat in the slovenly manner of the Purgunnah Sepoys, formerly in the Company's service, with the difference that none of the corps would appear to have any general uniform or appropriate colour; some among the company of guards which escorted me, appearing, for example, in red, some in blue, and others in green coats. They are all armed with muskets, but of those we saw, few appeared to be fit for service.

This regular force consists, at present, I understand, of from fifty to sixty companies of unequal strength, but containing, on an average, not less than 140 fire-locks; each being commanded by a Subadar with an undeterminate number of Jemadars, and other

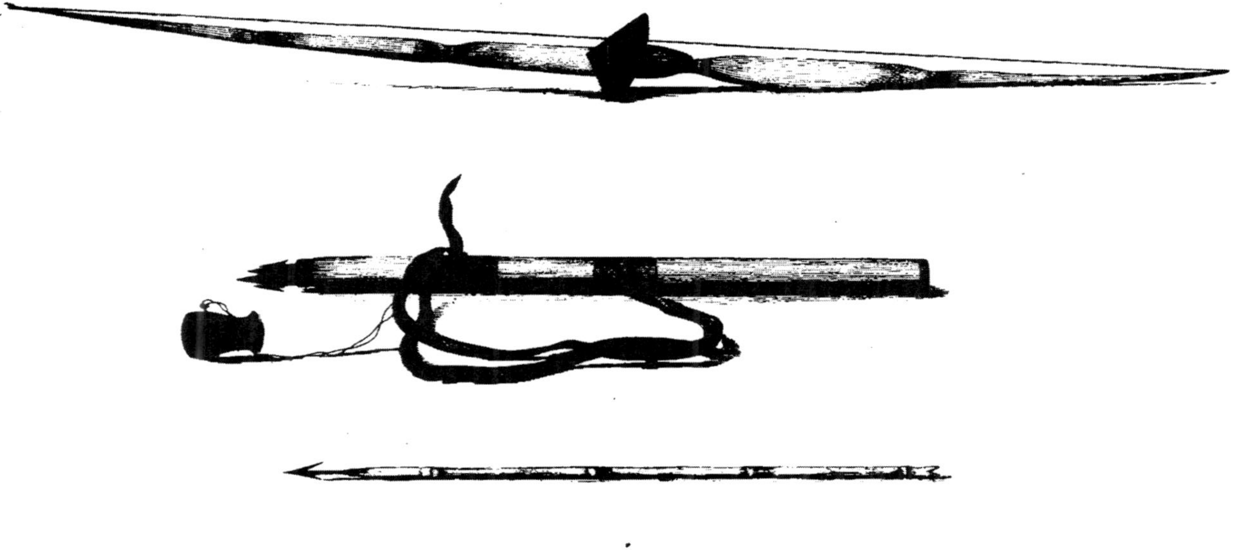

Drawn by A.W. Devis Esqr. Engraved by J. Greig.

Nepaul Bow, Arrow and Quiver.

Published by William Miller, Albemarle Street, January [illegible]

inferior officers under him. The Rajah of Nepaul has at present no corps in his service bearing the denomination of battalions. His guards are distinguished from the other companies by little else besides their having rather more officers, and their carrying the Jung-nishân, or war-standard, the ground of which is yellow, and exhibits an embroidered figure of Hunniman.

It is certain that the Nepaul regulars (if a fair judgment can be formed of the whole from the appearance of the guards) neither march nor carry their arms in a style any thing superior to that of the rabble ordinarily dignified with the title of Sepoys in the service of the generality of the Hindostan Powers, nor would their discipline appear to be much stricter, it being no uncommon practice among the officers (as I learned from two of them who were themselves examples of it) to throw aside their military garb, and even to absent themselves without ceremony from their corps, on any temporary disgust they may happen to conceive; but, with all their defects, I am disposed to think that they are on the whole no bad soldiers. They are brave, sufficiently tractable, and capable of sustaining great hardships, as was abundantly manifested in the return of the Nepaul army from Diggercheh, or Teshoo Loomboo, in the year 1790,* when, encumbered with the spoils of that city, they were induced by various considerations, though the winter was considerably advanced, to take the Khartah and Huttea route, instead of the ordinary one by Koote, at the latter of which passes, the commanders, it seems, were aware they should find it impracticable to elude the examination of the officers

* See Turner's Embassy to Tibet, p. 137.

stationed there, in order to take an account of the booty they had acquired. The perils to which they were exposed on this occasion were of a kind which it would be little imagined in Europe an Eastern army was either capable of supporting, or liable to encounter on the very borders, as it were, of Bengal. In short, it is an unquestionable fact, that in crossing that ridge of mountains which stretches in a south-east direction from the vicinity of Koote to the country of the Limbooas and of the Dewa Durmah, it was with the utmost difficulty and danger that they penetrated through the snow, with which their track was covered to a depth that proved fatal in several instances in the slightest false step. They were in this dreadful situation for five or six days, during which they were obliged to pass the night on the bare snow, after hardening it for that purpose, as well as they could, though their labour was sometimes scarcely over when a fresh fall would nearly bury them. The loss of the army in this retreat, which was conducted by Damoodur Paurdi and Bem Shah, is said to have amounted to upwards of 2000 men, great numbers of whom appear to have been frozen to death; the remedy so common and so effectual in the northern parts of Europe and America, in frost-bitten cases, was unfortunately unknown to these people, who, on our mentioning it to them, lamented bitterly that they had not been acquainted with it at this period, when many of their companions were daily obliged to be abandoned in this wretched condition, while others deemed themselves happy to escape with the loss of their fingers and toes.

The currency of Nepaul consists, principally, of silver pieces of eight annas, there are also some struck of sixteen annas; but the circulation of this last coin, which is called a Sicca, is confined to Nepaul proper, and is far from being common even there. The Sicca, indeed, has been known in this country only since the time of Purthi Nerain.

Besides the silver coins above-mentioned, they have one of so low a value as the two hundred and eighty-eighth part of a sicca, which is called a Cheedum. It may be easily conceived, however, that the pieces of this denomination are not in ordinary or general use, any more than the very minute gold coins which are sometimes struck at the mint of Khatmanda, and occasionally sent as presents by the Rajah to foreign powers. Even the ushrupee, or gold rupee, of Nepaul is to be considered rather in the light of a medal than of current coin.

The silver eight-anna piece, now called Mohr, and Addheeda, was formerly denominated Mehnder-mulie, after the Prince who first struck it, and by treaty established its currency in the neighbouring kingdom of Tibet; this prince would appear to have been one of the successors of Hur Sing Deo, and of the dynasty of Khatmanda, which city is said to have exclusively enjoyed for some time the privilege of supplying Tibet with coin, a privilege the more singular as it was from this very country that Nepaul obtained her silver bullion. The origin of this practice is ordinarily referred to the superstitious reverence in which the valley of Nepaul, and more especially the north-west parts of it, (highly celebrated for their sanctity) has been wont to be held by the spiritual sovereigns of Tibet; but what ever may have been the cause of it, there is not a doubt that the present Nepaul government made the departure of the Tibetians from ancient usage in this respect the pretext for the war which it waged about four years ago against the confederated Lamas; as evidently appears from a memorial transmitted to me from Nepaul on this subject, an extract of which is given in Appendix No. II.

Besides the gold and silver coins enumerated above, they have a copper currency in Nepaul of two or three denominations, such as Chârdâms, Dodums, &c. thirty-six of the former usually going to the mohr, or eight-anna piece.

The Mehnder-mulie exhibited anciently a representation of Lehassa, on one side, and on the reverse the name, titles, and emblems of the reigning sovereign of Khatmanda. Since the conquest of Nepaul by Purthi Nerain, no allusion to Lehassa has been preserved, the mohr bearing on one side the following inscription:

Sri Sri Sri
Run Behauder Shah
Dewâ;

And on the other

Sri Sri Sri
Goorkhnâth
Sri Bhowâni,

with the year of the Soka, and certain emblems allusive to the Hindoo superstition, as the sun, moon, Trisool of Mahadeo, &c.

The weight and standard of the Nepaul sicca, mohr, four-anna piece, and gold rupee, appear severally in the following result of an assay made at my request by the mint-master at Calcutta:

Weight of 5 siccas, or whole rupees, 76 annas, sicca weight, that is, 15$\frac{1}{5}$ annas each.

Weight of 5 mohrs, or addheedas, 37 annas 7$\frac{1}{2}$ pice, Calcutta sicca weight, that is, 7 annas 6$\frac{1}{5}$ pice each.

Weight of 5 quarter mohrs, or 2-anna pieces, 9 annas 3 pice, that is, 1 anna 10$\frac{1}{5}$ pice each.

Weight of a gold rupee, or ushrupee, 15 annas.

The standard of the silver coins is 7 rupees 13 annas per cent. worse than Calcutta sicca standard.

The standard of the gold coin is 2 per cent. worse than that of the Calcutta mohur.

Time did not admit of my attending much to the state of learning among these people, yet the little information that it was in my power to acquire on the subject disposes me to think that the Pundits of Nepaul are not behind hand, in the branches of science usually cultivated by their fraternity, with those of any other Hindoo country whatever. Astronomy, or rather its degenerate offspring, and ordinary companion among superstitious nations, judicial astrology, appears to be their favourite study, and has so deeply, as well as undistinguishedly, infected every rank among them, that a stranger might be tempted to conclude that here the horoscope and ephemeris determined in most cases the line both of civil and moral conduct, and that the people, in short, were universally directed by their soothsayers. In fine, it is extremely probable that there is no place in India where a search after ancient and valuable Sanscrit manuscripts in every department of Brahminical learning would be more successful than in the valley of Nepaul, and particularly at Bhatgong, which would seem to be the Benares of the Ghoorkhali territories. In support of this opinion I may observe, that I was credibly informed of a single private library in that city containing upwards of fifteen thousand volumes.

Besides the Sanscrit, which would appear to be considerably cultivated by the Brahmins of Nepaul, the principal vernacular languages of this country are,

The Purbutti.
The Newar.
The Dhenwar.
The Muggur.
The Kurraute.
The Howoo, or Hyoo.
The Limbooa, and
The Bhootia.

The Pundits of Bhatgong date the introduction of the first Sanscrit grammar into Nepaul, from the time of Unghoo Burmah, of the posterity of Pussoopûsh Deo; but it is not easy to ascertain with any exactness at what period this prince flourished.

The Purbutti and Newar characters, as also that in use among

To face P. 220

The Purbutti Alphabet.

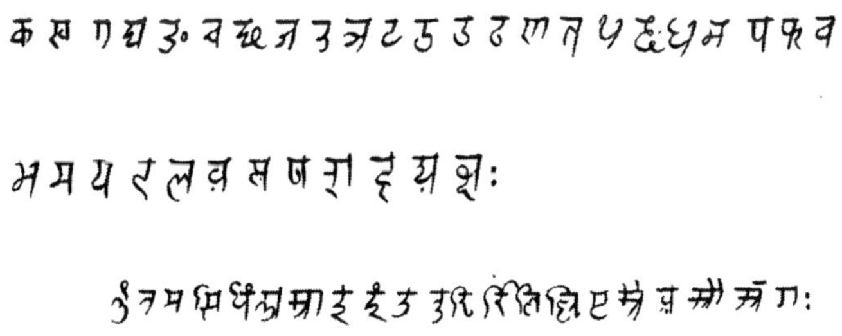

The Newar Alphabet.

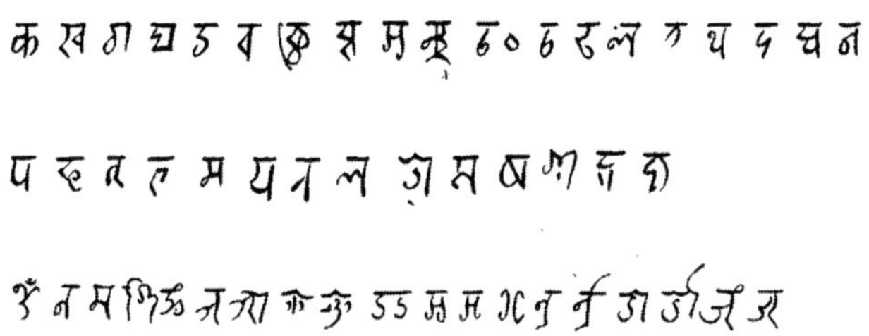

The Koithi Alphabet.

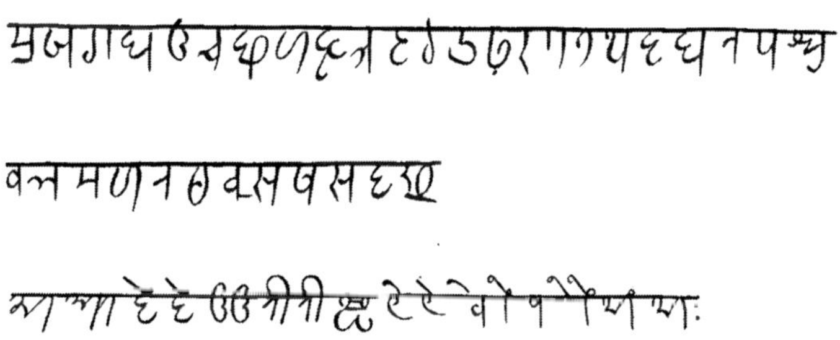

the Koiths of Nepaul, are exhibited in the annexed Plate. The character employed by the Purbutties, or mountaineers, (the restrained sense of which appellation has been already explained,) is, it will be seen, the Deonagur, from which the alphabet of the Newars is obviously derived, differing materially from it only in a few letters. The Koith character of Nepaul is almost exactly the same that is used in various parts of Hindostan.

The Purbutti dialect is evidently a derivative from the Sanscrit, agreeing very closely with the various idioms of Behar, Oude, &c.; but it is by no means so clear, that the Newar is a branch of the same stem, though it is certain that it contains several words of Sanscrit origin. I shall not, however, enter at present into any philological discussion concerning the origin and antiquity of the Newar or any of the other languages enumerated above, but content myself with presenting as copious specimens of each as circumstances have enabled me to collect.

Vocabulary of the Purbutti and Newar Languages.

	Purbutti.	Newar.
Mankind	Manis	Munnoo.
A man	Loagnia	Mujun.
A woman	Suâsni	Musa.
A hermaphrodite	Singharoo	Unnharam.
A child	———	Môcha, or Mucha.
An infant	Balik	Ngnı môcha.
A boy	Chhôra	Kay-môcha.

	Purbutti.	Newar.
A girl	Chhôri	Mhiau-môcha.
An elder brother	Dhajoo	Dhajoo.
A younger brother, a brother generally	Bhoe	Kheēnja.
An elder sister	Deede	———
A younger sister, or sister generally	Bhyne	Khehe.
A father	Baba	Boba.
A paternal or maternal grand-father	Brerajoo	Ajhajhoo.
A great-grandfather	Jujoo	Tapa Ajhajhoo.
A great great-grandfather	Chabjoo	Iya Ajhajhoo.
A mother	Ama	Mang.
A paternal grandmother	Bhajoo	Ujema.
A maternal grandmother	Bhajoo	Ujema.
A paternal uncle	Kañchow	Kukhajhoo.
An aunt by ditto	Kanchama	Ma-manjhoo.
A maternal uncle	Mama	Pajhoo.
An aunt by ditto	Moomani	Mullijoo.
An aunt (maternal)	Sani-ma	Chemanjhoo.
An aunt (paternal)	Phoophoo	Nuni-manjhoo.
An uncle by a maternal aunt	Sana-baboo	Chu-bhajhoo.

	Purbutti.	Newar.
The husband of one's sister-in-law, or wife's sister	Sarhoo	Khunja bhuta, Duda bhuta.
The sister of one's wife	Sale	Kehi bhuttoo, or bhutta
The brother of one's wife	Salô	Kunja bhuta, or bhuttâ.
The husband of one's sister	Bhunajoo	Jeleha dhaz-jhoo.
A son	Belah	Raij.
A son-in-law	Jooari	Jeleha.
A daughter	Bite	Mhean̄.
The mother of one's wife	Sasoo	Sussa mang.
The father of one's wife	Surooroo.	Sussa bhang.
A brother's wife	Bhujoo	Bhoucha.
A son's wife	Bhooari	Bhoumucha.
An old man	Bhoorhâ	Jheat.
A young man	Tendheau	Leamhô.
A full brother, sister, &c.	Sâk	Tho.
A half brother, sister, &c.	Soutaila	Chumma-myakai.
One's own akin	Apnoa	June.

	Purbutti.	Newar.
Another's, a stranger	Beranoa	Keeteekea.
The head	Kuppal	Chhun.
The hair	Row	Sir, or Sin.
The brains	Goode	Nyepoo.
The face.	Mookh	Khua.
The eyes.	Aukha	Mekha.
The eye-brow	Pemaila	Mipu Soñ.
The sight of the eye	Pooteele	Mekha-deo (or the Deoty of the eye).
The eye-lash	Ankhebhown	Mekha-poose.
The temples	Keenseere	Nyramoo, or Nyamoo.
The nose	Nak	Nyeka.
The nostrils	Natheera	Nhypwal.
The cheek	Gala	Nyukhô.
The forehead	Neendhar	Mhôhesa.
The whiskers	Koongar	Gwya.
The beard	Dharie	Chaker-gwya.
The lips	Oath	Mhutûshe.
The mouth	Mookh	Mhoojoo.
The chin	Choondea	Munnha.
The tongue	Jebre	Mye.
The palate	Taroo	Thankô
The teeth	Danth	Wah.
The gums	Dheenesa	Wahdhe.

	Purbutti.	Newar.
The windpipe	Lub-lubea	Kathoo.
The throat	Ghanthe	Keekoo.
The ear	Kan	Nhypeen.
The tip of the ear	Lôte	Nhypeen pooal.
The back	Kundhoo	Mhee.
The neck	Gurdun	Ghupa.
The back of the neck		Mekagha (or the root of the eyes).
The shoulder	Koombh	Bhôto.
The waist	Kumr	Shaulé.
The chest	Chhate	Noonggha.
The ribs	Kurren	Bhapee.
The nipples of the breast.	Doodth	Doodhoo.
The belly (generally)	Paith	Pooa.
The upper belly	———	Pooat.
The abdomen	Nytho	Chepooat.
The navel	Nabe	Tarphoo.
The rump	Phela	Peumpa.
The arm	Pakhura	Ludda.
The arm-pit	Kakhi	Yakô.
The hand	Kath	Laha.
The fist	Moothe	Mooth.
The finger	Ownla	Puching.

	Purbutti.	Newar.
The thumb	Boore-owntho	Mala.
The nail	Mung	Looshe.
The thigh	Tegra	Kheepa.
The knee	Ghoanda	Poole.
The leg	Pasoolâ	Che-chepate.
The ancle bone	Gole-ghantho	Goocha.
The foot	Ghora-paoom	Pole,
The sole of the foot	Pytalô	Paleto.
The heel	Kurkocha.	Gwale.
The heart	Moottoo	Nyoogosheing.
The kidney	Mugowla	Jhulausche.
The liver	Kullaijô	Sheing.
The lungs	Phoakso	Soo-ô.
The stomach	Bhoondre	Bhugga.
The gut	Andra	Ale-poote.
The body	Sureer	Mha.
A member	Joame	Saha.
Tears	Ansoo	Khobhe.
Blood	Ruggut	Khee.
Sweat	Pusseria	Chhôke.
A mole	Kohte	Teeh.
A wrinkle	Chhoure	Keykoong.
A wart	Moosô	Khye
The skin	Chhala	Chaingoo

	Purbutti.	Newar.
The flesh	Mashoo	Lahh.
A bone	Har	Khooeñ.
A vein	Neessa	Set.
The marrow	Mashe	Sheet.
The fat	Bôsô	Dak.
A disease	Roag	Loê.
A sick person	Roage	Loage.
A doctor	Bhyde	Bhyde.
Medicine	Oukhud	Waso.
The earth (the planet)	Bhoome	Bhoome.
The sky	Surug	Akas.
The moon	Chunduma	Looi-mella Deo, or the white Deoty.
The sun	Soorjeh	Soorjeh-deo.
A star	Fareh	Nugoo.
A cloud	Badul	Kheesoo.
Sun-shine	Gham	Nebha.
A storm	Burra-butas	Dhakoo.
A water	Pane	Leekh (Calenaudee-lua (Bhatgong), Luha, or Leha (Patn).
Fire	Ago	Mee.
Air	Butlas	Phye.
Earth (the elements)	Mate	Chat.

	Purbutti.	Newar.
Below	Ghurô	Kane.
Above	Ulgô	Thane.
A tree	Rookh	Sheema
A leaf	Pât	Sheeho.
A bough	Hanga	Sheema-dañ.
A root	Pura	Ha.
The root of a tree	———	Sheema-ha.
A bud	Koampla	Sooan-mukkoo.
A flower	Phool	Sooan
Fruit	Phul	Seesa-boosa.
Raw	Kacho	Kuché.
Ripe	Pakko	Nunggo.
Dryness	Sookheako	Gunggâ.
Moisture	Gulô	Dhoo-gego.
Heat	Tato	Tanô.
Cold	Cheesa	Shucho.
An animal	Pussoo	Pushoo-hunga.
A horse	Ghora	Synha.
An elephant	Hati	Kushi.
A tiger	Bhag	Dhun.
An ass	Gudda	Gudda.
A jackal	Seal	Dhoon.
A cat	Beralo	Bho.
A fox	Khukherea	———

	Purbutti.	Newar.
A he-goat	Bôka	Doogo.
A she-goat	Bakre	Chôlé,
A wether-goat	———	Budria.
A sheep	Bher	Phy.
A ram	Toombha	Bhea.
An ewe	Bhere	Ma-phy.
A cow	Gao	Sa.
A bull, or bullock	Ghoroo	Dhôho
A calf	Bhacha	Sa-cha, (or little bull).
A buffalo	Bhynsi	Mea.
A male buffalo	Ranghô	Tooméa.
A calf buffalo	Pakea	Mea-cha.
A dog	Kookhur	Kucha.
A bitch	Kookhurne	Ma-kucha.
A whelp or pup	Chownra	Kucha-cha.
A hog	Soor	Pha.
A sow	———	Mapha.
A boar	———	Bapha.
A pig	———	Pha-cha.
A fish	Macha	Gna.
A snake	Sap	Be, or Bey.
An ant	Kemula	Yareñ.
A fowl	Kookhûra	Goong-goo.
A pigeon	Purewa.	Busk-hooñ.

	Purbutti.	Newar.
An egg	Phool	Khañ.
A sparrow	Bhunggaina	Chukoocha.
A crow	Kowa.	Koakh.
A bee	Mahôu	Ha.
A bald head	Shaplea	Tealô.
A blind person	Kana	Kañ.
A squint-eyed person	Denô	Ya.
A deaf person	Bhyrô	Kenia.
A dumb person	Latoo	Lata.
A stutterer	Bhukbhukea	Khâkô.
Delicate	Patlô	Chukkbo.
Robust	Môtâ	Lohh.
Thin	Dooblô	Gyhi.
Tall	Uglô.	Taka.
Short	Pulkhea	Bawut.
Hump-backed	Kooborô	Dhooshe.
Lame	Khorundo	Khoo.
Sleep	Sootno	Dame.
Wakefulness	Jajno.	Dunne.
Hunger	Bhook	Petialô.
Thirst	Tukha	Peachalo.
Milk	Dood	Doodoo.
Sour-curd	Dhye	Dhow.
Butter-milk	Mhye	Kooatur.
Cream	Turs	Keheñ.

	Purbutti.	Newar.
A sort of clouted cream	Udhoutea	Takô doodoo.
Sweet curd	Khooroune	Khôa.
Butter	Noune	Loun.
Ghee, or clarified butter	Gheoo	Ghiô.
Oil	Tail	Chekun.
Honey	Maha	Kushte.
Salt	Noon	Ché
Salt-petre	Shoreh	Khache
Sugar	Khand	Sakhoo.
Sugar-candy	Mesre	Newéak.
Molasses	Ghoor	Chakô.
Pepper (black)	Murruch	Mulley.
Pepper (red)	Khoorsane	Mulley-bhata.
Garlick	Lishen	Labha.
Ginger	Udwa	Paloo.
Cardamum	Ullache	Yala.
Clove	Loang	Loang.
Nutmeg	Jaiphul	Jepho.
Cinnamon	Darcheeni	Lowntwai.
Saffron	Keysur	———
Woad	Darooa	Sheen.
Charcoal	Ungar	Yhanga.
A chest	Sundok	Dhansheta.

	Purbutti.	Newar.
A river	Nuddi, Kôla	Koushi.
A shop	Dooka	Pussul.
A street	Gully	Chow.
A road or path	Bâtô	Lan.
Straight	Soojhô	Tapéka
Crooked	Banggo	Baikô.
Hard	Sachô	Bulla.
Soft	Kownlô	Yatô.
Fine	Putalô	Cheekdhañ.
Coarse	Môtô	Towdhañ.
The morning	Bholee	Kunnij-sootha.
Noon	Dooepéhr	Bâne.
Evening	Sanjh	Sundhiaka.
Night	Raté	Chané.
Day	Diu	Nine.
A sensible person	Bhoodheman	Geane.
A blockhead	Moorukh	Ugeane.
Asleep	Solcakhochha	Déné.
Awake	Jagehha	Phetnachiné
Reason	Oothô	Dunni.
Sealed	Byseô	Somukachóne.
A friend	Mellap	Usta.
An enemy	Sutrô	Sutûr,
Joy	Hurka	Luslaya.

	Purbutti.	Newar.
Sadness	Bermad	Tungehaya.
A servant	Chakur	Sawruk.
A master	Saheb	Purman.
A cook	Bhansea	Sooa.
A horsekeeper, or groom	Chuwadan	Chulwada.
A dance	Naleh	Peakun.
A beggar	Cheehûck	Phôgin.
A musician	Banadar	Phanda.
A long drum	———	Khing.
A crucible	Hundeolo	Bhuncha.
A mould	Sanchô	Palung.
Colour	Runga	Rungah.
Warp	Tan	Yénka.
Woof	Bunnoo	Taika.
A loom	Loogabunné khawl	Taika.
A spinning-wheel	Chaka	Yant.
A distaff	Soorjuô	Natoo.
A gelding	Nukhus	Sone-walajan.
Glew	Sennish	Besum.
The new moon	Dootia.	Dootia.
The day following a new moon	Punewa	Purthe-putta.
A stage or day's journey	Bas	Bas.

	Purbutti.	Newar.
Snow	Heeon	Châwapoo.
Hail	Asaina	Poon.
Ice	Toosarô	Pô.
Thunder	Genjo	Nugaloo.
Lightning	Bayole	Purpeessa.
Rain	Panepurcha	Wahgato.
Scales	Tôlô	Turazoo.
A quarter	Choutai	Chukunché.
A half	Adebha	Buché.
A third	Tessarahessa	Loanch Reen.
The whole	Poora	Chukoat.
Cotton	Rouroô	Keeppye.
Cloth	Keepra	Kapoo.
Thread	Dhagoo	Ka.
Silk	Reeshum	Paka.
A needle	Jooyâ	Moolô.
Paper	Kageet	Bhouôut
A pen	Kulm	Lekheen
An inkstand	Mushaiene	Musma.
Ink	Mushee	Muss.
Red	Ratô	Yhaoun.
White	Seto	Tooyêe.
Black	Kalô	Hakô.
Green	Huryo	Waoon.

	Purbutti.	Newar.
Yellow	Phaijeelo	Mhasô.
Blue	Neelô	Wanehô.
A house	Ghur	Chhén.
A wall	Bhutô	Lôkha.
A door	Dylô	Khapa.
A roof	Chanô	Poo.
A floor cloth	Péchôna	Lasa.
A garden	Phoolware	Kaimba.
A wild, or forest	Bun	Goon
A plantation	Khait	Booñ.
Spring	Bussunt	Bussunt.
Autumn	———	Toala.
Winter	Jaro	Chella.
Summer	Gurme	Tannô.
Rainy season	Burkha	Burkha.
A mountain or hill	Purbut	Purbut.
A plain	Mydan	Khéô.
Stone	Dhoonga	Lôhôñ.
Lead	Sheesô	Mhañ.
Gold	Soon	Loon.
Silver	Roopoô	Wôhâ.
Copper	Lambo	Shuja
Brass	Peetul	Léy.
Tin	Justa	Justa.

	Purbutti.	Newar.
Iron	Phullam	Neek.
Ore	Dhaow	——
Bread	Rôtô	Madrie.
Wheat	Ghoaho	Chhô.
Barley	Jow	Tuchhô.
Rice (out of the ear)	Chowle	Jakhi.
Rice (in the ear, or Paddy)	Dhan	Wah.
Mash (a sort of pulse)	Mas	Mas, or ma-iye.
Moong (ditto)	Moonghe	Mooh.
Jooar or Jenora (a sort of grain)	Joonealo	——
Mussoor (or lentil)	Mussooroo	Moossoo.
Sanwa (a coarse species of grain)	Sama	——
Lobea, or Bhora (a species of pulse)	Bhôra	Bhoote.
Peas	Keraw	Kygoo.
Koolthe (a species of pulse)	Gaput	Khola.
Munroon (a coarse grain)	Kôdô	Doosee.
Kungne (ditto)	Kagnoo	——
Sugar-cane	Ookhoo	Too.

	Purbutti.	Newar.
A plantain	Kaira	Kaira.
A guava	Umba	Umbasi.
An orange	Suntôla, or Kòwnla	Sûntarrashi.
A walnut	Okher	Khoseng
A pine-apple	Kable Kuthan	Keethurr.
A mango	Amh	Amh.
A fig	Unjar	Doobûshe.
A mulberry	Toot	———
A grape	Dakh	Mushi.
A cocoa nut	Narewul	Nunkea.
A water-melon	Khurbooza	Khubuza.
The egg-plant	Bhua	Bhunta.
Fenugreek	Maithee	Maichor.
Spinage	Palunkhoo	Pullañ.
Toorye (a sort of pot-herb)	Tôrea	Poloo.
A pumpkin	Lowka	Jashe.
A vow	Bhôbe	Hâloo.
Speech	Koora	Kha.
Death	Murnoo	Shee.
Madness	Bhoulaha	———
Pain	Betha	Sheatô.
An itching	Lootô	Kyn.
Weakness	Nubuttyee	Pecoo.

	Purbutti.	Newar.
A wound	Ghaô	Ghaô.
A pimple	Phoûka	Poo.
A sear, or stain	Dogh	Ghakoo.
Pus (matter)	Peep	Whee.
An imposthume	Soonchô	Manoo.
A blister	Phouka	Yayatô.
A rash	Ghuñmôra.	
A gangrene	Syne katero	Sheephur.
Piles	Hursa	Ulla Rye..
Fainting	Moorchapurrea	Sutphaloo.
A cough	Khoke	Mooshô-woolô.
A defluxion from cold	Roogha	Shukkuncholô.
Costiveness	Mireend	Goombeylô.
A looseness	Pukhala	Puta jool malô.
Indigestion	Upuch	Ujerna.
A fever	Jarrô	Koampôlô.
The venereal disease	Beyrunge	Musaha.
A scalding	Sôzauk	Meheyôlô.
Small-pox	Bephen	Tou Ryê.
Vomiting	Oochal	Than woolâ.
A purge	Joolab	Kothewaseu.
A trade	Seep	Goon.
A tradesman	Seepaloo	Seañ.
A workshop	Karkarch	Jeasa.

	Purbutti.	Newar.
A goldsmith	Sunar	Sunar.
A brazier	Kâmee	Lumboat.
An ironsmith	Kamee	Kow.
A carpenter	Kurwee	Koune
A tailor	Dirmyñ	Shoojekar.
A ropemaker	Juhobatne	Khepanelema.
A confectioner	Hulwau	Mache kowme.
A butcher	Kussau	Nou.
A fisherman, or boatman	Manjhee	Hoorkia.
A shop-keeper	Puslea	Puslea.
A builder or bricklayer	Uwala	Weekeunni.
A washerman	Dôby	Dôby.
A carrier	Sarkee	Sarkee.
A potter	Koomhalea	Koomhal.
A barber	Naw	Nowû.
A painter	Chetterkar	Poon.
A dyer	Rungraiz	Chheepa.
A shoemaker	Chummar	Chummar.
A dealer, or merchant	Bypari	Bypari.
A stone-cutter	Lôhkurni	Lôhkurni.
A seller of spirituous liquors	Shoondhy	Soling.
A ploughman	Halle	———
A porter	Bhurrea	Bhalea.

	Purbutti.	Newar.
A thief	Choor	Chooñ.
A banker	Mahajun	Mahajun.
A speaker of truth	Sanchô	Suttea.
A liar	Dhauff	Asucha, or Usuchô.
Good	Ramro	Baula.
Bad	Nunacko	Bamala.
A water jar	Gagro	Dhaupô.
An earthen juglate	Bhougona	Lôta.
A pot	Bhañra	Thala.
A cup	Bhuttuko	Bhatcha.
A dish	That	Bhoo.
A bucket	Dhoal	Kumdal.
Rope	Jheeroo	Lackeput.
A well	Indar	Toon.
Grass	Ghas	Ghas.
Bamboo	Banse	Puff.
A knife or dagger	Kookheri	Chope.
A buckler	Dhaul	Suhen.
An arrow	Teer	Bala.
A bow	Gholell	Lépa.
A matchlock	Bundook	Toopiun
A book	Pooteu	Sañpoo.
An account, or calculation	Lékha	Léakha.
Balance	Baki	Lepee.

	Purbutti.	Newar.
Surplus, excess	Urkhialo	Oopur.
Peace	Melnô	Mellejood.
War	Jooddkea	Huttâi.
Question	Koora	———
Answer	Khunne	———
The foot of a hill	Phed, or Pehedo	Thankô.
A round peak	Thoomko	Tooapul.
A pointed peak	Choolhe	———
The ascent, or acclivity of a hill	Ookalô	Tañ.
The descent, or declivity	Oorhalô	Pak.
A precipice	Bhulkhandô	Gal.
A cataract, or cascade	Chhango	Jhoalla.
A rapid	Chhehuro	Chhôwah.
A depth, or pit of a rivulet	Ruhha, or Duhha	———
A ford, or passage	Junghar,orJoonghar	Khoo-ghaut.
The flat of a summit	Bhunjang	Bhunjang.
A month	Mas	Luchie.
January	Maugh	Maugh.
February	Phagun	Phagun.
March	Cheyte	Chyte.

	Purbutti.	Newar.
April	Bysack	Bysack.
May	Jeet	Jeeth.
June	Assar	Asar.
July	Sawun	Goonla.
August	Bhadun	Yenla.
September	Asin	Asen.
October	Karteek	Kateek.
November	Ughun	Mungsur.
December	Poos	Poos.
A week	Ek satho	Wa.
Saturday	Suneebar	Seneeber.
Sunday	Etwar	Adethéwar.
Monday	Soombar	Soomwar.
Tuesday	Mungulbar	Mungul.
Wednesday	Boodhbar	Boodh.
Thursday	Beesabar	Sookhwar.
Friday	Sukabar	Sookhwar.
Intelligence	Summachar	Summachar.
A rich or opulent person	Dhunne	Towme.
A beggar, or indigent person	Cheekûk	Phoongen.
A chief, or commander	Thoolômanûs	Punuan.
Sweet	Goolys	Chakô.

	Purbutti.	Newar.
Bitter	Teeto	Khayd.
Salt	Nomelo	Chayunagô.
Sour	Amelô	Paoon.
Insipid, tasteless	Ulunoo	Nealô.
A rupee	Roopea	Sahi.
A pice, or copper pice	Dhebooa	Dhiba.
Numerals		
One*	—	Sehee or Chee.
Two	—	Nuschee, or Nuchee.
Three	—	Soo-on.
Four	—	Pee.
Five	—	Nga.
Six	—	Khoo.
Seven	—	Nhy.
Eight	—	Chea.
Nine	—	Goo.
Ten	—	Sanuh.
Eleven	—	Surm-sehee.
Twelve	—	Surm-nuschee.
Thirteen	—	Surm-soo-ôn.
Fourteen	—	Surm-pee.
Fifteen	—	Surm-ga.
Sixteen	—	Surm-khoo.

* In the Purbutti dialect these numbers are the same as in the Hindooee.

	Purbutti.	Newar.
Seventeen	—	Surm-nha.
Eighteen	—	Surm-cha.
Nineteen	—	Surm-goo.
Twenty	—	Ngu-e.
Twenty-one	—	Ngu-nuchee.
Thirty	—	Sevee-e.
Thirty-one	—	Swee-sehee.
Forty	—	Pee-e-e.
Forty-one	—	Pee-e-chee.
Fifty	—	Nga-e.
Sixty	—	Khoo-e-e.
Seventy	—	Nhy-e-e.
Eighty	—	Chy-e-e.
Ninety	—	Goo-e-e.
A hundred	—	Suchee.
Two hundred	—	Nesul, or Ne-asul.
Three hundred	—	So-a-sul.
Four hundred	—	Pe-a-sul.
Five hundred	—	Nga-sul.
A thousand	—	Do-eschee, or Douhee.
Ten thousand	—	Jee dol.
A hundred thousand	—	Lak-sehee, or Lakchee.

	Purbutti.	Newar.
Ordinals.		
First	Phelo	Nappa.
Second	Doorsao	Won leppa.
Third	Terno	Somama.
Fourth	Chouthô	Peamana.
To be	Chhynoo	Dyô.
To come	Ounoo	Woe.
To go	Janô	Wane, Wône.
To do	Gurnoo	Yae.
To sit	Bumo	Chôné.
To rise	Ootho	Dhunni.
To eat	Khanâ	Nye.
To drink.	Peenô	Toone.
To sleep	Sootno	Dene.
To wake	Jaynô	Nhelmchakú hûné.
To laugh	Hasnô	While.
To cry	Roonoo	Khôé.
To give	Deenoo	Leu.
To take	Leenoo	Kâé.
To live	Joonoo	Mooun.
To die	Murnoo	Shé.
To play	Kaihlaoo	Mheté.
To learn	Dhumoo	Munúlô.
To set fire to	Dhurounoo	Munahachooe.

	Purbutti.	Newar.
To see	Daichhnoo	Sooé.
To show	Dikhaunoo	Kiné.
To bring	Beaunoo	Hruké.
To take away	Lejanoo	Jrouahoañ.
To send	Pathnownoo	Beachhooé.
To learn	Seikhnoo	Shené.
To teach	Seihanoo	Shunabi.
To talk	Boalnoo, Koocagurnoo	Khanally.
To flee	Bhagnoo	Beushé dooné.
To wash	Dhoonoo	Shélé.
To rub	Mulnoo	Thaé.
To grind	Pusnoo	Kilé.
To hear	Soonnoo	Niné.
To lie	Bandnoo	Chee.
To draw or drag	Juhhnoo	Sate.
To break	Bhanchnoo	Tothuwé.
To hang or suspend	Joundshounoo	Khayané.
To fear	Durnoo	Gyana.
To open (v. a.)	Khoalnoo	Khune.
To walk	Phurnoo	Ooshe, Henelivé.
To write	Laicknoo	Ukha, Chûe.
To fix or affix	Lownoo	Tai.
To fall	Khumoo	Dooloo.

	Purbutti.	Newar.
To mix	Millounoo	Paihya.
To blossom (v. n.)	Phooknoo	Wayato.
To rain	Purnoo	Wagato.
To hide	Choapnoo	Bhoosunachuwa.
To wish, desire	Chalea gurnoo	Muttink.
To pick (up) together	Teepnoo	Lé.
To move, stir	———	Nelambatô.
To leap	Phâl-palnoo	Tehe newe.
To dance	Nachnoo	Piakhanhwé.
To sing	Gounoo	Maihalé.
To play on an instrument	Bujanoo	Thué.
To lose	Hurrownoo	Tanô.
To sprinkle, diffuse	Jharnoo	Tha thoe.
To sow	Churnoo	Pie.
To grow, to sprout out	Oong-garnoo	Linachêwé.
To escape	Choottnoo	Tobello.
To seize hold	Summownoo	Jooné.
To run	Dugoornoo	Booiay.
To tear	Pharnoo	Phaey.
To sew	Shewoonoo	Sooe.
To lose (at play)	Harnoo	Joolumboote.
To win	Jeetnoo	Tiatô.
To beat	Marnoo	Dai.

	Purbutti.	Newar.
To taste	Chahhnoo.	Manasûé.
To smell	Soong-gnoo	Natuvé.
To sell	Baichnoo	Mu-e.
To buy	Kinnoo	Ing-gia.
To count	Gunnoo	Nin.
To cut	Katnoo	Dhiné.
To scrape	Tachnoo	Chhayajhooé.
To strike	Toahhnoo	———
To send for, to call to	Bullownoo	Soute.
To explain	Sumjhowna	Loomunké.
To make	Bunnounoo	Dyké.
To squeeze	Nichoarnoo	Taishé.
To dry	Sookhownoo	Ganô.
To want	Mangnoo	Phôné.
To commit to, to consign	Soampnoo	Biate.
To fight	Burnoo	Lôaé.
To tremble	Kampnoo	Thu-thu-nûyañ.
To kiss	Moeye-kanoo	Chûpanyé.
To rot	Gulnoo	Geetô.
To tumble	Lootnoo	Gôtuli.
To light	Ooja loo gurnoo	Muttoochia.
To know	Chinnoo	Shike.
To search	Khoajhnoo.	Malé.

	Purbutti.	Newar.
To glitter, shine, sparkle	Julkhnoo	Hulla pulla chea.
To swim	Pourhnoo	Tola wai.
To sink	Burnoo	Lokoombé.
To touch, feel	Choonoo	Shee-ee.

Specimens of the Limbooa and Muñgur dialects.

	Limbooa.	Mungur.
Fire	Mee	Mhie.
Water	Choqa	Die.
Rice (raus)	Scea	Jharoo.
Boiled rice	Jatt	——
Meat	Sa	Sia.
Wind	Summi	Ramsô.
Sun	Num	Namkhañ.
Moon	Laba	Giahoot.
Star	Kheseeba	Tooga.
Day	Lendik	Nams-in.
Night	Sendek	Nabhé.
House	Him	Yem.
Sword	Moodamphé	——
One	Chee, or Tchee	Katt.
Two	Nyaich	Nis.

	Limbooa.	Mungur.
Three	Loomchee	Seêm.
Four	Besi	Bûli.
Five	Ngachie	Banga.
Six	Tookehi	—*
Seven	Noochi	—
Eight	Yetche	—
Nine	Phungse	—
Ten	Thibo	—
Twenty	Niboang	—
Man	Nammi	Lainzha.
Woman	Mainchema	Mahaza.
Child	Hinja	Lainzazhu
Goat	Mailloo	Rahh
Sheep	Maindha	Look
Dog	Khiaba	Cheoo.
Cow	———	Nait.
Bird	Poo	Bhoorchiée.
Deer	Pewa	Kissi.
Tiger	Thirringba	Ranghoo.
Bear	Manghipa	Bholoo.
Wood, or forest	Lih, Thap	Nam.
Tree	Sing	Singaitoo.
Eye	Mikh	Nukh.
Nose	Nibô	Nha.

* The same as in the Purbutti.

	Limbooa.	Mungur.
Ear	Nikhô	Nakeep.
Mouth	Moola	Neeur.
Teeth	Hebbô	Shiak.
Hand, arm	Hookh	Hoot.
Fingers	Hookhijoo	Hoochhung.
Feet	Langy	Hil.
Head	Atakhi	Taloo.
Turban	Paya	Pugree.
Snow	Uha	Heooñ.
Frost	Phoan	Tosaroo.
Rain	Washi	Namas.
Lamp oil	———	Sude.
Image, idol	Mangee	Moorthi.
Hill, a mountain	Koaknia	Purbut.
River	Chooa	Gunduck.
Fish	Nga	Daisa.
Horse	———	Paisia.
Iron	Phenje	Phullam.
Copper	Tambah	Tambah.
Silver	Yoopa	Roopa.
Gold	Sumyung	———
Stone	Loony	Loony.
Earth	Khum	Dhurte.
Cloth	———	Burhin.
Sit down	———	Yooki.

	Limbooa.	Newar.
Get up	——	Sooki.
Sleep	——	Miski.
Laugh	——	Raitki.
Road	——	Tam.
To-day	——	Chinning.
To-morrow	——	Puhin.
Bring	Rakni	——
Go	Hooki	——
Come	Rakki	——
Mankind	Bhoormi	——
Bow	——	Meeañ.
Arrow	——	Be-e.

The Kerraute, Hyoo, and Dhenwar words that I have been able to collect are too few to be worth inserting; besides which, I cannot confidently answer for their correctness. I had hoped to have been able to present a copious specimen of the language spoken by the Kath Bhootiâs of that part of the Kuchar, or lower Tibet, lying directly to the northward of Nepaul, but have been unfortunately disappointed. It differs considerably, I understand, from the vernacular idiom of Lehassa and other parts of the upper Tibet.

It is proper to notice here, that in the preceding Vocabulary, the *a* is to be pronounced long as in *all*; the *g* invariably hard, as in *gun*; the *e* sharp as the French accented é; and that the *n* with a mark thus (-) over it, is to have the French nasal sound.

CHAPTER VIII.

HISTORICAL SKETCH OF NEPAUL.

CHAPTER VIII.

THE ancient history of the Nepaulians, like that of all other nations which affect to trace their origin beyond the date of authentic records, is clouded by mythological fables; the popular tradition that the valley of Nepaul was once an immense lake has already been noticed, and the probability of the fact maintained; nor is it, perhaps, necessary, on any physical grounds, to refer its subsequent conversion to a very remote period of antiquity. Their Pourans, especially those entitled Hurrumunt-khund and Ooter-khund, contain, I understand, copious details concerning this secluded region, during the time that it continued one of the favourite haunts of the Hindoo deities. At what æra to fix the commencement of its real history can only be determined after a close review of its annals at large, and with these I am as yet but superficially acquainted. For the present, therefore, we must be content with a bare chronological series of the princes who are said to have ruled over Nepaul since the epoch of Nymuni; from whom, it has been already observed, this country is supposed to have received its present name.

The term of the reign of the founder of this dynasty does not appear in my notes; but his son and successors are,

	Years	Months
Bhoorimahagah, who ruled	48	3
Jye Gupt - -	73	3
Perma Gupt - -	91	0
Sree Hurkh - -	67	0
Bheem Gupt - -	38	0
Munni Gupt - -	37	0
Bishen Gupt - -	66	0
Jye Gupt (2d) -	71	1
	491	4

The Raw of the Nymuni had not swayed the sceptre quite five hundred years, when Bhul Singh of the Rajepoot tribe, and one of the posterity of Mehip Gopaul, putting himself at the head of an army, levied in the country situated between Semroun Ghur and Janmukpore, invaded and subdued Nepaul, over which he ruled - - 49 0

When he was succeeded by his son, Jye Singh, who reigned -	21	7
And was succeeded by Bhowany Singh	41	0
	111	7

The kingdom of Nepaul, under the descendants of Mehip Gopaul, was bounded on the west by the Tirsoolgunga, and on the east by the Dhoodh-Kousi, to the north by the mountains of Neel-khent, and to the south by the valley of Chitlong. This dynasty, however, was put an end to, in the person of Bhowany Singh, by Yellung Kerraut, who invaded and conquered Nepaul with an army of Kerrauts, a tribe then occupying the country stretching from the Dhoodh-Kousi to the confines of Dewâ Durmah, and the remains of which are now scattered over the mountainous tract lying between that river and the eastern extremity of the valley of Nepaul. The reign of Yellung, it is pretended, lasted 90 years 3 months.

His successors were,

	Reigned Years	Months
Duskham - -	37	0
Ballancha - -	31	6
Kingly - - -	41	1
Hunnanter - -	50	0
Tuskhah - -	41	8
Sroopust - -	38	6
Purb - - -	56	0
Jetydastry - -	60	0
Punchem - -	71	0
King-king-king -	56	0
Soonund - -	50	8
Thoomoo - -	58	0

	Reigned Years	Months
Jaighree - -	60	1
Jenneo - -	73	2
Suenkeh - -	60	1
Thoor - -	71	0
Thamoo - -	83	0
Burmah - -	73	6
Gunjeh -	72	7
Kush Koon -	not known	
Teeshoo -	56	0
Soogmeea - -	59	0
Joosha - -	63	0
Gontho - -	74	0
Khembhoom -	74	0
Gully Jung - -	81	0
	1581	1

or 1630 years, allowing forty-eight for the reign of Kush Koon, which is considerably below the average of the reigns assigned to this dynasty: perhaps, however, it would be doing no violence to the probability of their history, to reduce the term of this dynasty of twenty-seven princes to half the period, or eight centuries, since it is evident that most of the reigns have twice, and some of them three times, the number of years assigned to them that the ordinary course of nature will suffer us to admit.

	Reigned Years	Months
The Kerrauts were dispossessed of their kingdom by Nevesit, a Chetree of the Soorej-bunsi race, who after conquering Nepaul reigned	50	0
Mutta Ratio -	91	0
Kaickburmah - -	76	0
Pussoopûsh Deo (formerly mentioned as the founder of Pusput-nath) - -	56	0
Bhosker Burmah (who extended his conquests southerly as far as Sagur) -	74	0
Bhoomy Burmah - - -	41	0
Chunder Burmah - -	21	0
Jay Burmah - - -	62	0
Breesh Burmah - - -	57	0
Surbo Burmah - -	49	0
Puthi Burmah - -	56	0
Jeest Burmah -	48	0
Koober Burmah - -	76	0
Hurry Burmah - -	76	6
Sidhe Burmah - -	61	0
Hurry Dutt Burmah (the founder of the temple of Seker-nerain) - -	39	0
Basso Dutt Bhurmah - -	33	0
Sreeputtry - - -	3	0
Seobreddy - -	77	0

	Reigned Years	Months
Bussunt Deo - - -	61	0
Deo - - -	57	0
Brikh Deo - - -	57	0
Sunker Deo - - -	50	0
Bhurma Deo - - -	51	0
Maun Deo (who is said to have had an interview with the god Sumbhoo, to whom he erected a temple) - - -	39	0
Mahe Deo - - -	51	0
Bussunt Deo - -	36	0
Oodey Deo - - -	47	0
Maun Deo (the 2d), in whose reign Nepaul was afflicted during three years with a severe drought, which ceased on the Rajah's propitiating the god Pusputty by an oblation of all his riches - -	45	0
Sookaum - - -	50	0
Seo Deo - -	41	6
Nurrender Deo - -	34	0
Bhem Deo Burmah - -	16	0
In his reign the Aheers, who were originally the sovereigns of Nepaul, recovered their dominions;		
Bishen Gupt, the conqueror, reigning	74	0

	Reigned Years	Months
Kishnoo Gupt - -	61	0
Bhoomy Gupt - -	40	0
	1877	0

Seo Deo Burmah, of the posterity of Nevesit, again subduing Nepaul, and expelling the Guptees, reigned - -	41	0
Unghoo Burmah - -	42	0
Kirtoo Burmah - -	18	0
Bheem Arjoon Deo - -	39	0
Nund Deo - - -	13	0
Seo Deo - - -	16	0
Nurrender Deo (who, as already noticed, established the Mutchender-jâtra) -	37	0
Bul Deo - -	17	0
Sunker Deo - -	12	0
Bhem Arjoon Deo (the 2d) -	16	0
Jye Deo - -	19	0
Sree Bull Deo - -	16	0
Condur Deo - - -	27	0
Jye Deo (the 2d) - -	42	7
Bul Deo (the 3d) - -	11	0
Ballunjoon Deo - -	36	7

	Reigned Years	Months
Ragheeb Deo - - -	63	0

This prince introduced the Tambul æra, or æra of Bickermajeet, into Nepaul, where, however, the epoch most in use at present among the Purbutties is the Saka. The Newars, on the other hand, have a style of their own, regarding the origin of which I know nothing certain, except that it appears to have been instituted about nine centuries ago; the year 914 of their reckoning beginning the 15th of Karteek, or 28th of October, 1793. Possibly, its commencement may bear some relation to the period of the first establishment of the Semroun dynasty in Nepaul, mentioned in the note in page 265.

	Years	Months
Seeker Deo - -	88	6
Soho Deo - - -	33	9
Bickrum Deo - -	1	0
Nurrender Deo - -	1	6
Goonakam Deo - -	85	6
Oodoy Deo - -	6	0
Nurbhoy Deo -	7	0
Bhaj Deo Budro - -	9	7
Letchmi Camdeo Dutt -	21	0
Jye Deb - - -	20	0

	Reigned Years	Months
(This last prince completely reduced the refractory tributary of Patn, Bhaskur Deo,) and		
Oodoy Deo - -	7	1
Bul Deo - - -	12	0
Puddiem Deo - -	6	0
This prince revived the custom of wearing crowns, which, it seems, had fallen into disuse since the time of Ballunjoon Deo		
Naug Arjoon - -	3	0
Sunker Deo - -	17	0
This prince erected an image to Mahadeo, to which he gave his own name of Sunker Deo		
Bam Deo - -	3	0
Sree Hurkh Deo - -	16	0
Seo Deo - -	27	7
Indro Deo - - -	12	0
Maun Deo - -	4	7
Nurrender Deo - -	6	4
It is pretended that there fell no snow in Nepaul before the time of this prince, who effected this change in the climate by certain religious rites.		
Rudro Deo - -	80	1
Omret Deo, (a great dearth) -	3	11
Soomeesur Deo - -	6	3

	Reigned Years	Months
Buz Caum Deo (the period of his reign unknown)		
Any Mull (a great dearth) -	31	9
Obhay Mull, (a great dearth, frequent earthquakes, and throughout an inauspicious reign) - -	48	2
Jye Deb - -	2	7
Unwunt Mull Deo - -	33	10
In this prince's reign, and in the Newar year 408, or Sumbuth 1344, many Khassias (a western tribe) emigrated to Nepaul and settled there; and three years after, or in the Newar year 411, a considerable number of Tirhoot families also planted themselves there.		
	2869	1

The names of Unwunt Mull's successors, but not the periods of their respective reigns, are specified in the notes at present in my possession. They are as follows:

Jye Nund Deo
Jye Singh Mull, and
Jye Ruero Mull, sons of Unwunt Mull.

These princes reigned successively after their father, but they all died without leaving any male issue. One of them, however, had a daughter, named Sutty Naik Deby, who was crowned Ranee, and afterwards married to Harrir Chunder Deo, the Rajah of Benares, by whom she had a daughter, named Raj Letchmi, afterwards distinguished by the lofty title of Debul Daiby Raj. Letchmi succeeded to the throne of her ancestors, but was soon deposed by a kinsman of the name of Jye Dub, who, however, had not reigned many days, when, in the month of Poos, in the year of the Saka 1245, (corresponding with the Newar year 444, or about the month of December, A. D. 1323), Hurr Singh Deo, Rajah of Semroun Ghur, and of the posterity of Bamdeb of the Soorej-bunsi princes of Oude, entered Nepaul, and completely subduing it, put an end to the dynasty of the Burmahs. Hurr Singh Deo's invasion of Nepaul was occasioned by his being driven out of his own possessions by the Patans; the reigning monarch of Delhi (who at this time was Secunder Lôdi) having been incited to this measure by the nephew of Hurr Singh.* Notwithstanding the disadvantageous circumstances under which this enterprize was attempted, Hurr Singh does

* According to another relation, Hurr Singh Deo's ancestors, for some generations back, had a certain footing in Nepaul, the entire reduction of which was reserved for Hurr Singh, upon the latter's being compelled to abandon his territories in the Turryani altogether. The account states that this establishment (whatever its extent may have been) was made in the year of Bickermajeet 901, by Nan Deo, at that time Rajah of Semroun, or (as it is also sometimes written) Summun Ghur. His posterity were,

Kanuck Deo.
Nersingh Deo.
Ram Singh Deo.
Bhad Singh Deo.
Kurm Singh Deo, and
Hurr Singh Deo.

not appear to have had the least difficulty in subduing Nepaul, the crown of which continued in his family till Purthi Nerain Goorkhali put an end to the dynasty of the Semroun Chetrees. The successors of Hurr Singh Deo were

Bullâl Singh.
Sri Deo Mull.
Nây Mull.
Assoke Mull.
Jestily Mull.
Jeit Mull.

The last of these princes, Jeit Mull, after providing for the maintenance of his army by distributing jaghires among the soldiery, has the credit attributed to him of having divided the rest of the lands throughout his kingdom in perpetuity among his subjects, whom, in addition to this immunity, he likewise released from the land-tax ordinarily levied before his time. He also established standard measures and weights, and considerably enlarged the city of Bhatgong, which was the seat of his residence. He was succeeded by his son,

Jye Ekshah Mull, or Jye Kush Mull, who is said to have annexed Morung, Tirhoot, and Gyah to his dominions, and to have conquered also Goorkha to the westward, and Sikarjoong of Tibet to the northward. He likewise completely subdued the refractory Rajahs of Patn and Khatmanda. He had three sons, among whom, at his death, he distributed his dominions as follows:

To Roy Mull he assigned the principality of Bhatgong, which at this period was bounded on the west by the Bhagmutty, on the east by Sangah, on the north by Kooti, and on the south by the forest of Medine Mull.

To Run Mull he gave the territory of Bunepa (a conquest made in the reign of Sree Bul Deo), which was bounded on the north by Sangachuck; on the south by the forest of Medine Mull, on the west by Sangah, and on the east by the Dhoodh-Kousi.

To Rutno, or Ruttun Mull, he left the kingdom of Khatmanda, bounded on the east by the Bhagmutty, on the west by the Tirsool-gunga, on the north by the mountains of Neel-khent, and on the south by the northern boundary of Patn, which, according to some accounts, fell to the share of a daughter of Jye Ekshah Mull; the limits assigned to this principality being, to the southward, the forest of Medine Mull; to the westward, the mountains of Lama-danda; to the northward, the southern line of Khatmanda; and to the eastward the Bhagmutty. The successors of Roy Mull were

Bhoo Bheen Mull.

Bessou Mull, who took Bunepa from the house of Run Mull.

Triloke Mull, from whom the house of Ruttun Mull seized Bunepa, Chunko, Sanka, and Kooti.

Juggut Johi Mull

Jye Jeta Metro Mull.

Bhuput Indro Mull, who considerably enlarged Theeme, Bhatgong, and Punhoti, the latter of which was a conquest from the house of Run Mull.

Runjeet Mull. This prince, who was the last of the Soorej-bunsi race that reigned over Nepaul, succeeded his father Bhuput Indro in the Newar year 842. He formed an alliance with Purthi Nerain Goorkhali, with a view of strengthening himself against the sovereign of Khatmanda, but this connexion, though for some time favourable to his views, ended in the total reduction of Nepaul by his ally. Runjeet Mull reigned forty years, losing his dominions in the Newar year 890, or, according to another computation, in 888.

I have given the names of the successors of Roy Mull, though unable to furnish any account of the transactions of their respective reigns, because I was desirous of exhibiting a complete series of Nepaul sovereigns from the earliest to the present time; but as such another meagre catalogue of the princes of the younger branches of Jye Ekshah Mull's house would answer no useful purpose, I shall pass over this part of the Nepaul chronology, with briefly observing, that during the two hundred years which appear to have elapsed between the partition of the kingdom by the last mentioned prince, and its conquest and reunion under Purthi Nerain, the grandfather of the reigning Rajah, although the power of the respective branches was constantly fluctuating, yet the ascendency, for the most part, appears to have been maintained by the elder one, or that of Bhatgong.

With regard to the Goorkhalis previous to their conquest of Nepaul, I have not been able to obtain any satisfactory materials towards even an abstract of their history; nor is it, indeed, probable, though it were ever so minutely known, that it would exhibit any features either interesting or important. The reigning family affects to derive its descent from the Rajepoot princes of Oudipoor, in the same manner that the founders of the Mahratta empire (or their historians for them) appear to have done. All, however, that we know for certain concerning this race is, that they have subsisted in the mountainous country bordering on the Gunduck, for a considerable period, during which they have gradually risen into power by successive encroachments on their surrounding neighbours. On their first coming from the southward* they appear to have established themselves at West Noakote, or Noakote of Ahudi Rolah, which is in the Palpa quarter; and whither they advanced through the Kemaoon mountains. From hence they stretched their dominion towards Lumjoong, adding, at some distance of time, the possession of Goorkha to their other acquisitions. Here they are said to have been fixed during six generations, till Purthi Nerain, the son and successor of Ner Bhopâl Shah, meditating further conquest to the eastward, crossed the Tirsoolgunga, and, as has been already noticed, seized on Bailkote and East Noakote, as preliminary steps to the reduction of Nepaul.

I was very gravely assured by Behadur Shah himself, that his

* The date of this migration I have not exactly learned, though some pretend to refer it to the period of Sultan Alla Udden Ghawe's invasion of Rajepootana, when various branches of the reigning family of that country, preferring exile to slavery, dispersed themselves over Hindostan.

father had invaded Nepaul at the earnest solicitation of the inhabitants at large, who were weary of the distracted government, and severe yoke of the Soorej-bunsi princes. This assertion, however, does not appear supported by the event, since Purthi Nerain met with such resistance in his enterprize as protracted its accomplishment for a period of more than twenty years. The fact indeed is, that he was invited in the first instance by the Rajah of Bhatgong to assist him in the prosecution of his ambitious schemes against the dominions of his neighbours: but Runjeet Mull soon discovering the views of his ally, concluded an accommodation with the sovereigns of Patn and Khatmanda, in conjunction with whom he endeavoured, though fruitlessly, to repel the artful Goorkhali. It was on this occasion that Captain Kinloch attempted to penetrate into Nepaul, Runjeet Mull having prevailed on the British government to aid him with a military force for the purpose of expelling Purthi Nerain. In the end, the Goorkhali successively acquired possession of Khatmanda, Patn, and Bhatgong.* Jay Perkaush, the sovereign of the former, did not long survive the loss of his dominions and liberty. Taiz Ner Sing, the Rajah of Patn, having rendered himself personally obnoxious during the war to Purthi Nerain, was treated with extreme rigour, if not actually put to death by order of the conqueror. With regard to Runjeet Mull, who surrendered his capital and person to his treacherous confederate, in the Newar year 888, or A. D. 1768, the Goorkhali affected to

* Some further particulars respecting Purthi Nerain's invasion of Nepaul will be found in Appendix No. II

carry himself towards him with extraordinary respect. This appearance of submission, however, did not prevent him from retiring, with Purthi Nerain's consent, to Benares, where he soon after died, leaving behind him a son named Abdhoot Singh, who for some time laboured to engage the British government in measures for reinstating him in his paternal dominions.

Purthi Nerain did not long enjoy the fruits of his perfidy and address, dying about three years after the final conquest of Nepaul, or in the year 1771. There are some apparent contradictions in his character which our imperfect knowledge of his history does not enable us to clear up: thus, notwithstanding the cruelty he manifested in his treatment of the inhabitants of Kirthipoor, in his ungenerous rigour towards the Patn sovereign, and on some other occasions, he is said to have disgraced one of his principal adherents for wounding one of the enemy while in the act of fleeing from the field of battle. In fine, we may conclude from the respect in which his memory is yet held by the Purbutties, and especially the military part of them, that whatever his conduct as a conqueror, or however severe his nature, may have been, he was not inattentive to the means of conciliating those on whose support he principally depended. He left two sons, Singh Pertaub and Behadur Shah, the former of whom succeeded him; and soon conceiving some jealousy of his brother (who is the present Regent of Nepaul) he seized and threw him into confinement, whence it was with some difficulty that Gusraje Misser (one of the hereditary Gooroos, or spiritual guides of the Goorkha family) obtained his release, with permission to carry him into exile.

Singh Pertaub reigned little more than three years, dying in the year 1775; he had added, however, before his death, somewhat to the conquests of his father, having, among other places of less consequence, seized on the districts of Tunnohi, Soomaisee, Jogimara, and Oopadroong, lying to the south-west of Nepaul. The Rajah of Tunnohi, Hurry Koomar Dutt, is still in possession of part of his patrimonial inheritance; and is also one of the Company's renters in the Circar Chemparun.

Singh Pertaub had only one legitimate son at the time of his death, namely the present Rajah, Run Behadur Shah,* who upon his succeeding to the kingdom was an infant in arms; but he left two illegitimate sons by a Newar woman; the eldest of them named Beedoor Shah, and the youngest Sheer Behadur, both of whom are still living. Beedoor Shah is older than the Rajah, but an obscure character, which is far from being the case with respect to Sheer Behadur (or, as he is more commonly called, Bâjoo Saheb,) who, though some years younger than Run Behadur, has exhibited such superior symptoms of genius as have induced the Regent to pay particular attention to the cultivation of his mind.

Behadur Shah, immediately on the death of his brother, returned

* It is necessary to observe, that the cognomen of this family is Sah, and not Shah; though the latter is very generally affected by them, on account of its royal import.

from his exile in Bettyah to Khatmanda, where placing his nephew on the throne, he took upon himself the administration of affairs as Regent; but it was not long, before Rajender Letchemi, the mother of the minor prince, who appears to have been very fond of power, contrived not only to supplant Behadur Shah, and to reassume the reins of government, but to secure the person of her rival. Gusraje Misser, however, again interposing his good offices, an accommodation between the parties took place, but which only lasted till Behadur Shah was enabled to seize and confine the Ranee in his turn. Neglecting, however, to conciliate the chief men of the state, who laid claim to greater rewards for past services than he was able, or perhaps disposed to grant, he soon discovered that they began once more to lean towards his antagonist, who at the same time professing a resolution to submit entirely for the future to the will of her brother-in-law, the latter judged it on the whole most prudent to restore her to liberty. The consequence was such as might have been expected, Behadur Shah found it necessary, not long after, to consult his safety by a second flight from Nepaul to Bettyah, whence proceeding to Patna, he fixed his residence in that city till the death of the Ranee, when he returned to Khatmanda, and reassumed the regency without any opposition. He has ever since held the reins of government, though latterly with some diminution of his authority, owing to the ripened age of his nephew, which makes it necessary for him to accommodate himself more than formerly, not only to the wishes of the young prince, but also to the views and opinions of his principal colleagues in the administration.

Although I am but slightly acquainted with the transactions of Nepaul during the regency of Rajender Letchemi, yet I am sufficiently informed of them to be satisfied that she was a woman of extraordinary character and talents. Her chief attention appears to have been directed to the improvement of the army, whence it may be inferred that she had extensive views of conquest. Short and troubled, indeed, as her government was, she subdued and annexed several petty states to the kingdom, among which were Palpa, Gurrumkote, and Kashki, all of them lying to the westward of Goorkha.

The acquisitions of Behadur Shah have been still more considerable, since he has either absolutely seized, or rendered tributary, all the states lying between Kashki and Serinugur, including both the territories of the Chowbeisia and the Bansi Rajahs, or the dominions of forty-six petty princes. These little states will be enumerated, and a general idea given of their situation, in the next chapter; it remains only to notice here, that the allegiance of all the tributary chiefs is secured either by hostages retained at Khatmanda, or by allegiances of marriage contracted between them and the reigning family. Thus Run Behadur is married to a daughter of the Goolmi Rajah, and Behadur Shah himself to a daughter of the Rajah of Palpa and Bootoul, or, as it is sometimes called, Bootwal.

With respect to the war in which Behadur Shah engaged some

years since against Tibet, and which, it must be owned, was terminated last year in a manner but little to the credit of his government, (having relinquished all his conquests in that quarter, and formally recognised the paramount authority of the Emperor of China over the Nepaul dominions,) it is unnecessary to say any thing in this place.*

* A summary account of its rise will be found in Appendix No. I.

CHAPTER IX.

Boundaries, Extent, and several Divisions of Nepaul.—Various Routes and Distances.

CHAPTER IX.

I SHALL now proceed, as formerly proposed, to close this Memoir with some account of the boundaries, extent, and several divisions of Nepaul, which, collectively considered, comprehends an immense tract of country stretching from Serinugur to the banks of the Teesta. Doubtless, however, nothing more than a slight sketch on his head will be expected from me, since it will be remembered that till the late deputation to Nepaul our knowledge concerning the dominions of the Goorkhali (by which appellation the successors of Purthi Nerain are usually distinguished) scarcely extended beyond the Cheerighati ridge of hills, and that my inquiries towards the improvements of this part of Asiatic geography must necessarily, for reasons already sufficiently insisted on, have been extremely circumscribed. Such, however, as these inquiries were, I shall here communicate their result, lamenting only that I am unable to furnish any satisfactory information relative to the natural history, produce, or population of a region which, owing to its situation with regard to Tibet, appears highly interesting to us in a commercial view. We have hitherto surveyed little more than the valley of Nepaul itself. Let us now run our eye, however superficially, along its dependencies, beginning with those lying to the eastward.

In this direction, then, the possessions of the Goorkhali are bounded by those of the Dewa Durmah, or Deb Rajah (to which we have exclusively, though improperly, appropriated the appellation of Bhoot or Bhootan), from which they are separated by the river Teesta. To the south-east they touch our districts of Betwea, Hazary, Rungamutty, and Cooch-behar, and to the north-east are divided from Tibet by the Kuchar, or alpine ridge in which the passes of Phullâk and Kooti are situated. The Nepaul frontier towards the Teesta is illustrated by the town and district of Seekhim, by the Morung principally in the south-east quarter, while the towns of Dhoalka and Lastie mark its limits on the north-east side; the former standing on the Kuchar to the west of Phullâk, and the latter immediately below Kooti. The country lying between Khatmanda and the borders just described is, with the exception of the Morung and other Turrye districts adjoining to it, entirely mountainous, giving rise or passage to several rapid streams, the most considerable of which are the Soan-Kousi, the Bhootia-Kousi, the Tambeh-Kousi, the Dhoodh-Kousi, the Arun, and the Teesta, which last springs from mount Chowurigolah, a branch or continuation of the snowy Phunijoong, and situated about one journey E.S.E. of it. This mountainous tract is inhabited by various uncivilized nàtions, differing considerably from each other in language and manners, but materially in point of religion. The principal of these tribes are the Kerrautes, the Hawoos, and the Limboos or Limbooas, whom the Nepaul government finds it no easy matter to keep in order, while it derives little or no advantage from them in any respect. They are all Hindoos, but of the meanest cast; Bheem Sein is the favourite divinity of the Limbooas; and appears indeed to be of great consideration among the mountaineers in general. These rude people subsist chiefly on fish, and wild fruits, though they also cultivate some species of grain; the hills occupied by the Hawoos or Hyoos producing Kagnoo, those of the Kerrautes several sorts of Ghya; and the Limboo mountains (which are situated close to Himma-leh, and much exposed to falls of snow) yielding a species of rice called Tâkmâro, which, it is not improbable, may be found to answer in the soil and climate of England.

To the southward the Nepaul territories are bounded by certain contiguous Purgunnahs of Durbungah, Tirhoot, and Chemparun; the towns which principally illustrate this frontier being Ummirpore, Janickpore, Bareh, and Persa, or Goolpussra. To the south-west lies Bulrampore of Goruckpore, adjoining to which is the tributary principality of Bootoul, or Bootwal; to the westward, the Nepaul borders, as they incline northerly, touch on various parts of Oude: and to the north north-west are divided from Pillibeat, Rampoor, Koshipore, Rodurpoor, and other districts of Rohilcund by the Kemaoon and Almorah hills, which are among the acquisitions of

Behadur Shah. In the north-west quarter they are bounded by the dominions of the Rajahs of Serinugur and Siremon,* and by Luddakh, Taklakhar, and Moostang of Tibet, all of them situated beyond the snowy ridge known by the general name of Himma-leh, but bearing different appellations throughout its immense extent. To the northward of this wide expanse of rugged but interesting territory lie Kheeroo, Joongah, and Manouphaut, belonging to the Lehassa dominions, but at present possessed in fact by the Chinese.

It will be seen by running the eye over Major Rennell's map, and describing on it, with the aid of the preceding detail, the general outline of the Nepaul territories, that while they include between their east and west limits no less a space than twelve geographical degrees, they are, on the other hand, in point of breadth, of no very considerable extent, no where extending two degrees in horizontal measurement from north to south, and for the most part exhibiting a slip of even less than a degree.

The tract lying between Nepaul and Serinugur, and in a direction from S. W. to N. W. of the former, comprehends the subjugated countries of the Chowbeisia (or twenty-four) and the Bansi (or twenty-two) Rajahs, together with the more recent conquest of Dhotee, Kemaoon, and Gherwâl, of which last Serinugur is the capital. Their exact position I am unable to determine, and therefore have not thought it worth while to enlarge the accompanying map, merely for the purpose of laying down places regarding which

* This is the name of the country of which Nahan or Nan is the capital.

my information was so imperfect. For the same reason I have not stretched its limits either to the northward or eastward so far as I might have done, had I been sufficiently satisfied with the materials I have collected respecting the geography of those quarters. It may not be amiss, however, to insert in this place the names of the Chowbeisia, or twenty-four Raaj or principalities constituting the Nepaul dominions immediately west of Goorkha, as, joined with some account of the routes which cross them in various directions, they may, in a certain degree, assist future inquiries, and in the mean time serve to convey a general idea of a country at present almost totally unknown; with the same view I shall also endeavour to throw some faint light on the geography of the northern and eastern parts, by presenting similar sketches of the roads leading from Nepaul proper to Joongah, Kooti, Beijapoor, &c. With respect to the Bansi, or twenty-two Raaj, all of which are situated still farther to the westward (lying between the Chowbeisia and Dhôtee) I have not been able to procure an accurate list of them. The whole of these forty-six petty states were formerly in a certain degree tributary to the Jumlah Rajah; who annually received from one, as a token of homage and subjection, a pair of slippers, from another, fish, &c. The princes at the head of them are, without exception, I understand, of the Rajepoot tribe.

List of the Chowbeisia.

Loomjoong

Kashki

Tunhoo, or Tunnohoo; these border on Goorkha. This Raaj has some of its districts situated in the Turrye; or to the southward of the first range of hills.

Gulkoat

Purbut, or Mulli-bum.

Noakote, or Nûwâkote.

Pyoon.

Luttohoon.

Bhurkote.

Gurhoon.

Reesing.

Ghering.

Dhoar.

Palpa, (the Turrye of which, called Bootoul or Bootwal, borders on the Goruckpore district.)

Goolmi (ditto).

Wighâ.

Khauchi.

Dang (comprehending some Turrye districts).

Moosi-kote.

Purthana (comprises some Turrye districts).

Jhilli.

Sulian, or Suliana (comprises some Turrye districts.)

Dhoor-kote.

Isma.

The following are enumerated among the districts lying to the west of Chowbeisia, and are all of them probably comprehended in the Bansi.

Jumlah.

Jajur-kote.

Cham.

Acham.

Roogûm.

Moosi-kote (2d).

Roalpa.

Mullijauta.

Bulhang.

Dyliek.

Suliana (2d).

Bamphi.

Jehari.

Kalagong.

Ghooria-kote.

Gootum.

Gujoor.

Darimeca.

ROUTES.

I.

Coss.

From Booloul (or Bootwal), 15 coss N. by W. of Goruckpore, to Beeni-shehr.

Bootoul to Palpa (the capital of Mahadut Sein, situated among mountains, the Gunduck passing below; the road for the most part through a thick forest. 5 munzils, or 37

To Durpoo-ghaut, on the Gunduck or Salegrami; this river separates the Palpa and Gurhoon territories; mountains, and woody - - 2 munzils, or 15

To Thaneh-choak; crossing the Audhi-kolah, or river Audhi, some parts very mountainous and woody 2 munzils, or 15

To Bhowareh, on the Audhi, a plain level road through a valley, dependant on Gurhoon - 1 munzil, or 8

To Khum-thathi, a place of great note, level good road, belongs to Gurhoon - - 1 munzil, or 8

To Lama-khait, crossing the river (I suppose the Audhi), a plain level road; dependant on Gurhoon 2 munzils, or 15

To the fort of Karki-nitta, situate on a hill; a place of note; hence the road strikes off to the north-west; belongs to the Rajah of West Noakote, one of the Chowbeisia. 3 munzils, or 23

From the fort of Karki-nitta to Keramaddun (a large fort); road strikes to the westward. Plain, no river; belongs to the Rajah of Suttohoo - - 1 munzil, or 8

	Coss.
To Pangleh; cross the Modi at Koosmachoor, 1 coss, and pass from the Suttohoo into the Purbut territory, otherwise called Mulli-bum. This Rajah is usually called the Purbutti Thakoor. From the Modi to Pangleh 14 coss. 2 munzils, or	15
To Lamba-khait, plain, belongs to Mulli-bum -	10
To Beeni-shehr, the capital of Mulli-bum, and standing at the confluence of the Salegrami, or Gunduck, and a small river called the Mehagde. (This city is sometimes called Beeni-jee, by way of pre-eminence) -	5
Coss	159

That part of Himma-leh directly to the north of Beeni is called by the descriptive name of Dhoulager, or the white mountains.

Four journies beyond, or northward of Beeni, is Mookhtinath (or Sri Mookhtinath) within half a mile of which the Gunduck takes the name of Salegrami, the consecrated stones so called abounding particularly in that part of its bed. The source of this river is said to be situated to the northward of Mookhti, in the direction of Moostang, and not far from Kagbeeni. Moostang is a place of some note in upper Tibet, or Bhoot, and twelve journies from Beeni-shehr. The breadth of the Gunduck is said not to exceed thirty yards at Beeni. Three journies beyond Mookhtinath is a celebrated spring or natural reservoir, called Dummodhur-koondeh.

II.

Coss.

Route from Bulrampore in Oude, 60 coss north of Lucknow, to Beeni.

To Patun Deby Bhowani; after travelling four coss, you reach the hills bounding the Turrye and the Vizier's country in this quarter; six cosses beyond which is Patun Deby Bhowani, belonging to Rajah Doulut Singh, one of the Chowbeisia. - - 10

To the fort of Jûkiâna, on a hill; wild rugged country intersected by streams or torrents; belongs to the Rajah of Khanchi, one of the Chowbeisia - 4 munzils, or 30

To the town of Khanchi, a fort on a hill; country as before, with many springs - 2 munzils, or 17

To the fort of Urghaloor, on a hill, a place of note belonging to one of the Chowbeisia Rajahs; road over hills and through valleys. The Rajah of Khanchi's territory terminates here - - 3 munzils, or 23

To the fort of Moosi-kote, belonging to one of the Chowbeisia; road as before. At 21 coss the Urghaloor territory ends. 4 munzils, or 30

To Gulkoat: for 9 cosses the territory of Moosi-kote; then you enter the Gulkoat country. Gulkoat is a considerable fort and town, the Rajah of it being one of the Chowbeisia. 2 munzils, or 15

	Coss.
To Tambeh-khan, where there is a copper mine, belongs to Gulkoat - -	10
To Bâgloo-choor, in a valley, a large town and fort, and very opulent and populous. First stage mountainous and woody, next plain. - - - 2 munzils, or	15
To Beeni-shehr (crossing the Gunduck or Salegrami, as before) 2 munzils, or	15
Coss	165

III.

Route from Khalmanda to Beeni.

To Noakote, by mount Bheerbundi.	
To Geerkhoo-tar, whence two roads strike off, one westerly to Mulli-bum, and another northerly to Tibet -	10
To Sumuri-bhunjan; road through a valley -	10
To Pourwa; half way through the former valley; rest mountains. - - -	12
To Sulian-tar; half way mountains, then cross by a bridge over a stream, and proceed in a valley. -	10
To Raghapoor; through a valley; cross a large river (I suppose the Gundi) by boats, the Goorkha mountains before you. - -	5
To Gaikhur-ford; at 1 coss, a stream; 6 coss beyond which is Gaikhur, belonging to Kashki.	7

	Coss.
To Poakhra; at 3 coss, cross by a wooden bridge the river Saite, very deep, but narrow; belongs to Kashki	8
To Buttola-choor, on the Saite. This place, which is surrounded by hills, is the residence of the Kashki Rajah.	3
To Surrung-koat, a large town, with a fort on a hill, belongs to Kashki. - -	5
To Kashki; very mountainous, both town and fort on a hill.	3
To Pangdhoor; mountainous; fort on a hill; belongs to Kashki. - -	10
To Koosmachoor, due west, mountainous. The Modi-nuddi passing within a quarter of a coss of Koosma, dividing Kaskhi from Mulli-bum. - -	5
To Pang, on the Salegrami, or Gunduck; road through a valley; belongs to Mulli-bum. -	10
To a small stream at the foot of a hill; all the way mountainous - - -	15
To a Deoralli; road through a plain or valley, well cultivated	10
To Chepia-nuddi, or the river Chepia, which was formerly the boundary between Goorkha and Loomjoong. Here the road to Tunhoo strikes off to the right, and that to Loomjoong to the left - -	5
To a Deoralli (the 2d), belonging to Loomjoong -	10
To the Mahdi-nuddi, over which there is a wooden bridge; road through a valley well cultivated with Shâli rice	10

	Coss.
To Puckbhuja, due west, a large fort, a road through a populous valley; belongs to Loomjoong -	15
To Ragho-pouwa, through a well cultivated valley, belonging to Kashki - -	10
To Lamba-khait (as before) - -	5
To Beeni-shehr (as before) - -	5
Coss	189

IV.

Route from Beeni-shehr to Chinnachin, the capital of Jumlah (west)

To Runbang, through a valley -	10
To Boordebang; mountainous and woody; belongs to Mulli-bum - - -	20
To Nusi-bhauji; mountainous, with some valleys, 7 journies, or	50
To Bholoo-ghaut (on the Surjeu, or Dewa) which separates the Jehari and Roogûm territories, mountainous and woody, 7 journies - - -	50
To the residence of the Rajah of Jhari, or Jehari, 1 journey	7
To Mount Chakhûra (or Chakooria) 6 journies -	45
Here the Jumlah territory commences.	
To Chinnachin (the capital of Jumlah) 10 journies	75
Coss	250

Jumlah is occasionally distinguished by the appellation of Bawe Pukuli, in allusion, it is pretended, to its extraordinary population and military force in ancient times, when the passage of the Rajah's army over two and twenty buffalo hides piled one upon another was sufficient to tread them into one mass. This symbol of power, however, is no longer applicable to the sovereign of Jumlah, his country being governed by a Goorkhali Soubah, and himself being under an honourable restraint at Khatmanda.

Chinnachin is situated in a valley, the north side of which is bounded by the mountains of Himma-leh. The town stands between the Chinnachin and Kurnâla rivers, which are said to unite at a point distant about six journies to the south-west of Chinnachin, and which would appear, from circumstances, to be the Doulu Bassender of Rennell. My information, however, respecting this remote and secluded region, is infinitely too vague to allow of my building more than a slight conjecture upon it.

The valley of Jumlah is described to be nearly of the same extent as that of Nepaul, but to be rather more contiguous to Himma-leh, and more chequered with low hills. The ridge of mountains immediately to the northward is called Seela-pahar, and makes part of the greater Himma-leh; for it is proper to observe, that the appellation of Himma-leh is very commonly bestowed on the Kuchar mountains; being strictly applicable, as well as the term Lungoor, to any mountainous tract liable to frequent or heavy falls of snow. To the north-west the valley of Jumlah is bounded by a mountain whose summit is perpetually covered with clouds. They sow their rice in Jumlah about the tenth of Bysack; reaping it about the tenth of Bhadoon. Behadur Shah, judging from the situation and climate of Jumlah, that the rice of that valley would be very likely to flourish in England, proposed to me that the experiment should be made, for which purpose he promised to forward to Calcutta a large supply of seed in proper season for dispatching to Europe.

The following route from Noakote to Acham, which would appear to be the western extremity of the Bansi is inserted solely with the view of conveying a loose idea of the general direction of the road, and of the relative situations of places. The distances are given in Ghurries (equal to $22\frac{1}{2}$ minutes) but are not to be relied on either in this or any of the other itinera. Besides, it would not be easy to fix, with respect to a country so little known to us, on any rule for converting time into road miles, while it would be altogether impossible for us to reduce these last (though we had ascertained them exactly) to horizontal distance.

V.

General Route from Noakote to Acham.	Ghurries.
To Noakote-sângô, i. e. the bridge over the Tirsoolgunga, which is rarely ever fordable	
To Samuri-bhunjan - -	6
To Pouwa - - -	$9\frac{1}{2}$
To Aukhoo-kola, or the river Aukhoo, which you cross,	14

	Ghurries.
To Sulian-tar, or Sulheyan, plain	1
To the passage over the Gundi (never fordable) -	2
To Sulian-kote, or Gong - -	4
To Goorkha - - -	5½
	42
To Goorkha-baisi, on the east bank of the Dhurrumdee (never fordable) - -	3
To the Bhooshni, or Khâr-kola - -	5
To Abou-wah-baisi - -	7
To Kurmi bhunjan, to the left, or south, of which stands Sig-by-thaneh, (or fort) - -	7
To Palsoong-tar - - -	3
To Chepia-kola, or the river Chepia - -	2¼
To Soobhoo-tar - -	3
To Tarkhoo-ghat, or the passage over the Mursiangdi (never fordable) - - -	6
To Lumjoon, or Lumjoong, by the direct road, which is very wild - - -	28
To Kurrapoo-tar - - -	29
To the bridge over the Phullia -	2
To Mahdi-ghaut, or the passage over the Mahdi, which gives name to Mahdi-baisi - -	25
To Phurha-bhirja-kote, which stands very high over Mahdi-ghaut - - -	4

	Ghurries.
To Rani-powah, on the Saite-nuddi -	25
To Kaiski-shehr - -	25
To Sulian-tar (the 2d) - -	26
To Mahdi, on the river of the same name -	3
To Kali-nuddi, or the great Gunduck -	3
To Shorah-kani, or the salt-petre works -	32
To Gulkoat-baisi - -	33
To Moosi-kote - - -	34

The Purthana Territory.

To Dhoor-kote - - -	32
To Bandicote, standing on the side of the Jhoomrukh-nuddi	31
To Purthâna-shehr - -	28
To Mahdi-kola (a small stream) -	29
To Ghiandi-kote - -	30

The Sulheyan or Suliana Territory, the Rajah of which is married to a sister of Behadur Shah.

To Bhâla-bang - - -	31
To Sulheyan-kote - - -	32
To the Behri-nuddi - -	30
To Jumri-kote - - -	28
To Bharia-kote - -	29
To Rangheya - - -	31

	Ghurries.
Urgho Rajah's Territory, now in the possession of the Goorkhali. The Gherjung-kote road to Jumlah is taken at that season of the year (the rainy especially) when the nature of the Kurna-kote road, (which lies through the Kuchar, or lower hilly tract, and is subject to the Owl,) renders it impassible.	
To mount Chakooria - - .	15
To Gurry-gong - - -	16
To Gherjung-kote - - -	26
Hence a road strikes off to Jumlah, which is north-west of Gherjung 14, 15 or 16 journies -	27
To the Chinnachin-nuddi - -	27
To Nagoom-kote - - -	32
The Jumlah Territory.	
To Boodhoong-gong - -	29
To Sathi-kote - - -	31
To Pathi-kote - -	27
To Kurna-kote (to the north of this lies Jumlah about 3 journies) - -	32
To the Kurnâli-kola - -	34
To Chham-kote - - -	31
To Acham - - -	32
	1010¼

General Route from Acham to Serinugur.	Ghurries.
From Acham to Dhotee they reckon twelve journies, which, one with another, may be stated at 24 ghurries, or 24 miles, making - - -	288
The greater part of this tract is a close forest lying at the southern foot of the mountains, and of course almost totally uninhabited. The forest commences about three journies west of Acham; and the Jumlah territory extends three days further west, or midway between Acham and Dhotee	
From Dhotee to Kemaoon, they reckon it fifteen days journey, or (at the same rate) - -	360
From Kemaoon to the borders of Gherwâl, they reckon eleven days, or - - -	264
And from the borders of Gherwâl to Serinugur, its capital, nine days, or - - -	216
	2138

According to the map the horizontal distance between Noakote and Serinugur is about 500 statute miles; so that, at this rate, four road miles give very little more than one horizontal mile. With respect to the road distance, it can hardly be reduced, when it is considered that the journey from Nepaul to Serinugur is uniformly between three and four months, and that the Nepaulians are very sturdy travellers, being generally in motion about two-thirds, at least, of the time between sun-rise and sun-set, and very commonly proceeding in that space from thirty to forty miles.

I would propose, therefore, (till we obtain more accurate information), assuming the horizontal distance as laid down by Major Rennell, and placing the intermediate stations (as enumerated above) according to the proportionate distance given by the route.

VII.

Account of some of the Rivers which occur in the preceding Route.

1. For an account of the Trisoolgunga see before.

2. The Aukhoo takes its rise from Mâlâ-bikh, north of Samuribhunjan, about three days, and disembogues itself into the Gundi a few miles from Sulian, and to the northward of the confluence of the Gundi and Dhurrumdee.

3. The Gundi, with the source of which I am not clearly acquainted, empties itself into the Kali-Gunduck (by which name what we call the Gunduck is usually distinguished, the word Gunduck being a general appellation for a river), at Salegrami Nerâini, in the district of Noel-ghurr, S. W. of Deo-ghaut eight good journies, south of Tunnohoo 3 journies, and south-east of Bootwal 3½ journies.

4. The Dhurrumdee rises in mount Takoo, north of old Goorkha 5 journies. It empties itself into the Gundi at Dhoorboongghaut, south of Sulian 2 journies.

5. The Bhoosni, or Khar-kola, takes its rise at Lâkha-joong, a mountain belonging to the Rooi Bhoat ridge, and north-west of Ghoorkha. It now runs into the Mursiangdi at Dhândhi-ghaut, south-west of Ghoorkha-baisi 7 or 8 miles.

Rooi (or snowy) Bhoat is the general name of a range of mountains to the northward of Old Loomjoong, and in which Luckwa-bussiari is situated.

6. Chepia-kola. This river issues from Siran-Choak, which lies three days north of Sig-sig. It empties itself into the Mursiangdi at Ghai-ghaut, which is about 13 miles south-west of Kurmi-bhunjan.

7. The Mursiangdi rises at Luckwa-bussiari (mentioned above), west of Munpang-baisi. It joins the Gunduck near Jogimara Oopadrong.

8. The Site, or Saite, rises at Mâchia Poochur, (or fish-tail snowy mountains). It empties itself into the Mursiangdi to the northward of Tarkoo-ghaut, or at Kâiphul-ghaut in Lakhajoong-baisi.

VIII.

CROSS POSITIONS.

W. by N. or W. N. W. of Tunnohoo, or Tunnohi, 17 or 18 ghurries, is Bussuntpoor.

N. W. of Bussuntpore 23 ghurries, is Ghainde-kote.

S. W. of Ghainde-kote, 1 day, or 29 ghurries, is Reesing.

W. S. W. of Reesing 30 ditto, is Ghering.

W. S. W. of Reesing, also 29 ditto, is Palpa.

W. S. W. of Palpa 1 day, is Bootoul, or Bootwal.

N. N. W. of Ghering, 1 day, or 29 ghurries, is Dhoulle-thaneh.

S. S. W. of Dhoulle-thaneh 16 ditto, is Murkote.

S. of Murkote 1 day, or 26 ditto, is West Noakote.

N. W. of West Noakote 12 ditto, is Urghaloor (in the Purbutty Rajah's territory).

S. W. of Urghaloor 29 ditto, is Suttohoo.

S. W. of Suttohoo 30 ditto, is Gurrohoo.

N. of Gurrohoo 12 ditto, is Assoor-kote.

S. W. of Gurrohoo 33 ditto, is Py-ying.

W. b. N. W. N. W. of Py-ying 5 ditto, is Ruri-ghaut, where the Kali-nuddi, or Salegrami, is crossed.

N. of Py-ying 28 ditto, is Urghâ.

N. N. E. of Urghâ 12 ditto, is Kanchi.

S. W. of Urghâ 28 ditto, is Assoor-kote (the 2d.)

W. S. W. of Assoor-kote 21 ditto, is Purthana.

S. of Purthana 28 ditto, is Oudepore.

W. of Purthana 16 ditto, is Poochi-ghaut, the passage over the Mahdi-nuddi.

W. of Purthana 25 ditto, is Chowghôra.

N. of Chowghôra 12 ditto, is Phâlâbang.

S. of Chowghôra 16 or 17 ditto, is Bhoommuri-kote.

S. W. of Purthana 32 ditto, is Soorma-kote, one of the boundaries of the Dang Sulheyan territory.

W. S. W. of Soorma-kote 28 ditto, is Dang Sulheyan-shehr.

N.N.W. of Dang Sulheyan 14 ghurries, is Behri-kote, on the Behri-nuddi, the passage over which is Chindra-ghaut.

W.S.W. of Dang Sulheyan 30 ditto, is Jagher-kote.

W.S.W. of Jagher-kote 15 ditto, is Jehari-kote.

N.N.E. of Jagher-kote 7 ditto, is Moosi-kote.

W. of Jagher-kote 25 ditto, is Jooalamookhi, or Soorujamookhi.

N. of Dang Sulheyan 14 ditto, is Banka-kote.

N.N.E. of Banka-kote, 13 ditto, is Ghurry-gong.

N.N.W. of Kurha-kote 30 ditto, is Sujapat.

N. of Sujapat 12 or 13 ditto, is Ghum-kote.

W.N.W. of Sujapat 8 or 9 ditto, is Hoomlah-kote.

S.W. of Hoomlah-kote 14 or 15 ditto, is Pangdhoor.

W.N.W. of Pangdhoor 15 or 16 ditto, is Dhoorlong.

S.W. of Dhoorlong 12 or 13 ditto, is Bajoong.

W.N.W. of Bajoong 21 ditto, is Bulliwa.

S. of Bajoong 35 ditto, is Noel-ghurr.

N.W. of Bulliwa 32 ditto, is Singana.

W. of Bulliwa 4 ditto, is Tagoom.

W.N.W. of Tagoom 32 ditto, is Dhoulle-thaneh (the 2d.)

W.S.W. of Dhoulle-thaneh 32 ditto, is Rakhoo-thaneh.

N.B. All this is included in what is called the Bansi.

S.W. of Kaiski-shehr 19 ditto, is Pheroâtâl, a considerable lake not less than a mile, or ¾ths of a mile across.

N.E. of Kaiski 29 ditto, is another large lake called Roopâtâl.

S.E. of Kaiski 15 ditto, is Bheâgamestâl, a third lake.

And N. W. of Kalski, 6 Ghurries, is Khahootâl, the smallest of the four lakes which enclose this territory.

The country around Kaiski-shehr is plain or level for the distance, in every direction, of about 15 or 16 Ghurries. It is included at present in the Nepaul dominions.

IX.

Route from Noakote to Joongah, &c.

	Ghurries.
To Dhyboon N. b. E. - -	20

You descend from the town of Noakote into Noakote-baisi, and then proceed along the east bank of the Trisoolgunga: at the foot of Dhyboon passes the Bettrouilli, which you cross, and then ascend Dhyboon The town of Dhyboon stands at some distance below the summit. There is no material ascent between Noakote-baisi, and the Bettrouilli, though the road is uneven and bad. The acclivity of Dhyboon from the Bettroulli is so good that a tolerable Tanyan may be safely rode the whole way. You are from 3 to 4 ghurries in reaching Dhyboon, after crossing the Bettrouilli. The Chinese general Thoong Thang did not descend below the town of Dhyboon, though part of his army did.

To Kabhria N. N. W. - -	12

From Dhyboon to Kabhria, there is neither ascent or

Ghurries.

descent deserving notice. The road, however, is winding. Near Kabhria the Nepaulians had an action with the Chinese.

To Ramcha N. b. E. or N. N. E. - - 10

There is an ascent between Kabhria and Ramcha, for three or four ghurries, but it is not of a difficult nature. This place is between Dhooncho and Kabhria.

To Sisnia-ooral, N. E. - - 25

The first three or four ghurries from Ramcha, the road winds round the mountain, after which the whole way is a descent till you reach Sisnia. The Sisnia-kola passes this place. It has its rise from the neighbouring mountains of Lawhribinna, and empties itself into the Trisoolgunga, but where I do not know. There is a cave here, from which circumstance the place is distinguished by the name of Ooral. There are many natural grottos or caves in these parts which, it is to be remembered, were the favourite haunts of Mahadeo and other Hindoo deities.

To mount Deoralli, N. N. E. - - 22

The first three or four ghurries, the road winds round Sisnia bottom. After which the whole way to Deoralli is an ascent. Mount Deoralli is one of the peaks of Himma-leh, and is among the loftiest of them. The road passes below it, at the distance of about 3 ghurries from the summit,

Ghurries.

and of course far below the region of snow. There is a Goopa, Ooral, or cave on the side of it, in which travellers rest. The Chinese had an obstinate action here with the Nepaulians, over whom, however, they prevailed, obliging them to fall back to Dhooncho (see next route), and from thence to Kabhria.

To Russooa, N.N.E. - - 15

This is a Bhootia village, and marks the present limits of Nepaul in this direction. The first two or three ghurries of this road is winding, the remainder a descent.

Under Russooa flows a rivulet bearing the same name, which is passed by a bridge. This stream joins the Trisoolgunga at Dhoonghia-sângô (Dhoonghia bridge) to the westward of Russooa. The Nepaulians disputed the passage of this bridge with the Chinese army during three days.

To Siaprie, N.N.E. - - 10

The greatest part an ascent and bad road (but out of the region of snow). The last ghurrie you descend to Siaprie.

To Tiburia, or Temuria, N.N.E. - - 12

Here there is a stream that bears the same name, and falls into the Trisoolgunga at Dhoonghia-sângô, as well as the Russooa rivulet. Here is a Bhootia village. For ten ghurries of this road you have a descent, and a very

Ghurries.

bad one. The Chinese army, in advancing from hence, was obliged to deviate somewhat from the common track, which exposed them considerably to the snow.

To Kheroo, N. by E. - - 15

The first five ghurries of this road is an ascent, part of which is bad and difficult; the remainder is plain, as you have now reached the table land of Tibet. Kheroo was once a large town, but is now rather inconsiderable, having been laid waste some years since in an incursion of the Kâla Soogpa Tartars, who occupy the country to the northward of Joongah, and who for some time possessed themselves of Lehassa.

North of Kheroo two or three miles, there passes a small stream, the bed of which is quite sandy like those of other plain countries.

You see no snowy mountains from Kheroo in the north quarter: but you observe them in the south (that is, behind you), in the west, and in the south-east quarters. The last of these is the Kooti ridge, beyond which, still more southerly, you descry a range running in the direction of Phullak and Sankia-goombah.

To Kerow-bari, due north - 19

Several villages on the road, which is all the way plain.

To Ghiaboo-ooral, due north - - 21

Ghurries.

You meet with two ascents in this journey, but of no difficulty. There are no villages, it would seem, on the road. Ghiaboo-ooral is a small village, near which passes the Soona-kola, which also has a sandy bed.

To Kookeer-ghautt, N.E. by E. - - 23

Roads rather uneven, but of no great roughness; a small stream passes this place, which would appear to be distinguished by the name of Ghautt, on account of its being a place of resort with the merchants, &c. and not in its more obvious and ordinary sense. The term Ghautt, I am told, is often employed in this quarter to denote a place of meeting. This was one of the camps of the Chinese army.

To Joongah, north - - 24

The road from Kookeer hither consists of several ascents. This would seem to be a wonderfully elevated spot, and is perhaps one of the very highest points of Tibet.

There is a lofty hill here on which a fort stands belonging to the Dalai Lama. It is said to be very strong, consisting of huge blocks of stone well put together. The Nepaul army once attacked it, but without success.

The sources of the Boora-gunduck (of the north) are near Joongah, from the vicinity of which place there would seem to run a ridge of mountains in a south-easterly

Ghurries

direction. It is from these mountains that the Boora-gun-duck springs, winding, in the beginning of its course, in such a manner as nearly to insulate Joongah. It joins the Trisoolgunga at Bhâlkoo (elsewhere Balchet), where it also yields its name to that river.

To Ghiboo-gounra, N. E. by E.	-	25

Between this place and Joongah the Seesa-kola passes; great part of the way is descent, the rest plain (there being no ascent at all).

To Munooaphaut, N. E. by E.	-	26

From Ghiboo hither the country is plain. At Munooaphaut is a Ghyang, or Lama's residence. *Phaut* signifies a plain. They grow here a great deal of the grain called *Munooa*, to which circumstance the place is said to owe its name.

Ghurries 279

The halting-stages in this journey are fixed, it not being possible to rest excepting at the places enumerated. It is, therefore, of necessity, a journey of sixteen days (though the distances are very unequal), unless you choose to join occasionally two days proper journey together, in which manner travellers sometimes pass from Noakote to Munooaphaut in ten, eleven, or twelve days.

From Munooaphaut there is said to be a good road to Tingrie

Mydoun, or the valley of Tingrie, which occurs in the route to Diggercheh, viâ Kooti.

The preceding is the route by which the Chinese army penetrated to Noakote in the year 1792.

The following routes to Neel-khent (called also Gussain-thân) are on the authority of a Brahmin who had visited that sequestered but greatly sanctified spot, twenty-one times.

I. *Road to Neel-khent from Khatmanda, by Nerjah.*

		Computed Coss.
1st day.	To Dherimsilli. N. W. (see Memoir).	2
2d day.	To Thansein (village of), to which you descend after passing over mount Kukauni, north -	5
3d day.	To Nerjah, due north -	5

In proceeding to Nerjah, you pass first the Syb-butty, or Lykhoo, and afterwards the Sooreybutty, or Tadi. These streams join a little way to the northward of the spot where the Rajah's camp was pitched at Noakote.

The Lykhoo has its rise at Linchoogong, issuing from the peak of the Sindoo. The Tadi (as before mentioned) issues from Soorey-koondeh, whence it derives its name of Sooreybutty. Nerjah stands towards the bottom of the north side of the hill, near the summit of which Luchungy is situated. The Tadi passes through the valley of Nerjah.

Coss.

During the violence of the rainy season they cross the Tadi here over a rope bridge, in preference to using boats, on account of the rocky bottom and rapidity of the stream. These bridges are called Joobingga.

4th day. To Yarsa, north - - $6\frac{1}{2}$

This plain at present belongs to Bhootan. In proceeding hither from Nerjah, you cross the Pharkoo, or Rachisi-nuddi of the Shaster. The Deoralli ridge runs to the northward of Yarsa.

5th day. To Dhoocho, N. N. E. - - 5

This is the name by which they distinguish the brows of a mountain where there is a Goopa, or natural cave, in which travellers put up. This sort of cave is called among the Purbutties, Ooral.

6th day. To Dhooncho, N. N. E. - 4

Descending from Dhoocho northerly you come to the Trisool-gunga, which is crossed here over a rude wooden bridge. From hence you proceed to Dhooncho, which is situated on the top of a mountain called Trisool Purput.

7th day. Neel-khent, due east - - 6

The road between Dhooncho and Neel-khent is represented as being quite level.

Computed Coss $34\frac{3}{4}$

About midway between Dhooncho and Neel-khent you come to

Chundunbari, about one coss to the eastward of which (or within two coss of Neel-khent) is a colossal statue or image in stone of Ghunnaisi. About another coss to the eastward of Ghunnaisi, (i. e. one coss west of Neel-khent) is Sersootee-koondeh, into which runs the water of Bhyroo-koondeh; as that of Neel-khent-koondeh does into this last. From Sersoote-koondeh issues the Trisoolgunga. Neel-khent-koondeh is supplied by three streams, or torrents rather, that come down from the superjacent hills, but their course from their springs is very inconsiderable, none of the latter being at a greater distance from Neel-khent-koondeh than a stone's throw. This lake is fabled to owe its formation to Mahadeo, who having, at the celebrated churning of the sea, swallowed something which stuck in his throat and occasioned the inflammation of that part, accompanied with a burning heat, retired to the snowy region of Himmaleh, where striking his Trisool, or trident, into the ground, he gave rise to the Trisoolgunga and its lakes. This god is called Neel-khent (or Blue-neck), in allusion to the effects of the poison abovementioned; and from the circumstance of his having stretched himself along the lake for the purpose of assuaging the fever he suffered from, originated those representations of Mahadeo under the name Neel-khent, which have been sometimes mistaken for the images of Nerayer.

This is the road to Neel-khent, according to the Shaster (I suppose the Hemmouret-kund is meant here); the following by Noakote was made by order of Purthi Nerain previous to his conquest of Nepaul, and while he resided either at Goorkha or Noakote.

II. *Road by Noakote from Khatmanda.*

		Coss.
1st day.	Rani-Powah, on the summit of Bheerbundy, north.	
2d day.	Noakote or Nowakote.	
3d day.	Dhyboon, N. W. - -	4
	The town of Dhyboon appears to be of some note, being well inhabited by Bhootias and Purbutties. Before you reach Dhyboon you cross the Pharkoo* (mentioned in last route), which falls into the Trisoolgunga below Dhyboon; there being at the confluence a Moorukt of Ramjee.	
4th day.	Ramcha-gong. This is a Bhootia village; the whole of the way to it from Dhyboon being described as an easy ascent. Ramcha stands upon a mountain which appears to be a continuation of the Dhyboon and Ramcha, and near the road is Khumhara-ghurr, north-west. -	2
5th day.	Gram or Gurram, east. - -	2
	The road through mountains; the Trisoolgunga winding below.	
6th day.	Bhugajoondo, east - -	2

* I suspect this to be the same with the Bettrouilli. It would appear that you may either cross or avoid the Trisoolgunga, which runs under Noakote, through the valley called Gheekhoo-târ. If you pass by the wooden bridge which is thrown over it, about two coss from Noakote, you have to ascend Dhyboon, I believe, by a different side from that which is mounted in proceeding by the higher road.

	Coss.
Between Gram and Bhugajoonda is a celebrated cave, under a considerable eminence, called Thara-ooral, or the cave of Thara. It is also known by the name of Bhumakagoopa. The Trisoolgunga passes below.	
7th day. Dheemcha, east - -	2
This is a Bhootia town, containing 700 houses. The Trisoolgunga passes on the north side of it.	
8th day. Dhooncho,* east - -	2
Here the Nerjah and Noakote roads meet. The Trisoolgunga passes below.	
9th day. Neel-khent, as before, east -	6
Coss	20

Almost due east of, but a little more elevated than Neel-khent, and at the distance of about 1 coss and a half (3 miles), is Soorey-koondeh, whence the Tadi has its rise.

Below Soorey-koondeh stands another lake called Bheerbhuddur-koondeh, the water of which has no outlet.

East of Bheerbhudder-koondeh, and situated rather high, is Chander-koondeh, a lake, the water of which is represented as communicating with Neel-khent-koondeh.

Due north of Soorey-koondeh, one coss, is Puncho-pândab-

* The Kheroo road (I am told) strikes off here to the right; they say it is four days easy march from Dhooncho to Kheeroo. See Route IX.

koondeh, the water of which gives rise to a river that passes on the west side of Kooti.

Due north again of the preceding, and at the distance of two coss, is Gouri-koondeh, which is the Durbar of Himally. Beyond Gouri-koondeh they pretend it is impossible to proceed, excepting through aid of the incantations of the Lama who resides here, and who must be propitiated for the purpose in the manner easy to be conceived. The water of this Koondeh or lake is stationary, having no communication with any other.

Upon the summit to Kerumboo, are five Poakhras (tanks or lakes), which are supplied with water from springs in an adjacent mountain called Husteemâchul, which is two coss north of Kerumboo, and of course situated somewhat higher. This place, though for the greatest part of the year covered with snow, produces rice, which, it is pretended, is sown and cultivated by Mahadeo Purbutty. It is ripe in Sawrun, which is the only time that travellers can pass, and though it is not produced in sufficient abundance to satisfy the cravings of the appetite, yet the devout pilgrims are very well satisfied in securing a few grains.

All accounts agree in representing that after you reach Dhooncho you have the greatest difficulty in drawing your breath, though you have no longer to ascend. They do not attribute this effect to the rarity of the atmosphere owing to the great elevation; but to the deleterious influence of the Bhyroo-pâte, Soan-pâte, and other plants which grow under and about the snow.

There is a third road to Neel-khent, or Gussain-than, from Nerjah, by Tambeh-Sillar. It is much more direct than the others, inclining more easterly, but it is so difficult that it is rarely travelled, and known only to the Bhootias of that quarter, without having some of whom for guides, &c. there is no attempting it. It is one day's journey from Nerjah to Tambeh-Sillar: and thence another day to Neel-khent, this road joining the rest at Bhyroo-koondeh.

The cold of Neel-khent, even in the month of August, is too severe to admit of the pilgrims resting there beyond a single day. Avalanches are common in this road, and sometimes exceeding dangerous; glacieres both of ice and frozen snow occur also in various parts of this alpine region. When it is considered that Neel-khent is visited in Sawrun (or July, August); that the road is then passable but with great difficulty, owing to the depths of snow lying on and at either side of it (but particularly in the hollows which border on it); that the traveller is subject to fresh and heavy falls at this time; that the mountain (Jibjibia) inclosing Neel-khent to the southward, or towards Nepaul, is covered with snow to a considerable depth, from its summit to about midway down on the Neel-khent side; and that this mountain is not situated in a higher latitude than 28, we cannot suppose it to be less elevated than the Peak of Teneriffe. It is not extraordinary that the valley of Nepaul should be discernible from this eminence; but what must we conclude concerning the elevation of Himma-leh, when we consider that some of the peaks of this alpine ridge, which here appear interminable, and to be heaped one upon another, seem, according to the united testimony of several travellers, to be even higher from this point of view than Jibjibia itself does from Noakote or Nepaul.

Route from Khatmanda to Diggercheh or Teeshoo Loomboo, by Kooti.

Gooje-serri, near Pusputnath, or Deopatun.

Sankoo, E. N. E. from Khatmanda, about 9 road miles.

Deopoor. This place is situated on a mountain E. by N. of Sankoo, from 12 to 15 ghurries journey of a person lightly equipped. There passes near it a pretty considerable stream, called the Indiani, which rises in Himma-leh and disembogues itself into the Soan-Kousi at Dholat-ghaut. I compute this distance to be about 14 road miles.

Seepa. This place also stands on a hill E. by N. of Deopoor, distance 12 or 13 ghurries, i. e. about 13 road miles; you cross the Indiani in proceeding hence to

Jhari, which is nearly in the same direction, and only 2 ghurries from Seepa, say E. by N. 2 road miles; a small stream occurs here.

Choutra, E. N. E. or N. by E. 12 to 15 ghurries, or about 14 road miles.

Koobindiah, where a little rivulet passes.

Bullephee. Here a larger stream occurs. You then ascend to

Phyria, which is from 12 to 15 ghurries from Choutra; say

E. N. E. 14 road miles. This place is situated on the side of a mountain called Laick-pâtti.

Phaldoo. N. N. E. 12 to 15 ghurries, or 14 road miles.

Laisti. N. N. E. 8 ghurries, 7½ or 8 road miles; the present boundary of Nepaul towards Kooti.

Dhoogna. N. N. E. 10 ghurries, 10 road miles. Leaving this place you cross the Bhootia-Kousi over an iron bridge. This river issues from Himma-leh, and joins the Soan-Kousi at a town called Pullânti.

Khûsa, or Khussa-goombah, N. E. 20 ghurries, say 19 road miles. You cross the Bhootia-Kousi two or three times in this day's journey.

Chosiong. N. N. E. 12 ghuries, 12 road miles.

Kooti. N. N. E. 12 to 13 ghurries, 12 road miles. The Bhootia-Kousi runs on the east side of Kooti, and is hereabouts joined by the Ghuttia-kola, a stream that comes from the westward. Crossing the Ghuttia you proceed to

Soona-goombah. E. by N. from 10 to 12 ghurries, say 11 road miles.

Mathie-goombah. N. E. from 14 to 15 ghurries, 14 road miles. The Bhootia-Kousi winds near the road during the last two days journey.

Lungoor-phede (or the foot of the passage through the Himma-leh), east 12 ghurries, i. e. about 12 road miles. The snowy mountains take hence a very southerly direction. The source of the Bhootia-Kousi is said to be at no great distance from hence, and not far from the springs of the Arûn or Aroon, rising at different sides of Himma-leh. The course of the Bhootia-Kousi is at first about west, and afterwards generally S. S. W. The Arûn takes, in the beginning, a direction nearly N. E. and describes an astonishing circuitous course before it discharges itself into the Kousi. The elevation of the pass over which you proceed through Himma-leh is very inconsiderable, consequently those stupendous mountains must tower sublimely over the traveller's head. Descending its eastern side you proceed to

Lung-kote, E. from 16 to 18 ghurries, or 17 road miles, and about N. by E. for the last 4 ghurries, or 5 miles. The whole distance about 21 ghurries, or 22 road miles.

Tingri, due east 10 or 11 ghurries, 12 road miles. This place is situated in the Tingri-mydân, or the valley of Tingri, and stands upon the Arûn. From hence the road to Diggercheh (the Sgigatchi of Major Rennell) is quite level, and tolerably direct. From Tingri, the Nepaul army, in its invasion of Tibet a few years since, proceeded to a station to which, on account of its bad water, they gave the name of

Ghuttia-pany, due east 15 ghurries, 18 road miles. The Arûn passes also under this station, where its channel is very broad, though it was not middle deep at the time the Nepaulians passed this way. From hence they advanced to

Neeka-pany, east 4 ghurries, or 5 road miles. This also was a nameless station, which the Nepaulians called Neeka-pany, on account of the goodness of its water. The road during this space lies along the Arûn.

Koona-goombah, or Kona-gong, east 16 or 18 ghurries, about 16 road miles. This place obtained its name from the circumstance of its being situated in the elbow of a small stream. The Arûn passes near it to the northward.

Shikar-goombah, N. 2 ghurries, or 3 miles. The army encamped at Shika-doobhan, or the confluence of the Arûn, and another river that comes from the Shikar-goombah quarter.

Shikar-doobhan, due east (from Koona-goombah), 10 ghurries or 4 computed coss, i. e. not above eight miles. From Shikar-doobhan, they proceeded to a station which they called Dhain-baitra Katrakagong (from the circumstance of their having caught here a great many sheep), due east 10 ghurries, or 10 miles. This place is situated on the south side of the Arûn.

Chho-goombah, east 4 ghurries, or 4 miles. This is a place of considerable note. It contains a goombah so large, that a company of sepoys which encamped in it were said to be in a manner lost.

Choor-balooa, east 4 ghurries, or 3 miles. This is a plain formed of a kind of quick sand, or, perhaps, quagmire. It is enclosed between the Arûn and another stream, which unite at its extremity; the Arûn afterwards pursuing a very southerly course. The army did not halt here, but continued its march to

Saita-goombah (so named by the Nepaulians on account of the

white colour of its edifice), east 16 ghurries from Choor-balooa, and 20 from Chho-goombah, 16 miles.

Bhyria-gong (or Willow Town), north, 10 to 12 ghurries, 12 miles. The Nepaul people gave the name of Bhyria to this village on account of its abounding in willows.

From Bhyria-gong proceeded to within 1½ ghurry, or 1¼ mile of Sankia, east from 10 to 12 ghurries, or 11 miles, encamping in a valley. From thence marched beyond Sankia, east 3 ghurries, or 3 miles, near a stream.

Ekela-goombah, east 7 or 8 ghurries, then turning north for 8 or 9 ghurries, on the whole 16 or 17 ghurries, or 18 miles. This place obtained its name from the Nepaulians, on acoount of its standing alone.

Shangooko-baisi, E. by N. or E. N. E. 12 or 13 ghurries, or 14 miles. This place is near a large stream (name not mentioned), over which there is a wooden bridge, from whence it derives its name.

Lollpehar, east 10 or 11 ghurries, 12 miles. There is a little ascent to Lollpehar (so named from the red colour of its soil), after passing which you have a fine plain all the way to Diggercheh.

Kaghez-goombah, east 15 coss, 25 miles.

Diggercheh, or Teeshoo Loomboo, east 8 or 9 ghurries, 10 miles. North of Diggercheh, or Teeshoo Loomboo, at the distance of about 3 miles, runs the Berhampooter.

125½ computed road miles from Chho-goombah.

186½ from Tingri.

257½ from Kooti.

398½ from Khatmanda.

Route from Khatmanda to Kooti and Shikargong, the same, in point of general direction to Kooti, as the preceding, but exhibiting some different stages.

	Ghurries.
To Châbêhal, on the west bank of the Dobi-kola (cross it).	3
To Sankoo - - -	8
To Deopoor (Mount), N. E. descent -	3
To Indiani-nuddi (cross) - -	4
To Seepa (Mount), ascend from the Indiani -	15
To Jhari-kola (descend, cross) - - -	3
To Bhootia-Seepa, or Choutra, (ascend) -	16
To Miangdia-kola (cross) - -	10
This river issues from Mount Dooskoon, south-east of Bhootia-Seepa.	
To Phyria-ghaut (road along the bank of the Miangdia)	12
To Kunsa (ascend) - - -	3¼
To Laick-pâtti, 5 or 6 ghurries (ascent, rest winding, and a little descent) - - -	16
To Phaldoo (descend) - -	4
To Laisti-kola (road through a valley) -	3
To Dhara-puni-gong - -	10
To Dhoogna-gong - - -	9
To Bhootia-Kousi (cross over an iron bridge) -	9

	Ghurries.
The Bhootia-Kousi rises in Bhâg-Bhyroo, or Bhyroob Lungoor. It joins the Soan-Kousi at Ramcha-goomany, a village to the south-east. Bhâg-Bhyroo is to the N. E. of Kooti.	
To Khussa-goombah (ascend 5 ghurries, 2 or 3 winding)	8
To Salia-ooral (or goopah) ascent, winding, and descent	7
To Bhysia-kola (cross) - -	8
Rises east of Dhoomung Mount, north-east of Bhootia-seepa, not properly in Himma-leh. It most probably falls into the Bhootia.	
To Kohunnia-burri-ung (named from the extraordinary difficult nature of the road) - -	5
To Chosiong village, moderate - -	3
To Rani-ooral, or goopah, ditto - -	4
To Old Kooti (an ascent all the way) -	4
To Bheemal-Deoralli (chiefly descent) -	2
To Kooti proper (partly an ascent) - -	3
To Ghuttia-kola (passes to the north-west of Kooti)	1
No place appears to be so difficult as Kooti, all round is below it. It flows from the bottom of Kala-Bhyroob mount, which is not two days from Kooti. It is in Himma-leh.	
To Ghuttia-ghurry, on the west side of the Kola, then cross the Ghuttia	

	Ghurries.
To Bheemul-ghurry (some ascent) - -	$1\frac{1}{4}$
To Soona-goombah, 3 or 4 ghurries ascent, afterwards some plain - - -	8
To Chaprong, or Suabrong-goombah	10
2 ghurries ascent, 6 or 7 ditto winding, and 2 ditto descent.	
To Dheramsilla-phede, a kind of Serai at the foot of Kala Bhyroob ridge (road moderate, mixed) -	21
To Kala Bhyroob Lungoor Bhenjang (or hollow)	16
This is the passage through Himma-leh; all the way ascent; if you rest here it must be in a cave. From the Bhenjang you have the Himma-leh on your right and left (the face to Lehassa, and back to Khatmanda), whose peaks appear just over the head. There is sometimes, as you pass, snow lying on the Bhenjang, but not usually. The ridge on the right runs towards the Deb Rajah's country, that on the left comes from Kheeroo, &c.	
To Shikar-goombah, moderately easy road; a stream called Reenoo passes to the westward of Shikar, which is passed in proceeding to Shikargong. It issues from the north-east of Sankie-goombah	17
To Shikargong (a fort), a plain -	17
To the west of Shikargong passes a stream. The road to Lehassa, Diggercheh, &c. strikes off from Shikar-goombah.	
Ghurries	$263\frac{1}{2}$

Route from Khatmanda to Bejapour.

	Ghurries.
The Bhagmutty - -	3
To Teemi - -	2
To the Munnokra-nuddi - -	3
To Bhatgong - -	6
To Bhatia-dekhûra - -	1½
To Sanga-bunjan - -	1¾
To Bunepa - -	3
To Dhoolkill - -	4
To Bhouwerkote - -	6
To Pallângchoki-baisi - -	3
To Mookhpa - -	4
To Dholat-ghaut (over the Soan-Kousi) -	3
Dholat is two short journies S. S. E. of the conflux of the Soan and Bhootia Kousi. Here the Indiani joins the Kousi	
To Ukhurria-ghaut (Soan-Kousi) -	4
To Aumchoak-ghaut (Soan-Kousi) -	3
To Teemûl-baisi - -	4
To Mujhoowa-ghaut (Soan-Kousi) -	5
To Dhoomjah-baisi - -	3
To Jubaka-ghaut (Soan-Kousi) -	5
To Sitki-ghaut (Soan-Kousi)	6
To Pooch-hi-ghaut - -	7

	Ghurries.
To the confluence of the Tambeh-Kousi with the Soan-Kousi (at Beni) - - -	5
To Koorkoat-ghaut - -	4
To Hurdiani-ghaut - -	6
To Kang-sang-ghaut - -	7
To Soroong-baisi - -	8
To Jallookiani-ghaut - -	5
To Namdhoo-ghaut - -	3
To Nepaul-târ - - -	7
To Lubsi-ghaut - -	4
To Cheebhoo-târ - - -	8
To Seroong-baisi (the 2d) - -	7
To Teen Patn - -	3
To the confluence of the Dhoodh-kousi (at Koosumptâr)	4
To Sarsoo-baisi - -	5
To Hurdiani-ghaut (the 2d) - -	5½
To Seering-ghaut - -	5
To Puncha-kunnia-deepha (a remarkable rock in the bed of the Kousi) - - -	5
To Ghoomounia-ghaut - -	4
To Ohdhang-ghaut - -	7
To the conflux of the Arûn and Soan-Kousi -	7
To Ukhurria-ghaut (the 2d) - -	5
To the Tumboor (i. e. the confluence of the Tumboor and Soan-Kousi, at Tambra-phede) -	26

	Ghurries.
To Kôka-kola - - -	28
To Barah-chattra - -	28
To Chattra-ghaut (on the Kousi) -	5
To Bejapour - - -	16
	$294\frac{3}{4}$

In favourable weather this is a 10 or 12 days journey at a medium.

Route from Bejapour to Dalimcote.

To Sângoori-ghuny - -	16
To Dunh Koota (1 day) - -	32
To Chhoomling - -	34
To Lebhoora - -	16
To Aukhibooi - -	16
To Chinepoor - - -	13
To Noondhâki (1 day)	
To Chânggya (1 day)	
To Phoong-goora-ghaut (1 day), on the Tumhoor	
To Taplejoong - - -	16
To Khanwa-kola - -	16
To Chhung-tâpoo (1 day) - -	30
To Sree-limbhâ (1 day) - -	30
To Kelekhma-kola - -	18
To Sikhem - - -	16

	Ghurries.
To Chakhoom (1 day) - - -	32
To Nânghia-labhia - -	21
To Gundhoop - - -	18

At the confluence of the Dewa and Teesta; the conflux is to the south-east.

The Dewa issues from Phunijoong, a snowy mountain, situated S. S. E. of Tingri, about 16 or 17 ghurries. E.S.E. of Phunijoong one day, or 25 ghurries, is Chownri-golah mountain, a continuation of the former, whence the Teesta rises, and also the Tumhoor. The Teesta comes from the north-east, and the Tumhoor from the south of the mountain. S. E. of Chownri (9 or 10 ghurries) is Ecrony-golah, a great mart: and S. S. E. of Ecrony, 12 or 13 ghurries, is Singhi Maligda, near the Bengal frontier, another considerable mart.

Going by Gundhoop, you have to cross both streams separately; proceeding below Gundhoop you cross only the united streams, under the name of Teesta

From Gundhoop to Dalimcote - -	32

Though Dalimcote appears near from Gundhoop

	336

The Kousi is navigable from Dholat-ghaut to Khoorkut-ghaut, which is within three hours journey of Bejapour. It may be ascended even against the stream, the banks being in some places either so low, or having such good pathways along the brink of the river, as to admit of tracking, while in other places there is so little current, that oars and luggus* may be used. Between Khoorkut-ghaut, and the junction of the Soan and Dhoodh Kousi, there are some cataracts which render the further navigation impracticable.

* These are long bamboos, by means of which the boatmen push the boats along in the shallow water.

ITINERARY,

Containing the Bearings and Distances of the various Towns, Villages, &c. &c.; which occurred in Colonel KIRKPATRICK'S *Route from Munniary to Khâtmândû, and from thence back to Segouly.*

1793, February.	Names of Places.	Distance.	Bearings.	Rivers.	Course.	Barom.	Remarks.
		M. F.					
	Munniary						
	Russelpore	2 4	N 10 E				
	Bhâgmutty R.	1 5	N 75 W	Bhâgmutty	S 22 W	. .	Fordable in the dry season.
13th.	Kurrurbunna	1 0	N 76 W	. . .	. .	29.94	
		5 1					
	Purtai or Butlay	0 5	N 37 W				
	Chandnouti	1 2	N 37 W				
	Patra	1 1	N 37 W				
	Peepra	1 0	N 60 W				
	Bukkia river	2 0	N 60 W	Bukkia	. .	. .	Fordable
	Beeriay	2 0	N 79 W				
	Chynepoor	3 0	N 51 W				
14th.	Kuchoorwa	2 0	N 47 W	. . .	. .	29.96	
		13 0					
	Surajepoor	1 4	N 15 W	Loll Bukkia	. .	. .	Fordable, runs under Kuchoorwa on the East.
	Bowanpore	2 4	N 11 W				
	Jumni Nulla	1 4	N 10 E	Jumni	S 58 W	. .	Fordable
	Putra	1 7	N 11 E				
15th 16th	Bharra-ghurry	3 3	N 10 E	. . .	. .	29.85	
		10 6					
17th.	Soophye	3 3	N 23 E	Jumni		29.84	The Nulla is twice crossed, once a little to the north of Bâreh, and a second time about a mile from Soophye.

1793. February.	Names of Places.	Distance.	Bearings.	Rivers.	Course.	Barom.	Remarks.
		M. F.					
18th.	Jhurjhûry	10 0	N 5 W	Billarie	. .	29.63	The Billarie winds along the south side of the Forest.
	Small rivulet	2 0	N 40 W				
	Bed of the Sukti	4 0	N 56 W				
	Beginning of Pass	1 3	N 17 E				
19th.	Camp	2 4	N 67 E	Sukti	S 67 W	28.91	
		9 7					
	In the bed of the Sukti	1 0	N 22 E				
	Commencement of the ascent and spring of the Sukti	1 4	N 45 E				
	Top of the Hill	1 4	N 56 E				
	Kurra Nulla	2 0	N 45 E	Kurra	W 20 S	. .	Fordable.
	Muckwanpoor-mâri	0 4	N 46 E	. . .	. .	. .	N 75 E of this place, and at the distance of 3 miles, is the fort of Muckwanpoor, situated on the summit of a mountain.
	Nulla	1 4	N 45 E				
	Nulla	1 0	N 79 W				
	Kurra Nulla	1 2	N 48 W	Kurra	W 10 S	. .	Fordable.
20. to 22. inclusive	Etonda, or Hettowra	1 6	N 42 W	. . .	. .	28.55	Variable weather.
		12 0					
	Rapti 1st passage	2 0	N 16 E				
	2nd	0 5	N 6 E				
	3rd	0 4	N 9 E				
	4th	1 1	N 5 E				
	5th	0 2	N 10 E				
	6th	0 4	N 11 E				
	7th	0 5	N 55 W				
	8th	0 2	N 32 W				
	9th	0 3	N 31 W				
	10th	0 1	N 10 E				
	11th	0 2	N 32 E				
	12th	0 2	N 29 W				
	13th	0 1	N 87 E				
	14th	0 2	N 18 E				
	15th	0 4	N 86 E				
	16th	0 2	N 80 E				
	17th	0 5	N 76 E				
	18th	0 4	N 20 E				
	19th	0 7	N 16 E				

1793. February.	Names of Places.	Distance.	Bearings.	Rivers.	Course.	Barom.	Remarks.
		M. F.					
23rd.	Camp	2 6	N 50 E	. . .	. . .	27.41	
		12 6					
	Summit of Dhoka-phede	1 6	N 69 E				
	Bheem-phede	1 2	N 74 E	. . .	. . .	26.40	
	Cheesapany fort	2 4	N 16 W	. . .	. . .	24.63	
	Cheesapany spring	0 4	N 29 E	. . .	. . .	24.43	
	Summit of the Mountain	1 1	N 30 E	. . .	. . .	24.13	estimated; the summit of the pass over the mountain is here meant.
	End of descent	2 4	N 41 E	Kan-kola	N 41 W		
	Tambeh-kan, or Kowli-kan Vil.	0 6	N 40 E	. . .	. . .	25.50	
24th.	Camp	1 0	. .	Kan-kola	N 53 W		
		11 3					
	Rising Ground	0 5	N 53 E				
	Markhoo	0 4	N 10 E				
	Small Hill and Nulla	0 6	N 20 E	Kan-kola, or Markhoo-kola			
	Beginning of ascent	0 7	N 14 W				
	End of the Hill and Nulla	2 5	N 41 E	Branch of Kan-kola	E 10 S		
	Village	0 2	N 40 E				
	Chitlong Town	1 1	N 14 E	. . .	. . .	25.32	Chandraghiri mountain, bearing N 44 E.
25th 26th	Camp	0 6	N 13 E				
		7 4					
	South foot of the Doona-baisi mountain	0 4	N 4 W	branch of do.	S		
	End of 1st Ascent	1 2	N 1 W				
	End of 2nd Ascent or summit of Doona-baisi mountain	1 0	. . .	. . .	. . .	22.50	estimated.
	Commencement of the descent	0 4	N 4 E				
	Vil. on the Hill	2 6	N 6 W				
	Carried over	6 0					

1798. February.	Names of Places.	Distance.	Bearings.	Rivers.	Course.	Barom.	Remarks.
		M. F.					
	Bt. over	6 0					
	2nd Village	1 2	N 4 W				
	Bottom of the mountain	0 3	N 5 W	Nulla	W		
27th	Camp in the Doona-baisi	0 1	N 5 W	. . .	. . .	26.50	(estimated) The village of Pussân-kheil S 15 W of Camp 1½ furlong.
		7 6					
	Shoulder of 1st Hill	0 4	N 45 E				
	Mahaise R., and commencement of the Ascent	1 6	N 22 E	Mahaise	W 9 S		
	Village	0 6	N 15 W				
	Summit of the Hill	1 0	N 17 W				
28th.	Bottom of ditto	1 2	N 22 W	Kolpoo	W 5 S		
	Camp	0 6	N 11 E				
		6 0					
	Beginning of the ascent of Mt.-Koombara	0 2	N 24 W				
	Top of 1st Hill	1 4	N 25 W				
	Beginning of 2nd Hill	1 2	N 15 E				
	Summit of ditto	0 7	N 16 E	. . .	. . .	24.22	estimated
March	End of 1st descent	1 6	N 30 W				
1st.	Camp in the Bailkote valley	2 4	N 17 E	Small Nulla	N 5 E	. .	The village of Bailkote bore from Camp W N W 1 mile on the top of the mountain.
		8 1					
	Bottom of the Hill	1 2					
	West pt. of Muddenpoor Hill	0 6	N 42 W				
	Tadi River	0 4	N 36 E	Tadi	W 15 S		
2d to 15th inclusive	Camp in the Noakote Valley	2 0	N 34 E	. . .	. . .	28.24	The town of Noakote on the top of the Hill N 8 W 1¼ mile.
		4 4					

From NOAKOTE *to* SUMBHOO-NATH.

1793. March.	Names of Places.	Distance.	Bearings.	Rivers.	Course.	Barom.	Remarks.
		M. F.					
	Tadi River	0 4	S 64 E	Tadi	W 20 S		
	Sindoora Nulla	0 4	S 57 E	Sindoora	W 17 S		
	Beginning of ascent	1 2	S 51 E				
	Custom House	1 6	S 61 E				
16th.	Mâhâ-rany-ka Powah	3 0	S 31 E	. . .	. . .	24.28	Summit of Mount Bheerbundy.
		7 0					
	Angle of the Hill	1 0	S 56 E				
	Summit of ditto	1 4	S 48 E	. . .	. . .	. .	W. of this half a mile is Kowhila Peak.
	House on the top of 2nd Hill	2 4	S 43 E				
	Beginning of descent	1 4	S 9 E				
	End of ditto	0 6	S 20 E	Bishnmutty	W 10 S		
	Dherim-tulla	1 6	S 21 E				
17th.	Bâlâ Neel-khent	1 4	S 11 E	Bishnmutty	. . .	25.80	
		10 4					
18 to 23 inclusive	Temple of Sumbhoo-nath	1 4	S 12 E	. . .	. . .	25.87	

From SUMBHOO-NATH *to* SEGOULY, *on the return.*

	Bishnmutty R.	0 4	S 52 E	. . .	S	
	Khâtmândû	0 2	S 52 E			
	Bhâgmutty R.	1 2	S 12 E	. . .	W 10 S	
24th.	Patn or Pâtun	1 0	S 14 E	. . .	. . .	25.70
		3 0				
	Nukhoo Nulla	0 6	S 20 W	. . .	W	
	Small Village	1 2	S 19 W			
	Koakna Village	0 4	S 5 E			
	Bhâgmutty Hill	0 2	S 20 W			
	Bhâgmutty Ford	0 6	S 39 W			
	Village	1 6	S 50 W			
25th.	Phurphing	1 6	S 80 W	. . .	. . .	25.00
		7 0				

1793. March.	Names of Places.	Distance.	Bearings.	Rivers.	Course.	Barom.	Remarks.
		M. F.					
	Small nulla	0 6	S 70 W				
	Top of 1st Hill	1 0	S 71 W				
	Foot of ditto	0 6	S 75 W				
	Top of 2nd ditto	1 0	S 70 W				
	Foot of ditto	1 0	S 61 W				
	Top of 3rd Hill	0 6	S 75 W				
	Top of 4th Hill	0 4	S 76 W				
	Gow-thân	0 3	N 22 W				
26th.	Camp in the See-bhoo-dhoal Val.	0 5	. . .	. . .	. .	24.48	
		6 6					
	Top of 1st Hill	0 7	N 59 W				
	Foot of ditto	0 4	N 23 W				
	Khargoo Village 2nd Hill	0 6	N 56 W				
	Top of 3rd Hill	1 0	S 42 W				
	End of 1st descent	1 1	S 22 W				
	Ditto of 2nd do.	0 4	S 42 W				
	Trees	0 3	S 38 W				
	Last descent	0 5	S 20 W				
	Tambeh-kan N.	0 4	N 45 W				
	Former Ground	0 2	S 50 W				
	Village of Tambeh-kan	0 7	S 54 W				
27th.	Camp at N. foot of Cheesapany	0 6	. . .	. . .	. .	25.50	
		8 1					
	Summit of Cheesapany Hill	2 4	S 40 W				
	Cheesapany Spr.	1 0	S 29 W	. . .	. .	24.63	
28th.	Ditto Fort	0 4	S 29 W				
		4 0					
	1st precipice	1 0	S 25 E				
	2nd ditto	1 0	S 20 E				
	Bheem-phede	0 4	S 45 W				
	Dhoka-phede	1 4	S 75 W				
	Old Encampmt.	1 4	S 70 W	Rapti	. .	. .	Crossed three times.
29th.	Nimboo-târ	2 4	S 53 W	. . .	. .	27.60	
		8 0					
	Crossed Rapti 1st time	. .	. . .	. . .	. .	. .	Close to Camp.
	2nd	1 0	S 15 W				
	3rd	0 4	S 20 W				
	4th	0 6	S 78 W				
	5th	0 3	W 8 N				
	Carried over	2 5					

1793. March.	Names of Places.	Distance.	Bearings.	Rivers.	Course.	Barom.	Remarks.
		M. F.					
	Bt. over	2 5					
	6th	0 4	W 5 S				
	7th	0 2	S 20 W				
	8th	0 1	W 3 S				
	9th	0 2	S 30 E				
	10th	0 1	S 30 W				
	11th	0 1	S 11 W				
	12th	0 2	S 33 E				
	13th	0 4	S 33 E				
	14th	0 3	S 56 E				
	15th	0 4	S 11 W				
	16th	0 3	S 9 W				
	17th	1 0	S 4 W				
	18th	0 5	S 10 W				
30th.	19th	0 4	S 5 W				
	Hettowra	. .	. .	. . .	. . .	28.55	
		8 1					
	Separation of the road	0 2	S 10 E				
	Kurra Nulla	0 6	S 10 W				
	Dry Nulla	1 0	S 20 W				
	Rising Ground	0 4	S 10 W				
	Dry Nulla	1 2	S 70 W				
	Entrance of Pass	1 2	S 25 W				
	Springs and end of Pass	1 4	S 28 W				
	. . . . .*	2 5	S 28 W				
	Semul Bass	2 0	S 17 E				
	Joona Nulla	0 6	S 63 W				
	Purrewa-bheer	0 3	S 62 W				
	. . . . .	0 3					
31st.	Camp at Bechiacori	0 6	S 23 W	. . .	. . .	28.85	
		13 3					
	Commencement of the Forest	0 2	S 25 W				
	Nâgsoti Nulla	2 6	S 82 W				
	. . . .	1 2	S 20 W				
	Dry Nulla	1 2	S 40 W				
	Addha-bhâr	1 0	S 4 W				
	Paunchgaucby	1 6	S 8 W				
	. . . .	1 0	S 5 W				
	. . . . .	0 4	S 80 W				
	Semul Bass (2d.)	2 0	S 65 W				
	Gurooka	1 6	S 30 W				
April 1st.	Goorpussra	0 6	S 65 W	. .	. . .	29.57	
		14 2					

* A distance is occasionally given without the name of a place, merely to shew the variations of bearing.

1793. April.	Names of Places.	Distance.	Bearings.	Rivers.	Course.	Barom.	Remarks.
		M. F.					
	Amouli	1 0	S 35 W	Nulla			
	Persa	1 0	S 26 W				
	Pinnera	1 0	S 15 W				
	Village	1 0	S 9 W				
	Bank of the Dehar	2 0	S 8 W				
	Beheera R.	1 4	S 17 E				
	Ullown Fort	0 3	S 17 E				
	Ditto Village	0 6	S 11 E				
	Ekdurra	2 4	S 17 E				
	Jakiany	1 4	S 4 W	. . .	. . .	. .	The last village in the Nepaul territory.
2nd.	Dhoulye Denher	3 2	S 22 W	. . .	. . .	29.55	
		15 7					
	Tillâwé	2 0	S 17 W				
	Large Tank	2 0	S 34 W				
	Bela	0 4	S 9 E				
	A Jheel or Lake	2 2	S 21 W				
	Boori Gunduck	2 0	S 15 W				
3rd	Segouly	1 0	S 15 W	. . .	. . .	29.58	
		9 6					

APPENDIX.

APPENDIX. No. I.

Extract from a Memorial of the Court of Khatmândû, relative to the Origin of the War with Tibet.

In ancient times there subsisted a close union between the Rajahs of Nepaul and Bhoat (i. e. Tibet); when the pure Mehnder-mulli of the coinage of the former country, was the current money of the latter. During the respective reigns, however, of Rajah Jy Purkaush Mull, the sovereign of Nepaul, and of Rajah Runjeet Mull, the ruler of Bhatgong, the Mehnder-mulli became much debased, the consequence of which was, that at the period Nepaul passed into the possession of the Goorkha, Bhoat was full of this base coin. The Maharajah (i. e. Pirthi Nerain) immediately put a stop to this improper practice, sending, at the same time, a friendly deputation to Bhoat, for the purpose of stating the mischievous consequences that would ensue, were it persisted in; and of engaging the Lamas to revert to the ancient usage, by giving circulation only to a pure currency.

To this representation the rulers of Bhoat replied, that the amount of base Mehnder-mulli then in their country was very considerable; that the suppression of it would consequently be attended with great loss to their people; and that therefore they could not agree to the introduction of the pure Mehnder-mulli proposed by the Maharajah, but must desire that the Goorkhas would continue to supply them with the adulterated coin.

Nine or ten years elapsed in this negociation between the two governments, without their being able to fix on any plan of accommodation. At length the Goorkha envoy proposed, that, as they could not stop the circulation of the base coin with which they had been supplied, they should, at least, establish a just rate of exchange, between the base and pure coinage, to the end that the merchants of either country might stand, in their commercial transactions, on the same footing as formerly. The Bhootias, however, would by no means consent to such a regulation; but, on the contrary, absolutely directed, that the base and genuine money should be considered, in all negociations of trade, as one and the same; the consequence of which was, that for three or four years there was no sort of traffic carried on between the two countries. The circulation of the Nepaulian coin accordingly ceased (i. e. in Tibet). The Goorkha, nevertheless, continuing to retain his friendly disposition towards the Bhootias, endeavoured to prevail on them to depute some respectable person to the common boundary, there to meet, and, in concert with, deputies from Nepaul, devise some arrangement for the mutual benefit of the two states, as, without a speedy adjustment of the matter, it was evident that the trade of the two countries must inevitably be ruined. The Bhootias, however, were so far from listening to this reasonable proposal, that they, on the contrary, sent word vauntingly to the Goorkha, that they had constructed a new road through the plain or valley of Tingri; that they were establishing a post on the common frontier; that they had assembled an army of 125,000 men, and that, if the Goorkha wished for war, he was welcome to advance.

Notwithstanding, however, their obstinate refusal to settle this point amicably, and the menacing countenance which they had assumed, the Goorkha, aware of their dependence on China, and, on that account, considering that it would be improper to commence hostilities against them, determined to transmit a representation of the whole to the Emperor, which accordingly, together with letters to the Chinese governor, or resident of Lhasseh, and to the Lamas of Diggercheh and Sankia, he dispatched to Lhasseh, whence, however, the bearers of these letters were not permitted by the rulers there to proceed, but, together with the memorial for the Emperor, were sent back to Nepaul.

Hereupon the Goorkha again addressed the Bhootias, informing them, that however desirous he was of avoiding hostilities, yet, as their dispositions were very different, he had determined to meet them, and would therefore send his army into their country, where, if they pleased, they might fight it; and, in fact, teazed by the provoking conduct of the Bhootias, he did accordingly send a force to invade Bhoat; into which, after some opposition, they penetrated as far as Shikargong, which being a place of strength, detained the Goorkha army before it; during which period the Bhootias attempted its relief three or four times, but without success, being repulsed by the Goorkhalies on every occasion.

In this conjuncture, some persons of rank on the part of the Teeshoo Lama, and Sankia Lama, came into the Goorkha camp, saying that they would accommodate the disputes with the Bhootias; and desiring that hostilities might cease. The Goorkha commander replied to these deputies, that his government had originally wished for nothing so much as a firm union with the Bhootias; but that the Lhasseh people being of a different mind, had occasioned the Goorkhali's army being where they found it. He added, that if the Lamas wished to mediate a peace, it was well; and that, to bring about such an event, the best means would be to engage the Lhasseh government to send a respectable deputation, either to Kooti or to Kheeroo; where being met by the deputies on the part of the Goorkha, the existing disputes might be amicably adjusted. The two Lamas engaging to this effect, the Goorkha army raised the siege of Shikargong, and retired in separate bodies to Kheeroo, to Kooti, and to Phullak, where they took up their quarters.

In the mean time the Emperor of China, being advised of these occurrences, in detail, the consequence was, that Chânchoo, a military commander, with three or four Umbas, or general officers, and a large force, arrived at Lhasseh, when the Pootla Lama of Lhasseh, and the Lamas of Diggercheh (*i. e.* Teeshoo Lûmboo) and Sankia, represented to him candidly, that they had been in fault; that they were on the point of accommodating matters with the Goorkha, and of deputing to Kheeroo, for that purpose, some of their principal people. They therefore proposed to him to remain, in the interim, where he was; upon which he said unto them, "Dispatch this business immediately." Accordingly several persons of distinction, to the number of fifteen or sixteen, among whom were the father of Teshoo Lama, the Sankia Lama, the great Kâji, or minister of Lhasseh (viz. Kâji Dhooreen), and the Khuzanchie, or treasurer, Dybuk, repaired to Kheeroo, where they were met on the part of the Goorkha by Shamerpa Lama, Bem Shah, Tuksali Hurrihur Opadiah, Ner Singh Sehai, and four or five other men of rank; Chânchoo about the same time entering Shikargong.

The negociations commenced, by the Nepaul deputies representing that it had been entirely owing to the unreasonable proceedings of the Bhootias that the Goorkha army had penetrated into Tibet; that this measure had been attended with great expense to the Goorkha; besides which, lacks of rupees had been lost to the Nepaul state, owing to the communication with Bhoat having been shut for the last eight or ten years; during which period there had been a stop both to the operations of trade and of the mint. They concluded with demanding, as a preliminary, satisfaction or security for the amount of these losses. The Bhootias confounded by these just representations, replied, it was exceedingly likely, that their mutual disputes had occasioned the expenditure of large sums; for which, however, it was not in their power to make any restitution. On this the Nepaul deputies urged it strenuously to the Lamas of Diggercheh, and Sankia, and to the Shamerpa Lama, to decide who was in fault; binding themselves, should they be pronounced to have been the aggressors, to reimburse Lhasseh all its expenses; Lhasseh stipulating, on the other hand, to reimburse the Goorkha, provided the Bhootias were found to blame.

The end of these discussions was, that the Lhasseh government was convicted of being the aggressors; and even acknowledged itself in the wrong: pretending, however, that they had not the means of making the Goorkha the compensation demanded, they required him to abate of his demands, when they would satisfy him. Hereupon the Goorkha deputies proposed to accept fifty lacks, on payment of which, the ancient boundaries of the two states should be re-established. In the event of their being unable to pay this sum, is was proposed that Lhasseh should cede to the Goorkha all the countries south of Lungoor (*i. e.* the snowy mountains*) which had fallen into his hands. In case neither of these proposals should be acceptable, the Goorkha deputies agreed to receive an annual tribute of one lack of rupees from Lhasseh. Not one of these several propositions would the Bhootias accede to. Hereupon Chânchoo deputed Mon Tajeen and Tank Tajeen, with a military force, to Kheeroo, where, when these two Umbas arrived, they set about investigating the merits of the quarrel between the Goorkha and Bhootias. The result was, that the Bhootias were again convicted of being the aggressors, that the Chânchoo was incensed against them, and that the Lhasseh government consented to pay the Goorkha annually fifty thousand rupees, executing a written instrument to this effect, and calling upon the gods to witness the engagement. The Umbas, upon the conclusion of this treaty, repaired to Lhasseh, whither also the Kâji of Lhasseh and the Lamas of Diggercheh and Sankia returned, after paying the first year's tribute into the Goorkha's treasury, from which they took a formal receipt. Hereupon the Bharchdars of the Goorkha evacuated Kheeroo, Kooti, Joongah, and Phullak, and returned to Nepaul; at which time the Goorkha sent a deputation, consisting of Hurry and Bhulbudder Khuwâs, and five and twenty others, with presents, and an Arzee to the Emperor of China. When this deputation passed through Diggercheh, Chânchoo dispatched along with it an Umba of his own family; the whole arriving at Pekin the sixth month, and remaining there five and forty days, in which period they were admitted fifteen times to an audience. At the end of forty-five days they were all honourably dismissed with suitable presents; and charged with a Firmaun to the Goorkha, conveying to him a title and dignity, together with a splendid dress, and honourable presents. This deputation was absent (reckoning from the day of its departure from Nepaul to the day of its return thither) just fourteen months.

This is not the place to offer any comment on the preceding narrative. It is sufficient to observe here, that the Bhootias soon dis-

* See the Map.

continued to pay the tribute settled by treaty, never, indeed, discharging more than one year's amount. The consequence was a renewal of the hostilities, which terminated in the invasion of Nepaul by a Chinese force, and the subsequent submission of the Goorkha to the Emperor's authority.

APPENDIX. No. II.

OFFICIAL PAPERS AND LETTERS, RELATIVE TO COLONEL KIRKPATRICK'S MISSION TO NEPAUL.

A.

Particulars relative to the Origin of the War between the Emperor of China and the Rajah of Nepaul. From a paper (in Persian) communicated by Mr. Duncan.

THE Teshoo Lama having, towards the end of Mr. Hastings's government, proceeded to Pekin, at the invitation of the Emperor of China, and dying soon after his arrival there, Sumhur Lama, his brother, on receiving the intelligence, was much alarmed, and fled from Lassa, taking with him a considerable quantity of treasure, and went to Nepaul: the Rajah of Nepaul bestowed a Jaghire on him, and received him under his protection. Sumhur Lama informed the Rajah of Nepaul of the particulars of the Chinese empire, and communicated to him the position of the gold and silver mines, and other mines, in the neighbourhood of Lassa (or Lhasseh). Thus having excited the avarice of the Nepaul Government, he informed people to accompany the Rajah's troops, and they marched towards Lassa. These troops went to the distance of twenty days journey from Nepaul towards Bhoat, and were victorious in several battles which were fought. When the officer commanding the Bhoat troops saw that he was worsted, he made peace through a chief belonging to the Emperor of China, and a tribute of three lacks of rupees from the Lassa country was settled for the Rajah of Nepaul; and as it had before been customary to stamp the coin at the mint of Lassa with the name of the Rajah of Nepaul, the

* i. e. Tibet.

present treaty provided for the continuation of this practice. After the peace was concluded, the Nepaul army returned home. In consequence of the superiority which had prevailed in favour of the Nepaul troops over those of Lassa, the rulers at Lassa sent a deputation to Calcutta during the administration of Sir John Macpherson, and demanded assistance. This request, however, was not complied with; doubtless, this will appear on the proceedings of Council. Sumhur Lama, working on the avaricious disposition of the Rajah of Nepaul, last year prevailed upon him to send troops to Diggercheh,* and 18,000 men went there and plundered the treasure belonging to the Lama of that place, who is also one of the priests of the Chinese Emperor; taking away with them, as a prisoner, a Vizier of Lassa, who came to make peace. The Emperor on learning the news of this plunder, sent his Vakeel with letters in the month of January 1792, to Nepaul. He arrived there two days after Abdûl Kâdir Khan reached Nepaul. The Vakeel wrote to the Rajah of Nepaul, while at the distance of two days march, to inform him that he was deputed by the Emperor of China, and as he had the Emperor's letters with him, it was necessary that the Rajah should come out to meet them. The Rajah replied, that he should not pay them any honours, that he was welcome, if he chose to come, if not, that he might return. The Vakeel seeing no alternative, came into Nepaul, but was received with little kindness. At length the day that he was introduced, paid his respects, and returned, the Rajah sent his Chobdar† to him for the letter which was brought. In it was written that he should refund 52 crores of rupees which he had plundered of property belonging to the Lamas, and must release the Vizier of Lassa, whom he had made a prisoner, and send Sumhur Lama, who, having put himself under his protection, had been the cause of all the disputes. The Rajah refused to comply with these requisitions, and wrote to the Emperor to proceed as soon as he pleased in the manner he thought proper, and the Vakeel took his departure in fifteen days from his arrival, without succeeding in the

* Or Teeshoo Lûmboo.

† An attendant on men of rank in India, usually distinguished by a large silver mace which he carries.

objects of his mission. On his arrival in China, and relating the result of his embassy, the Emperor, on hearing the insolence of the Rajah, and of the plunder of Diggercheh, with the forts and temples there, which is a place of religious respect in the consideration of the Emperor, he sent a large force under a chief of his own, with the name and title of Sund Fô, that is to say, a possessor of seven Soubahs. Sund Fô first came to Lassa, from whence he wrote to the Rajah of Nepaul, desiring that he would seize and send to him Sumhur Lama, the instigator of the disputes, who resided with him, together with the Lassa Vizier, whom he had taken prisoner. The Rajah of Nepaul replied that Sumhur Lama was the same as himself, and that he should not send him, but that, on condition of peace, he would send the Lassa Vizier. Sund Fô openly carried on a correspondence, and secretly divided his troops, 70,000 men, into two divisions; one of 30,000, and the other of 40,000 men, and with a dispossessed Zemindar of Nepaul, sent them first several marches to the eastward. When the Rajah of Nepaul heard first of their march, he was much agitated, and detached Damodur Pande Bukhshy to Chunga. The Bukhshy, on his arrival there, meeting no other force than the garrison, attacked the place, and carried it, where leaving a few troops, he began his march back, and on the way made other detachments from his army, leaving some with Perpierra Takoor at Kan Rowan. The division of the Chinese army of 40,000 men passed to the eastward under the hills to Trisool-Gunga, and arrived on this side of Kan Rowan, where they were discovered. Perpierra Takoor was two marches distant on the other side. The Chinese troops coming towards Nepaul, Perpierra Tokoor heard of them, marched against them, and a battle ensued, in which he was wounded, and many of his people killed. When the Rajah of Nepaul heard of the defeat of his troops, he resolved on giving up Sumhur Lama, but the Lama poisoned himself. He sent in, however, the Lassa Vizier with his attendants to the Chinese army; they received him, but did not make peace. The Chinese defeated the Nepaul troops repeatedly, and proceeded to Noakote, distant 13 coss from Khâtmândû. In a few days they will also take Nepaul. To this period, the 4th of September, 1792. There are about 200 soldiers in Nepaul,* and the Rajah's treasure is conveyed to Muckwanpoor, where he is probably himself; and it is ascertained that the Chinese Sund Fô is arrived at Kurree Kuttu, distant ten marches from Khâtmândû.

B.

From the Dalai Lama at Pootla Lassa, to Lord Cornwallis. Received 3rd August, 1792.

By the favour of God I am in good health! The tranquillity of mankind is the object of my wishes; may God fulfil them! I hope also for your Lordship's health. I at this time address you on the affair with Goorkhali Rajah, whose country is contiguous to this. This man's father, and he, have to this time reduced all the Rajahs round about Nepaul, and also Nepaul itself; and from his craving disposition, wants to engage in hostilities with others. Thus, in the year 1203 (1789), and the present, he has excited disputes with me. I have shown no disposition to contend with him, but he, from the blackness of his heart, will act hostilely against me. Accordingly he has attacked my Zemindars in several places, and had it in view to come to this quarter. But by the favour of God this country has the protection of the Emperor of China; accordingly, two deputies always remain here for my protection; they wrote information of this circumstance to the Emperor, who detached a large army under the command of his officers to this country. When this intelligence reached the Goorkhali troops, they quitted my territory and fled to Nepaul. It is the resolution of the officers sent from China, by the favour of God, to exterminate the Rajah of Goorkhali and the other chiefs. Accordingly they pursued the fugitives, and got possession of several places of the Goorkhali territories. The Emperor, by the influence of his good auspices, will certainly soon obtain possession of Nepaul and Goorkhali. The

* By Nepaul, Khâtmândû appears to be here meant.

Rajah, however, to promote his object, proposes asking assistance from your Lordship, and will write lies and calumnies that the Emperor has detached a large army against him, and that therefore he requests aid; that should your Lordship not depute a force to assist him, the Emperor will rise up hereafter against your Lordship's government, as he has against his. Let not your Lordship act agreeably to his artful insinuations, for the Emperor is not hostile to any except the Goorkhali: and it is a maxim of his majesty to take measures against him who first commences hostilities. If any of the chiefs or companions of the Rajah should fall into your Lordship's hands, be pleased to seize and deliver them up to the Emperor's officers, or, though you should not deliver them up, do not allow them to return to their country. The officers will write their sense of your Lordship's kindness in so acting, to the Emperor, to whom it will afford satisfaction. I request on my own part also that your Lordship will conform to what I have written. Your Lordship is a protector of the Ryots, and the dispenser of justice: wherefore the Almighty has exalted you. The Ryots under your Lordship's government live in ease and happiness. I hope your Lordship will gratify me by letters.

I have sent your Lordship one pair of Khauduck, 33 Tolahs and 4 Maashas weight of gold dust, and a piece of Cochin (silk); be pleased to acknowledge the receipt thereof.* *Dated 7th of Rajal,* 1206, *from Poolla (Lassa.)*

C.

From Lord Cornwallis to the Rajah of Nepaul. Written 15th September, 1792.

I HAVE the pleasure to acknowledge the receipt of your letters. The contents of these letters, representing the disturbances now subsisting between you and the Rajah of Lassa, dependent on China, have given me

* The original of the above letter is written in the Bhootia language.

great concern, because, as friends to the Company, I am extremely desirous that unanimity, and the utmost harmony, should have continued between you.

It cannot have escaped your observation, that the English Company have nothing more at heart than to maintain the most cordial and friendly terms with all the Powers in India; and particularly with those whose countries lie contiguous to their own: and sensible of the policy and wisdom of this conduct, they are careful not to infringe the rules of friendship, by interference in a partial manner in the disputes of others, except when self-defence, or wanton attacks oblige them. But, however this line of conduct is in general the policy of the English government; the connexion that has been formed with the Emperor of China renders a due observance of it still more necessary. The English Company have for many years carried on extensive commercial concerns with the subjects of the Emperor of China by sea, and have actually a factory established in his dominions. I am confident that this argument will satisfy you that a compliance with your request, to assist you with a military force against the Rajah of Lassa, who is dependent on the Emperor of China, would be not only an infringement on the general policy of the English government, but also a measure inconsistent with the connection that has so long prevailed between the Company and the Emperor. Desirous, however, that harmony and peace should be preserved among those who are the friends of the Company, I shall be very happy if my amicable interference can in any shape contribute to re-establish them between the Lassa and you, and shall be ready to use it in the way of a friend and mediator between you. As the present season of the rains, however, will not admit that any steps towards such a mediation be adopted, I shall postpone my intention until the rains are over, when I will depute a gentleman in my confidence to you, who will communicate my sentiments fully, and by his endeavours I hope that peace will again reign between you and the Lassa, and the intimacy and friendship between each other be increased.

D.

From Lord Cornwallis to the Dalai Lama at Pootla Lassa. Written 25th of September, 1792.

I HAVE received several letters in the Tibet character, accompanied by a Persian translation, the contents of which, I have fully understood,* with several articles in token of friendship, all of which came safe to hand, and have contributed much to the improvement of the intimacy subsisting between us.

The contents of this letter, representing the disputes still prevailing between the Rajah of Nepaul and you, have given me great concern: because, as friends to the Company, I am extremely desirous that unanimity and the utmost harmony should have been established between you.

It is a matter of great concern that I have been able to comprehend only the Persian paper, accompanying the several letters; and can therefore only, for the present, reply to its contents. The other letters, however, are sent to Benares, in the hopes that persons may be found there who can explain them: and, in the mean time, I consider it incumbent on our friendship, and good neighbourhood, to inform you of my sentiments in regard to the contents of the Persian letter, without delay.

Although, as is presumed in that letter, the Goorkhali Rajah has written to me on the subject of the disputes which have long prevailed between you and him; yet, as the English Company have nothing more at heart than to maintain the most cordial and friendly terms with all the powers in India, and sensible of the wisdom of this conduct, they are careful not to infringe the rules of friendship, by interference in a hostile manner in the disputes prevalent among foreign powers, except when self-defence, or wanton attacks, oblige them, I have answered his letter accordingly.

It cannot be unknown to you that a friendship has long subsisted between the English and the Rajah of Nepaul; and also between the

* Vide Letter, p. 348.

Emperor of China (whose protection extends over you), and the Company. The English have for many years carried on commercial concerns with the subjects of the Emperor, and have actually a factory established in his dominions. On account of this connexion with the Emperor, knowing you to be held in high veneration by his Majesty, and considering you desirous of the Company's friendship, I am anxious that your government should continue in peace, and that an end should be put to war, which ultimately contributes to the misery and distress of our subjects. With this view, therefore, I shall be happy if my amicable interference can in any shape contribute to re-establish harmony and peace between you and the Rajah of Nepaul, and shall be ready to use it in the way of a friend and mediator between you. As the present season of the rains, however, will not admit that any steps towards such mediation be adopted, I shall postpone my intention till the rains are over, when I will depute a gentleman in my confidence to that quarter, who will communicate my sentiments fully. By his endeavours, I hope that peace will again reign between you and the Rajah of Nepaul, and the intimacy and friendship between each other be increased. That gentleman being in my confidence, will be accompanied by a few sepoys, intended as a guard and protection to himself and his servants. I mention this to you, to prevent the bad effects of fallacious reports.

I shall avail myself of that opportunity, to send a few articles to you in testimony of my regard, and flatter myself that they will contribute to our friendship.*

* Letters of the same tenor and date as the above were also addressed to the Chinese Vizier, and to Teshoo Lama (Rajah of Teeshoo Lûmboo).

E.

From Lord Cornwallis to the Rajah of Nepaul. Written 30th September, 1792.

In consideration of the friendship and close connexion between you and the Company, and the intimacy so much increased by virtue of the commercial treaty entered into by you with Mr. Duncan, so highly for the benefit of the subjects of both governments, I have experienced great concern in learning the disputes that prevail between you and the Rajah of Lassa; and did myself the pleasure of writing to you, that, influenced by a strong desire that peace should be re-established, I should be happy to effect it by my amicable interference, for which purpose I would depute a gentleman in my confidence, who would explain my sentiments to you, and endeavour to effect so desirable an object, as to reconcile the differences existing between those who are the friends of the Company.

Considering the season favourable to undertake the journey, Captain Kirkpatrick has taken leave of me, and will proceed to your quarter without delay. I request that you will consider him as enjoying my implicit confidence, and knowing every argument which he may use to be my desire, and tending to the prosperity of your government and to the increase of our friendship. I trust that you will pay due attention to what he says, and I hope that the result of his deputation will be the re-establishment of peace and quiet between you and the Rajah of Lassa; and an increase of the benefits expected from the commercial intercourse established between the subjects of our respective dominions.

Captain Kirkpatrick will deliver you a few articles in token of friendship, which I hope you will accept as such.*

* A similar Letter was also transmitted to the Minister.

From Lord Cornwallis to the Dalai Lama, Teshoo Lama, the Chinese Vizier, and the Rajah of Teeshoo Lûmboo; written 15*th October*, 1792.

I FEEL much concerned, in consequence of the friendship and intimacy subsisting between us, that differences and disputes should exist between you and the Rajah of Nepaul: and a few days ago I did myself the pleasure of writing to you expressive of my readiness to interfere in an amicable manner between you and the Nepaul Rajah, and to endeavour by that interference to adjust matters, and to renew the unanimity formerly existing between you, by the establishment of peace; and I mentioned my intention to depute a gentleman in my confidence to that quarter, that he may communicate my wish to you, and by his exertions re-establish peace and unanimity between those with whom the Company are on terms of intimacy.

The season being at hand for travelling, Captain Kirkpatrick, in whose abilities and disposition I have great confidence, and who is a gentleman high in the estimation of the Company and myself, has taken leave of me for this purpose. I request that you will consider this gentleman in my stead, and what he urges in conversation as coming from me, replete with friendship, and tending to increase the prosperity of our affairs mutually. I entertain great hopes that, through his means, peace and harmony will be renewed between you and the Rajah of Nepaul. I have availed myself of this opportunity to send you a few articles as presents; and rely on your friendly disposition to accept them as tokens of regard.*

* This letter was addressed, mutatis mutandis, to the other persons mentioned above.

F.

From Colonel Kirkpatrick to the Right Honourable Earl Cornwallis, K. G. Governor General, &c. in Council.

My Lord,

I have the honour to acquaint you that I arrived here yesterday, having left Bankapoor on the 7th instant, according to the determination which the Nepaul deputies came to on receipt of your Lordship's letter; and of which I duly advised Mr. Cherry, for your Lordship's information.

I was met yesterday, at the distance of about three miles from hence, by Roodur Beer Sâh, at the head of two or three hundred sepoys; and by Zorawur Khunâs, the Governor of the Western Turrye. The former is a younger brother of the Dewan Bem Sâh; and, together with his military party, was lately dispatched from Nepaul, for the express purpose of waiting my arrival there, and of escorting me to the court of his master.

The form of my reception, on my approach to this place, was of the most honourable kind; and, indeed, it is incumbent on me to say that I have observed, from the moment of my crossing the Bhâgmutty, the most earnest and uniform solicitude in my conductors to afford me, in all respects, the completest satisfaction.

As the transportation of our baggage from hence, must, of necessity, be transferred to the hill-carriers, it will probably be the day after to-morrow before the requisite arrangements can be made for prosecuting our journey: and as the Rajah's court is removed to Noakote for the purpose of celebrating the Hooly, I think it is likely I shall be invited to proceed to that place, which is situated, I understand, about five and twenty miles N. W. of Khâtmândû.

It is proper I should mention to your Lordship, that Bem Sâh and the Rajah's brother, Bajoo Seer, having, on their return from Ghyah, indicated a wish to view the European corps at Dinapoor, and the artillery at Moneer; Lieut. Colonel Johnstone and Major Green were so obliging, at my desire, as to enable me to gratify their curiosity in the best manner that circumstances would allow. They appeared to be highly pleased with what they saw, as well as very sensible of the attentions shown to them; and have since taken more occasions than one of testifying the strong impressions they have received of our amicable disposition towards them, during their late short sojourn in the Company's dominions. The alacrity and unreservedness, however, with which the artillery officers explained whatever appeared to attract the notice of Bem Sâh, promise, in particular, to have the effect of producing in him, at least, a correspondent spirit of confidence, and perhaps, through his influence, in the rest of his countrymen.

I have the honour to be, &c.

Bharra-ghurry, 16th February, 1793.

G.

From the same, to the same.

My Lord,

I had the honour of addressing you under date the 26th ultimo, from Chitlong.

I have now the honour to inform your Lordship, that, arriving on the 1st instant at Bailkote (a place about five miles to the southward of this), I was there rejoined by the Dewan Bem Sâh, who made me some apologies in the name of the Regent, on account of the fatigues I had been exposed to by the difficult nature of the country, the badness of the roads, and the prolongation of my journey so far beyond Khâtmândû; concluding the compliment, with the observation, " that if I had suffered more incon-

" veniences, I have also been gratified with a fuller view of his miserable " possessions (as they here pretty commonly affect to style them), than I " might have expected."

The 1st instant had been pronounced by the astrologers as a propitious day for my introduction; but as I had foreseen that neither myself nor party would be in a situation to go through this ceremony immediately after passing over the Koomhara mountain, it was fixed that my interview with the Rajah should take place on the 4th, being the nearest following day suited to the occasion.

Accordingly, on the 3d, I moved from Bailkote, and took up my quarters here, at a convenient distance from those of the Regent, being met about half way, and conducted to my tents, by Gujrâj Misser, and two or three of the principal officers of this government, respectably attended.

Last night, myself, and gentlemen of my party, proceeded to the Durbar, the Rajah and Regent advancing about the same time to meet us. They received us in the customary manner, at a short distance in front of the Kennauts inclosing the tent of audience, the young Rajah leading me, between two rows of armed and other attendants, to a chair placed on the left of his musnud, on which himself and uncle seated themselves together, the Regent taking the right hand of his nephew. Our entrance into the tent was announced by an irregular discharge of artillery.

I think it is unnecessary to trouble your Lordship with a detailed account of the conversation which I held with Behadur Sâh on this occasion, as it was, for the most part, of an immaterial nature. It will be sufficient to observe, that the Regent (for the Rajah himself, though certainly of an age to take a share in such concerns, was wholly silent) expressed, in general terms, the desire of his nephew to cultivate the friendship of the Company; and that I, in return, declared the confidence I entertained that the present meeting would, by its effects, very soon ripen to perfect maturity the intimate connexion so happily and wisely commenced under the auspices of Gujrâj Misser, and so successfully seconded by the conciliating conduct of Bem Sâh, Deena-nâth Opâdiah, and the other officers who had been deputed from hence for the purpose of escorting me hither.

Your Lordship's letters to the Rajah and to the Regent, with which I was charged, were delivered by Moulavee Abdûl Kâdir, previous to my introduction: the nature of their contents, owing to the change of affairs since my departure from Calcutta, not making it necessary for me to present them myself.

The time for my visit being returned is not yet fixed, but I imagine that an early day will be appointed for the purpose.

I have the honour to be, &c.

Noakote, March 5th, 1793.

H.

From the same to the Most Noble Marquis Cornwallis, K. G. &c. Governor General in Council.

My Lord,

I had the honour of addressing you under date the 5th instant from Noakote.

On the 7th the Rajah returned my visit, attended by the Gooroo (Gujrâj Misser), Srikishen Sâh (the Choutra, or under Regent), and other principal officers of his court. Previously to his taking leave of me, he informed me, through the Gooroo, that being obliged to return immediately to Khâtmândû, his uncle would discourse with me on matters of business in his stead. He accordingly set out for his capital the following day.

On the 9th Behadur Sâh visited me, having been prevented, as his message to me on the occasion imported, both by business and a slight indisposition, from accompanying the Rajah on the 7th. This visit, like the preceding one, being merely ceremonious, passed in conversation too immaterial to be noticed. The presents which I made severally to the Rajah and the Regent will appear from my account of disbursements for the current month.

The ensuing day being proposed to me for the commencement of business, I attended Behadur Sâh accordingly for that purpose.

I had, it is proper to observe to your Lordship in this place, previously ascertained from Gujrâj Misser, that my continuance in Nepaul beyond the end of the present month, was a matter altogether out of the contemplation of this Durbar. I had suspected as much from certain hints that had, for some time past, been occasionally dropped, which determined me to engage the Gooroo to open himself freely to me on the subject, that I might regulate my conduct accordingly; this he did in a very unreserved manner, on the morning of the 10th, his information satisfying me, that although the Regent was entirely sensible of the advantages which were likely to result to his country from the cultivation of an intimate intercourse with our government, and had all the dispositions for that purpose which could be wished, yet he had been at length compelled to yield to the obstinate resistance of a certain powerful party, which could not, by any means, be reconciled to the idea of my remaining even for a few months at Khâtmândû. This party had all along violently opposed my being invited to proceed from Patna: nor could they, it seems, be now induced to consent to my residence, notwithstanding the opportunity which had been already afforded me of judging of the strength or weakness of this country constituted, according to their own account, the principal objection to the reception of the deputation, which might, therefore, be considered as having already produced the evil they professed so much to dread. It may not be amiss to mention by the way, that at the head of this party, adverse to the improvement of the connexion between the two governments, are Srikishen Sâh, the Choutra or deputy of the Regent: Bulbhudder Sâh, a brother of Srikishen, Jeoo Sâh, a brother of Bem Sâh; and the Dewan Dhowkel Singh, all of them possessing considerable authority in this Durbar. Bulbhudder Sâh, it may be proper to add, is the same who lately, in company with Bem Sâh, and the Rajah's brother, Bâjoo Seer Behadur, performeda pilgrimage to Ghyah, where he refused the proffered indulgence of an exemption from duties, obliging, by his example, Bem Sâh to do the same. It was his indisposition towards us, that also determined him not to visit me while at Patna, although I did not ascertain this point, till my arrival at Noakote.

Great as the power and credit of Behadur Sâh are, I nevertheless discovered from the Gooroo's conversation, that they are not sufficient to render him altogether regardless of the remonstrances or wishes of such persons as those I have just named. I could also perceive, that, little as the Rajah troubles himself, at present, with the affairs of government, and averse even as he seems to be engaged in any kind of business, his uncle is not totally free from solicitude, lest factions, or ill disposed men, should seek some occasion of persuading the young prince, that it was time for him to assume the reins of government: and that, perhaps, none would be more likely to be seized, with this view, than an attempt on the part of Behadur Sâh to detain me in opposition to the decided opinions of his coadjutors in the administration. It hence appeared, that although the Gooroo's influence with the Regent continued undiminished, yet it could not any longer be exerted in regard to the deputation, with any effect, or, at least, without the hazard of consequences of too serious a complexion to be either risked by one so attached as Gujrâj Misser is to Behadur Sâh, or to be urged by me in contradiction of what I so well knew to be the spirit of your Lordship general administration, as well as of the particular views of Government in my deputation.

Thus instructed by Gujrâj Misser with regard to the inclinations of this Durbar, I proceeded to my appointment with the Regent, who, after the first compliments were exchanged, began the conference with a review of the circumstances which had led to my present visit to Nepaul, in the course of which, he recapitulated the principal incidents of the war with China; acknowledged the wise and friendly advice which the subsisting connexion between the governments had induced your Lordship to offer him, touching the imprudence of his prosecuting hostilities against so mighty a power, and your kindness in deputing me for the purpose of mediating and bringing about an accommodation between him and the Chinese. This discourse, however, contained nothing material that had not been already stated over and over, in the correspondence which had passed on its several topics, excepting a distant hint that it conveyed of the expectation he had entertained, when he applied to your Lordship for military aid, having been somewhat disappointed. He concluded with adverting to a passage in one of your Lordship's letters, that intimated my being charged with a message of a particular and confidential nature; the allusion to which was evidently designed to draw from me its communication.

As I was apprized that the tenor of this address was framed in a great measure in conformity to the wishes of the adverse party, I judged it right to adopt my reply accordingly.

I therefore observed, that although it must be unnecessary, in addressing a person of his sagacity, to enlarge on the nature of the connection which had subsisted between his government and that of the Company, previously to the period when, owing to the activity of Mr. Duncan, seconded by the good offices of Gujrâj Misser, the foundation of a firm and beneficial intercourse had been for the first time laid in the treaty of commerce concluded about a twelve month ago, by the agency of Moulavee Abdul Kâdir Khan: yet I would use the freedom of observing, that, till then, the communication between the two governments had consisted in little more than the occasional intercourse of letters, the trade having languished so much, in consequence of impolitic restrictions, as scarcely to merit notice. I next proceeded to state, that although, through the blessing of God, the good understanding of our respective governments had been augmented considerably in consequence of the treaty referred to, yet it could not be said to have attained the perfection of which it was capable, when your Lordship received his application for military assistance; I nevertheless (I added) would refer it to his candor to pronounce, after duly considering how recently any thing like a cordial intercourse had sprung up between the two states, and how inviolable a rule it had always been with your Lordship to observe the strictest neutrality in all disputes arising among the neighbouring powers, excepting in cases respecting the honour or rights of the Company, or of their allies, whether your answer to that application, and the measures which you had immediately taken on the occasion, did not manifest the most sincere desire on the part of your Lordship to cement, by every means in your power, the growing friendship of the Company's government and that of Nepaul? The Regent acknowledged the affirmative, and applauded the wisdom which had dictated the sentiments conveyed in your Lordship's letters on the occasion; insinuating even that those sentiments had had such credit with him, as to influence him in a great degree in the accommodation which he had entered into with the Chinese, at a conjuncture when the army of the latter was reduced nearly to the last extremity.

After complimenting him on the sound judgment and moderation which his conduct on this occasion had evinced, I observed, that with respect to the particular, or confidential message which he had alluded to, he would recollect that the passage in question was contained in a letter that had been written by your Lordship during the existence of the misunderstanding between him and the Chinese; and at the moment when you had determined to interpose your good offices as a mediator. These differences having been long since happily adjusted, he would perceive, I added, that it was no longer necessary for me to enter into any exposition of your Lordship's particular sentiments, or instructions to me upon that subject.

On his noticing that, subsequent to his accommodation with the Chinese, your Lordship had seemed, in one or two of your letters, to continue to point to some particular communication which I was charged to make, I replied, that as it was very certain that your Lordship, independently of your desire to be instrumental in healing the differences which had arisen between him and the Chinese, had been uniformly anxious to improve, as far as rested with you, the good understanding which had lately grown up between the Nepaul government and the Company, so it was true that, notwithstanding the original and more immediate object of my mission had passed by, you nevertheless continued to be actuated by the same amicable sentiments, and to think it likely that I might, by means of being the instrument of an easy and unreserved communication between him and your Lordship, contribute greatly to the strengthening of the friendship of the two governments, and to the advancement of the interests and prosperity of the countries severally dependent on them. I added, that among the points which your Lordship conceived to fall under this description, were the equitable adjustment of all questions respecting boundaries, and the increase of the commercial intercourse of our respective dominions, which last, I slightly remarked, seemed to me already to be open to much improvement: and would, I doubted not, on future observation, and better knowledge, prove capable of a still greater augmentation (to the equal benefit of both governments), than could at present appear. I concluded with remarking, that these, however, as well as other topics, connected with the ultimate object of my mission;—namely, the perfecting of the friendship of the two states, could properly be discussed only as occasions presented, which would depend on the duration of my visit, as that also must on circumstances of convenience, and the final pleasure of your Lordship and of this Durbar.

I received only a vague reply to these observations, the Regent contenting himself with declaring that he was ready to demonstrate the force and sincerity of his amicable dispositions towards the Company, in any manner that might be required; pointing particularly, however, though obliquely, to the rendering us military assistance whenever it should be demanded: and that, with regard to the productions of the country, whether of a commercial, or any other kind, nothing more was requisite to obtain them than the applying for them; every thing it contained being entirely at your Lordship's command. I answered, that these declarations certainly evinced both his cordiality and his wisdom: but that it appeared to me, as I persuaded myself it would to him, that none of these were points that admitted of being adjusted precipitately. The conference closed with my saying, that it would not become me to urge the topics I had barely glanced at any farther at present: that it rested with him to give what I had mentioned the consideration it was entitled to; and that I was well assured that his resolutions on the occasion would be suitable to his elevated station, and to his reputation for political knowledge and experience.

Besides Gujrâj Misser, who, for the most part, delivered the sentiments of the Regent, in the course of this conference, there were present on the occasion Srikishen Sâh, Bem Sâh, Nersingh Tuksali (or the master of the mint), and Deena-nâth Opadiah. None of these, however, took any part in the conversation. Of Srikishen's adverse disposition I have already spoken; Bem Sâh, I believe to be very well inclined, though I do not imagine he is an active friend; the Tuksali, I have reason to think, would be well pleased to see an intimate correspondence established between the two governments. With respect to Deena-nâth Opadiah, I need scarcely remark to your Lordship, that his jealousy of the influence of Gujrâj Misser, operating as it has done, to the diminution of his own consequence as a Vakeel, renders him secretly hostile to the maintenance of any intercourse that is not conducted by himself, although, for the most part, he has dissembled his sentiments on this point with no inconsiderable address.

On the 12th instant I had another interview with Behadur Sâh, on which occassion, after going over again nearly the same ground as at our preceding conference, he intimated with sufficient plainness, though with due delicacy, that he had reaped, in the accomplishment of the long wished for meeting between us, whatever had been latterly proposed as the object of my visit to Nepaul. He touched on the desire which had, in former periods, been so often manifested by the English government for his reception of a deputation from Calcutta; observing at the same time, that matters not having then been ripe enough for so confidential an intercourse on his part, it had been reserved for your Lordship to remove completely the veil which had hitherto been held up between the two states, and to inspire him with that reliance on our honour, good faith, and friendly dispositions, which had led him to expose unscrupulously the nakedness of his country to us.

With respect to what I had glanced at in our last conference on the subject of commerce and boundaries, he remarked, that he was not less solicitous than your Lordship to have those points arranged on the most solid and beneficial footing for both parties: but that the season was approaching fast, when almost all intercourse between Khâtmândû and the circumjacent countries would cease, and of course any effectual enquiry concerning their productions, in a commercial view, become impracticable; and that the trade of Bhootan and Tibet was at present totally suspended, owing to the late hostilities with the Bhootias and Chinese, and could not, for some time, be either restored to its proper channels, or be susceptible of any improvement. As to the question concerning boundaries, he remarked, that as he was far from wishing that the Company should sustain the least detriment by any adjustment of that point, so he was perfectly certain that your Lordship would have the same regard for his interests; and under this confidence was willing to refer the settlement of it entirely to the equity and friendship of our government.

I had now ascertained with sufficient certainty, that my residence at this court was not to be hoped for. It therefore, I conceived, only remained for me to consider upon what footing, and in what manner, it was most advisable that my mission should be closed.

In revolving this matter in my mind, it appeared to me, that although much had not perhaps been gained by the deputation, yet something certainly had; since, independently of the knowledge which had been acquired of the face (to say no more) of a most interesting country, till now unvisited by any Englishman, the barrier which had so long, with the most unremitting jealousy, been opposed by this government to our obtaining any accurate idea concerning it, might be considered, if not totally, at least in a great measure, removed. The repugnance of a certain party to the cultivation of an unreserved intercourse with us, prevented, at present, it is true, our deriving all the advantages from my mission which it had been proposed to reap from it; yet it seemed to me, that either that repugnance might, with proper management, and in due season, be subdued, or the persons acting under its influence cease to enjoy the credit and authority they now possessed. Under these circumstances, I judged it would be right to submit to the necessity, which had imposed a certain constraint even on the Regent himself, with such a grace as should carry a fair appearance to the world; effectually prevent any idea of my quitting this court with the least dissatisfaction, and thereby preclude from the minds of the persons composing it, every apprehension of their having given offence that might hereafter operate against a revival of the unreserved communication which, though not completed, had, nevertheless, under your Lordship's auspices, happily made a rapid and considerable progress, and which, I was disposed to think, might, at no great distance of time, become renewable with every effect that could be expected from it.

These reflections made me determine, with the entire concurrence of the Gooroo, to avail myself of the opening afforded by Behadur Sâh in the course of our last conference, for demanding my early dismission. This I have since done in such terms as I thought best calculated to answer the ends I had in view; and of which I will only report at present, that the Regent appeared to be very well satisfied with them, observing significantly, but privately, to the Moulavee, that I had understood him exactly in the manner he had wished me to do.

If I have been drawn into greater prolixity in this address, than your Lordship may judge to have been necessary, I can only excuse it by attributing it to the necessity I considered myself to be under of stating in the fullest manner all the circumstances connected with a transaction, which, on account of the interesting object of my mission, will no doubt attract your Lordship's particular notice.

I expect to leave this in a few days on my return to Patna, where I shall wait your Lordship's further commands.

I have the honour to be, &c.

Khâtmândû, 19th March, 1793.

I.

From the same, to the Most Noble Marquis Cornwallis, K. G. &c. &c. Governor General in Council.

My Lord,

I had the honour of addressing you under date the 19th ultimo, when I mentioned generally, that I had applied to the Regent of Nepaul for my dismission, and expected in consequence to leave Khâtmândû on my return to Patna in a few days.

An accidental occurrence had rendered it necessary for me, instead of visiting Behadur Sah myself, for the purpose of executing the resolution I had taken, to employ Moulavee Abdûl Kâdir Khan on the occasion. He accordingly, on the 15th ultimo, attended the Regent, to whom he delivered himself in nearly the terms I had dictated to him: and the substance of which was, "that having well weighed what had passed on his (the "Regent's) part at our conference, I could not but allow that there was a "great deal of reason, as well as of candour and kindness in what he had "stated: that I felt as he had declared himself to do; namely, that in "effect, the main end of my mission had been obtained in the satisfaction "which I had derived from my personal interview with the Rajah and "himself: that it clearly appeared to me, from the facts he had so obligingly set forth at our last meeting, that my longer stay at present in "Nepaul was not likely, under the existing circumstances, to contribute to "the advancement of the commercial objects of my deputation; that I did "not consider myself, in this case, to be authorized by your Lordship to "prolong my visit indefinitely: but that, happily, this point was of the less "consequence now, as the cordial understanding and confidence recently "established between the two governments having at length removed "every other bar to their unreserved intercourse, my visit might be repeated at some future period." To this the Moulavee added, on my part, some protestations of my personal respect and attachment, concluding with saying, that as the unhealthy season was approaching fast, it was my request that I might have my audience of leave on as early a day as should be conveniently practicable.—The Regent, in his answer, expressed great concern at the necessity which I appeared to think there was for my early departure: and lamented that circumstances were so unfavourable to the gratification of the desire he had to cultivate my friendship. He should yield, however, he said, with whatever reluctance, to my wishes: but not without indulging the expectation of making himself ample amends on some future occasion, for his disappointment in the present instance.

The following day (the 17th March) we set out for Khâtmândû, where, on the 21st, myself and the gentlemen of my party dined in the palace by invitation of Behadur Sâh, who sat in the room with us during our repast: and when it was over, conducted us through the garden and other adjoining parts, with every mark of the politest attention. In the course of the evening he touched generally on what had passed between us relative to my departure; regretted that circumstances should compel me to leave Nepaul so quickly: openly expressed his hope and wish that an early occasion might offer, favourable to the renewal of the personal intercourse which had been (so agreeably to him) commenced between us, and signified his desire to be informed particularly what powers our government was in amity with, or otherwise, to the end that, having now determined to esteem the friends and enemies of the Company as his own, he might regulate his carriage towards them accordingly. To this point I thought it sufficient to reply, that I was persuaded so strong a manifestation of his good will towards the Company's government would be highly gratifying to your Lordship; and that as, happily, there no longer existed any reserve between him and your Lordship, he would doubtlessly be occasionally furnished with the kind of information he required. Towards the close of this visit it was settled that I should have my audience of leave on the 24th following. It may be proper to notice to your Lordship in this place, that the Rajah was not present on this occasion.

On the 24th we accordingly took our leave, the Rajah bearing a part in this ceremony. Behadur Sâh reiterated his former professions of friendship and attachment, expressing, however, at the same time, some solicitude, lest, as opinions were liable to be at variance on such questions, the Company's government in this country should not always consider him in the amicable light which your Lordship had done. I answered, that as the maintenance of the Company's true interests must at all times be the primary object of those entrusted with the management of their affairs; and as the cultivation of a friendly intercourse with Nepaul was manifestly blended, in an intimate degree, with that object, he might be assured that, on such a point, there could never be but one opinion entertained by the British administration in India.

Previous to our departure, some presents were sent to me for your

Lordship, and a few for myself: an account of which I shall transmit to the Persian translator.

It is a justice I owe to the gentlemen who attended the deputation, to assure your Lordship, that during our short stay in Nepaul, they seconded with zeal, and I have reason to think with considerable success, my endeavours to conciliate all ranks among the natives, and to inspire them with respect and regard for our nation. It gives me pleasure to be able also to add, that the whole of our followers conducted themselves on all occasions in the most unexceptionable manner.

We left Khâtmândû on the 24th ultimo, and were escorted to that town by Roodur Beer Sâh, at the head of the Rajah's company of guards. From thence to the borders of Nepaul (which we passed yesterday) we were attended by Zorawur Singh, the governor of the Western Turrye. The attentions which we experienced from both these officers (more especially from the former, who, as I have before noticed to your Lordship, is a brother of the Dewân Bem Sâh, and a kinsman of the Rajah), joined to the more than ordinary kindness and respect with which we were uniformly treated by the inhabitants of Nepaul in general, while they have impressed us all with the liveliest satisfaction, have a claim to my most particular acknowledgments, which I have accordingly in some measure conveyed to the Rajah.

I arrived at this place to-day, and expect to reach Choprah by the 12th, when I shall immediately dismiss all my extra servants; a few, who accompanied me from Calcutta, excepted.

On my arrival at the Presidency, I shall submit to your Lordship an account of the measures which I took, with the view of obtaining the information required of me by your Lordship's instructions; and of the extent (inconsiderable as it has been) to which I have been able to fulfil them.

I have the honour to be, &c.

Segowli, April 4th, 1793.

K.

To the Most Noble Marquis Cornwallis, K. G. &c. &c. &c. Governor General in Council.

My Lord,

I had the honour of apprising you, under date the 4th of April, that it was my intention to submit to your Lordship the result of the few observations on Nepaul, which the short duration of my visit to that country had qualified me to make.

I accordingly, soon after my return to the Presidency, began to arrange the notes which I had made with this view, and had advanced considerably in my task about a month ago, when I was seized with a fever which obliged me to lay it aside, and from the effects of which, I am only now recovering.

I lament the interruption the more, as I could have wished to have acquitted myself of this task before your Lordship's departure for Madras, which I must now despair of being able to do: though I shall resume it immediately, and prosecute it with as little delay as possible.

I have the honour to be, &c. &c.

Calcutta, 5th August, 1793.

To the Honourable Sir John Shore, Bart. Governor General, &c. &c. in Council.

Honourable Sir,

Having at length thrown together, in the best manner time would allow, the observations that occurred to me in my late short visit to Nepaul, as well as the result of the enquiries that circumstances permitted me to make, concerning that and the neighbouring countries, I have now the honour to submit the same to your indulgent consideration, entertaining little other hope of this essay proving acceptable, besides what rests on the novelty of its subject, which, I trust, will in some measure compensate for the imperfect and hasty manner in which it is treated.

I had intended to illustrate some passages of the Memoir with a few views and other drawings, of which I have been unfortunately disappointed. I shall endeavour, however, to supply this deficiency hereafter.

I am, &c. &c.

Fort William, 10th November, 1793.

L.

Memorandum respecting the Commerce of Nepaul: delivered to the Governor General.

THERE is good reason to believe, that, could a free and secure communication be opened between Bengal and Tibet, the woollen staples of Great Britain might be disposed of to the inhabitants of the latter country to a very considerable amount.

Both the Tibets are extremely elevated regions, and therefore excessively cold. It is to the upper Tibet, however, that we must principally look on this occasion; *that* being an infinitely more extensive and populous country, than the Kuchâr, or lower Tibet, which separates Nepaul and the mountainous tract, stretching to the eastward of that valley, from the upper, or Tibet proper.

The cold is so extreme in Tibet that the inhabitants, for want of woollens of a proper kind, are said to be obliged to encumber themselves to such a degree with the clothing ordinarily in use among them, as absolutely renders it difficult for them to move under the load.

They manufacture, it is true, some coarse woollen stuffs of the rug kind: but these would not appear to be either well suited, in point of warmth, to the severity of the climate, or to be made in any great quantity.

Be this as it may, I understand that our woollens, both fine and ordinary, are bought up in that country, whenever the Beoparies* carry them thither, with great avidity. The two-coloured cloths (particularly those having red on one side, and blue or yellow on the other) are preferred by the superior classes, to whom, it is probable, warm flannels of the finer sort would also be highly acceptable. For the poorer descriptions perhaps nothing would answer so well as our blanketing.

This is a traffic, however, which hitherto has never been engaged in excepting on a very inconsiderable scale; and even on such a scale but very rarely.

The reason of this is to be particularly sought for in the jealousy of the states between us and Tibet, and in their ignorance of the true principles and advantages of a free commerce. Something, perhaps, ought also to be referred to the distrustful character of the Chinese, who of late years have assumed pretty openly the entire government of Tibet. It would seem, at least, to have been owing to that court, that the attempts of Mr. Hastings to open a free commercial intercourse with Tibet were defeated.

But besides this obstacle to a direct communication between Bengal and that part of Upper Tibet, of which Lehasseh (or Lassa) is the capital, there has always, perhaps, existed another (no less serious), in the unfavourable circumstances which are opposed to commercial enterprize in this quarter by the country of the Deeb Rajah, which separates Tibet from Bengal. These consist partly in the rugged nature of that country; but possibly more in the wretched policy of its sovereign, by whom, I have been assured, such heavy imposts have been usually laid on the trade as almost amount to a prohibition of it. But to whatever cause the fact is to be attributed, it is pretty certain, I believe, that adventurers from Bengal prefer the circuitous route to Tibet by Nepaul, to the nearer one by the country called by us Boutan.

* Travelling merchants.

It may, nevertheless, still be practicable to engage the Deeb Rajah sooner or later to enter into a commercial treaty with our government, on a basis of reciprocal advantage.

A convention of this kind, however, would not make it the less proper for us to endeavour to find out other channels for the conveyance of the staples which have been mentioned to Tibet. For though Lehasseh and those parts lying directly to the northward, and to the eastward of that city, might perhaps be most readily supplied with our commodities by the way of Boutan, yet if we wish to push our commercial speculations into the western parts of Tibet (which would seem to promise us as good a market as the eastern), we must for this purpose turn our eye towards Nepaul: from whence too it might possibly appear, that the eastern trade could be carried on with great advantage.

Let us suppose Khâtmândû to be the centre from whence our staples are to be distributed throughout Tibet. The merchandize would proceed as high as Segouly, situated on the Boori Gunduck, by water. Hence it would pass to Hettowra, on carriages or bullocks, in four or five days. From Hettowra it would be transported by hill-porters, in three or four days, to Khâtmândû. These porters are capable of carrying bales weighing from eighteen to twenty-four Dhârnies, or from forty-five to sixty Seer, Bengal bazar weight:* and consequently, from 10 to 15 pieces of yard-wide broad cloth. They receive for the trip from Hettowra to Khâtmândû from $1\frac{1}{4}$ to $1\frac{1}{2}$ rupee, according to the season of the year, and the weight of their load.

At Khâtmândû, the merchants or caravans will disperse. Those having goods intended for the Lehasseh, or eastern market, would convey them by porters to Listee, the Nepaul frontier town on that side, and only three days distance from Kooti, a considerable town of Tibet. This journey may be performed with ease in eight days.

The Nepaul mart or entrepot for supplying Diggercheh or Teeshoo Lûmboo and the adjacent parts, would be Dhoalka, with is situated below the pass of Phullak, whence Tibet may be entered with greater ease than by Kooti. Dhoalka is not above five easy days journey from Khâtmândû.

* Being from about 230 to 305 lb. weight.

The merchandise intended for middle Tibet, or that part of Tibet lying directly to the northward of Nepaul, would be transported to Russooa, the frontier town of Nepaul in that quarter. This would take 7 or 8 days.

The articles designed for the supply of the north-west parts of Tibet, would have to proceed to Joomlah, or rather to its capital, Chinachin. Chinnachin is pretty near a month's journey for a caravan from Khâtmândû, to the north-west of which it lies. This is the frontier station of Nepaul in the Taklakhar quarter. Taklakhar is a town of Tibet of considerable note. It is about 12 journies from Chinachin, but much nearer to the borders of the Joomlah district. Chinachin might also be approached by the way of Almorah: but as, to take this route, merchants would have to advance far up into Rohilcund, it would not answer, probably, so well for the staples in question as the Khâtmândû road: though, doubtlessly, it would seem to be the properest channel for the exports of the Vizier's country, and perhaps of Benares. We are here, however, considering only of the best routes for the British staples.

It may be thought there would be no necessity for our merchants limiting their enterprises or speculations to the Nepaul borders; but though there should really be no serious obstacles to their pushing their expeditions into the interior parts of Tibet, yet I am inclined to believe that they would find it equally advantageous to dispose of their commodities severally at Listee, Dhoalka, Russooa, and Chinachin to the Tibet traders, who, if not restrained by their Chinese masters, would most probably be very ready to repair thither for the purpose of dealing with them. It is true that they would not obtain at these marts so high a price for their goods as they would yield in the interior parts; but, on the other hand, it is to be considered that their risk would be less, the return quicker, and their security (being under the protection of the Nepaul government) greater.

Our merchants would at these places receive from the Tibet traders, in exchange for their woollens, &c. gold dust, gold ingots, borax, and musk principally. There are probably some other articles, as munjeet, antimony, &c. which might be advantageously imported hither for the European market. Munjeet, however, is the produce chiefly of the lower Tibet, and southern hills, and is therefore almost entirely in the hands of the Nepaulians.

It might not be amiss, in the infancy of the trade, to abolish all duties on woollens of British manufacture exported from Bengal to Nepaul, whether for the use of that country or the consumption of Tibet.

Admitting all the preceding remarks and suggestions to be well founded, it remains to consider how any commercial scheme built upon them is to be carried into effect.

If, on the one hand, the Nepaul government were sufficiently intelligent to discern, and sufficiently energetic to promote its own best interests, and the Chinese officers, on the other, raised no obstacles in the way of the Tibet speculators, there would be no difficulty in the matter. There are perhaps a few members of the former (and at their head, I believe, is Behadur Sâh himself) who are not ignorant of the advantages which their country would derive from its becoming the channel thoroughfare of such a commerce as might be carried on between these provinces and Tibet; but the majority being of a description which holds trade in a very cheap light, the superior understanding of one or two individuals has not been able to counteract the effects of that obstinate jealousy with which those people are so well known to have regarded all sorts of intercourse with us till within the last two or three years. It is not necessary in this place to enquire how far we have, during this period, succeeded in our endeavours to remove this distrust. It will be sufficient to observe, what certainly is not to be denied, that though we no doubt have accomplished a good deal, yet we have not inspired them with the degree of confidence necessary to actuate them, before we can reasonably expect to derive all those commercial advantages to which a solid and cordial connection with the Nepaul government seems capable of leading.

By a due and watchful attention, however, to this point, it is highly probable that we shall, sooner or later, attain our object. Perhaps, indeed, no better opportunity for the purpose could possibly offer at any time than that which presents itself at this moment.

In a letter delivered to Lord Cornwallis by Deena-nâth Opadiah on the eve of his Lordship's departure from Bengal, the Rajah of Nepaul refers to his Vakeel and to me for an explanation of his wishes on a certain point, towards the accomplishment of which he solicits his Lordship's good offices. The object alluded to is the obtaining of the Pergunnahs of Rodurpoor, Kâshipoor, and Kewulpoor from the Vizier, in farm. These Pergunnahs constitute the Turrye, or low lands of Kemaoon, which last belongs to the Rajah of Nepaul, and the possession of them on any terms, is a point that the Nepaul government has very much at heart, the grain they produce being of the utmost consequence to the maintenance of the troops which the Rajah is obliged to keep on foot in the Kemaoon quarter. The possession of these districts would also open to them an easier communication with their westernmost frontier than they have at present.

If our government should see no objection to their being gratified in this particular, it is not improbable that they would not only accept it under any stipulations that might be judged necessary, with a political view to the prevention of future encroachments, or other disagreeable consequences of neighbourhood, but also consent, in return, to the establishment of a commercial intercourse with Tibet on the plan slightly delineated above; and to the residency of a British minister in Nepaul, for the purpose of watching over the interests of the merchants; of promoting the extension of the trade; and of improving the friendship and good understanding at present subsisting between the two governments.

In the different conversations which I have had with the Vakeel, on the subject of his court's wishes relative to Kâshipoor, &c. and to which application time did not allow Lord Cornwallis to give any answer, I have not scrupled to declare pretty plainly, that I did not see how so delicate a request could be urged either with propriety, or any probability of success, till the mutual confidence and good understanding of the two governments should be so firmly and unequivocally established, as totally to remove any sort of reserve. When his master, I observed, should have manifested the sincerity of his desire to improve his connection with the Company, by co-operating cordially with the government in the measures necessary to the effectual introduction of a free commercial intercourse between the two countries there was nothing which he could reasonably solicit, or the Company properly comply with, which he might not hope to obtain.

The Vakeel appearing to be convinced by the reasoning, and to be desirous of ascertaining what I conceived remained to be done for accomplishing the object I had insisted on, I presented him with a paper, of which the following is a translation, and which he promised to transmit immediately to Behadur Sâh, seconded by such explanations and arguments as should occur to him on the subject.

In the event of the Nepaul government's manifesting a disposition to enter upon a formal discussion of these propositions, the necessary negociation may be conducted either at the Presidency, or by the agency of the person whom Government may select for the station of resident in Nepaul, and who might be deputed to Khâtmândû in the first instance, for the express purpose of settling the new treaty of commerce.

Should the business assume this desirable aspect, it may be necessary to request Lord Macartney's* exertions towards facilitating the successful operation of the new treaty, which would very materially depend on the conduct which the Chinese government in Tibet should pursue upon the occasion.

Upon the final adjustment of this affair to the satisfaction of our Government, there are two or three points of inferior importance, in which it would perhaps be right to gratify the Rajah of Nepaul, but which it is not necessary to state in this place, as I have mentioned them on other occasions to the Governor General.

Heads for the Improvement of the Treaty of Commerce with the Nepaul Government, as submitted to Behadur Sâh by Deena-nâth Opadiah.

1. The Maharajah duly to consider the terms of the commercial treaty of March, 1791: to weigh well the advantages likely to result to his own government, as well as to the Company's, from a cordial and regulated

* Lord Macartney was, at the date of this paper, in China.

pursuit of the objects of it: and to evince his regard for the English, and his desire to cultivate their friendship, by promoting to the best of his power, the extension of their woollen trade, in particular, into such parts of Tibet as shall appear to be most easily accessible through the territories of Nepaul.

2. To agree, for this purpose, to the following stipulations in favour of the English commerce, in addition to those already fixed by the aforesaid treaty.

3. To engage generally to take all traders from the Company's possessions under his protection: and to afford them every security and indulgence during their stay in his country, that the interests and nature of his government will allow: understanding by the traders here mentioned, such as may from time to time enter the territories of Nepaul for commercial purposes under Rówannehs (or licenses) regularly obtained from the custom-house officer of Manjie.

4. To facilitate the mercantile operations of the aforesaid traders, by consenting to the occasional or constant residence (as circumstances may render necessary) of one or more native Gûmashtahs, or agents, at each of the following places, situated near the common borders of the Nepaul dominions and Tibet;

viz. 1. At Listee in the Kooti quarter.

2. At Dhoalka in the north-east quarter.

3. At Russooah in the Kheeroo and Joongah quarters.

4. At Beenishehr (of Mullibum) in the Luddack and Moostang quarters.

and 5. At Chinachin in the Taklakhar quarter.

5. To take the proper measures for securing to such Gûmashtahs and their servants suitable accommodations for themselves and merchandize; the Gûmashtahs defraying the expenses of the same, and yielding, in all respects, during their residence, due obedience to the authority of the Maharajah's officers governing in the several places enumerated.

6. To engage that the aforesaid Gûmashtahs, Beoparies, or traders, shall be permitted to expose their merchandize to sale at the several places recited above, and to deal without any restraint with such Bhootia Beoparies,

or traders, as may repair to the said frontier stations, for the purpose of purchasing or bartering their commodities.

7. To promise that the aforesaid Gûmashtahs or Beoparies shall be liable to no demands of any kind, or on any pretence whatsoever, from the officers governing at the frontier stations specified, or from any other officers of the Nepaul government, save and except the duties settled by the treaty of March 1791, and such other additional moderate Dustoor, or fees, on the actual realised amount of their sales (whether the same be in gold, or silver, or articles of barter) as shall hereafter be fixed to be paid to the commanding officers at the frontier places enumerated, on their receipt from the said officers of passports or Rowannehs to Khâtmândû.

8. To agree to the substituting in lieu of the frontier places above mentioned, any others that may hereafter appear to be more favourably situated for the commercial purposes in view.

9. To engage to regulate the duties to be levied on the returning trade from Tibet, whether this consist of silver or of gold, or of raw or manufactured materials the produce of that country, on equitable principles, and in a manner calculated to guard the merchants especially from the inconveniences and losses liable to result from vexatious delay, and ill-regulated imposts.

10. To consent, finally, to the residence of an English gentleman and suitable retinue in Nepaul, for the combined purposes of facilitating and aiding the operations of the traders; of watching over and controlling their conduct, of endeavouring to extend the general commerce, and of improving the friendship and beneficial connection so happily commenced between the Maharajah and the Company's government.

W. K.

APPENDIX. No. III.

Some Account of the Invasion of Nepaul by Purthi Nerain. Extracted from Father Giuseppe's "Account of Népál," in the Second Volume of the Asiatic Researches, p. 315.

AFTER the death of their sovereign, the nobles of Lelit Pattan nominated for their king Gainprejas, a man possessed of the greatest influence in Népál; but some years afterwards they removed him from his government, and conferred it upon the king of B'hatgán;* but he also, a short time afterwards, was deposed; and, after having put to death another king who succeeded him, they made an offer of the government to Prit'hwínáráyan,† who had already commenced war. Prit'hwínáráyan, deputed one of his brothers, by name Delmerden Sáh, to govern the kingdom of Lelit Pattan, and he was in the actual government of it when I arrived at Népál; but the nobles perceiving that Prit'hwínáráyan still continued to interrupt the tranquillity of the kingdom, they disclaimed all subjection to him, and acknowledged for their sovereign Delmerden Sáh, who continued the war against his brother Prit'hwínáráyan: but some years afterwards, they even deposed Delmerden Sáh, and elected in his room a poor man of Lelit Pattan, who was of royal origin.

The king of B'hatgân, in order to wage war with the other kings of Népál, had demanded assistance from Prit'hwínáráyan, but seeing that Pri'th-wínáráyan was possessing himself of the country, he was obliged to desist, and to take measures for the defence of his own possessions; so that the king of Górc'hà,‡ although he had been formerly a subject of Gainprejas, taking advantage of the dissensions which prevailed among the other kings

* Bhatgong. † Purthi Nerain. ‡ Goorkha.

of Népál, attached to his party many of the mountain-chiefs, promising to keep them in possession, and also to augment their authority and importance; and, if any of them were guilty of a breach of faith, he seized their country, as he had done to the kings of Marecajis, although his relations.

The king of Górc'hà having already possessed himself of all the mountains which surround the plain of Népál, began to descend into the flat country, imagining he should be able to carry on his operations with the same facility and success as had attended him on the hills; and, having drawn up his army before a town, containing about 8000 houses, situated upon a hill, called Círtipur,* about a league's distance from Cat'hmândú, employed his utmost endeavours to get possession of it. The inhabitants of Círtipur receiving no support from the king of Lelit Pattan, to whom they were subject, applied for assistance to Gainprejas, who immediately marched with his whole army to their relief, gave battle to the army of the king of Górc'hà, and obtained a complete victory. A brother of the king of Górc'hà was killed on the field of battle; and the king himself, by the assistance of good bearers, narrowly escaped with his life by fleeing into the mountains. After the action, the inhabitants of Círtipur demanded Gainprejas for their king, and the nobles of the town went to confer with him on the business; but, being all assembled in the same apartment with the king, they were all surprised and seized by his people. After the seizure of those persons, Gainprejas, perhaps to revenge himself of those nobles, for having refused their concurrence to his nomination as king, privately caused some of them to be put to death; another, by name Danuvanta, was led through the city in a woman's dress, along with several others, clothed in a ridiculous and whimsical manner, at the expense of the nobles of Lelit Pattan. They were then kept in close confinement for a long time: at last, after making certain promises, and interesting all the principal men of the country in their behalf, Gainprejas set them at liberty.

* Kirthipoor. † Khâtmândû.

The king of Górc'hà, despairing of his ability to get possession of the plain of Népál by strength, hoped to effect his purpose by causing a famine; and with this design stationed troops at all the passes of the mountains to prevent any intercourse with Népál; and his orders were most rigorously obeyed, for every person who was found in the road, with only a little salt or cotton about him, was hung upon a tree; and he caused all the inhabitants of a neighbouring village to be put to death in a most cruel manner: even the women and children did not escape, for having supplied a little cotton to the inhabitants of Népál; and, when I arrived in that country at the beginning of 1769, it was a most horrid spectacle to behold so many people hanging on trees in the road. However, the king of Górch'hà being also disappointed in his expectations of gaining his end by this project, fomented dissensions among the nobles of the three kingdoms of Népál, and attached to his party many of the principal ones, by holding forth to them liberal and enticing promises; for which purpose he had about 2000 Brahmens in his service. When he thought he had acquired a party sufficiently strong, he advanced a second time with his army to Cirtipur, and laid siege to it on the north-west quarter, that he might avoid exposing his army between the two cities of Cat'hmândú and Lelit Pattan. After a siege of several months, the king of Górc'hà demanded the regency of the town of Círtipur; when the commandant of the town, seconded by the approbation of the inhabitants, dispatched to him by an arrow a very impertinent and exasperating answer. The king of Górc'hà was so much enraged at this mode of proceeding, that he gave immediate orders to all his troops to storm the town on every side; but the inhabitants bravely defended it, so that all the efforts of his men availed him nothing; and, when he saw that his army had failed of gaining the precipice, and that his brother, named Surúparatna, had fallen wounded by an arrow, he was obliged to raise the siege a second time, and to retreat with his army from Círtipur. The brother of the king was afterwards cured of his wound by our Father, Michael Angelo, who is at present in Bettía.

After the action the king of Górc'hà sent his army against the king of Lamji (one of the twenty-four kings who reign to the westward of Népál) bordering upon his own kingdom of Górc'hà. After many desperate engagements, an accommodation took place with the king of Lamji: and the king of Górc'hà collecting all his forces, sent them for the third time to besiege Círtipur; and the army on this expedition was commanded by his brother Surúparatna. The inhabitants of Círtipur defended themselves with their usual bravery; and after a siege of several months, the three kings of Népál assembled at Cat'hmândú to march a body of troops to the relief of Círtipur. One day in the afternoon they attacked some of the Tanas of the Górc'hians, but did not succeed in forcing them, because the king of Górc'hà's party had been reinforced by many of the nobility, who, to ruin Gainprejas, were willing to sacrifice their own lives. The inhabitants of Círtipur having already sustained six or seven months siege, a noble of Lelit Pattan called Danuvanta fled to the Górc'hà party, and treacherously introduced their army into the town. The inhabitants might still have defended themselves, having many other fortresses in the upper parts of the town to retreat to; but the people of Górc'hà having published a general amnesty, the inhabitants, greatly exhausted by the fatigue of a long siege, surrendered themselves prisoners upon the faith of that promise. In the mean time the men of Górc'hà seized all the gates and fortresses within the town; but two days afterwards Prit'hwínáráyan, who was at Navacúta (a long day's journey distant) issued an order to Surúparatna, his brother, to put to death some of the principal inhabitants of the town, and to cut off the noses and lips of every one, even the infants, who were not found in the arms of their mothers; ordering at the same time all the noses and lips which had been cut off to be preserved, that he might ascertain how many souls there were, and to change the name of the town into Naskatápur, which signifies the town of cut-noses. The order was carried into execution with every mark of horror and cruelty, none escaping but those who could play on wind instruments; although Father Michael Angelo, who, without knowing that such an inhuman scene was then exhibited, had gone to the house of Surúparatna, and interceded much in favour of the poor inhabitants. Many of them put an end to their lives in despair; others came in great bodies to us in search of medicines; and it was most shocking to see so many living people with their teeth and noses resembling the skulls of the deceased.

After the capture of Círtipur, Prit'hwínáráyan dispatched immediately his army to lay siege to the great city of Lelit Pattan. The Górc'hians surrounded half the city to the westward with their Tanas; and, my house being situated near the gate of that quarter, I was obliged to retire to Cat'hmândú to avoid being exposed to the fire of the besiegers. After many engagements between the inhabitants of the the town of Lelit Pattan and the men of Górc'hà, in which much blood was spilled on both sides, the former were disposed to surrender themselves, from the fear of having their noses cut off, like those at Círtipur, and also their right hands: a barbarity the Górc'hians had threatened them with, unless they would surrender within five days. One night all the Górc'hians quitted the siege of Lelit Pattan to pursue the English army, which, under the command of Captain Kinloch, had already taken Sidúli, an important fort at the foot of the Népál hills, which border upon the kingdom of Tirhùt: but Captain Kinloch not being able to penetrate the hills, either on the Sidúli quarter or by the pass at Hareapur, in the kingdom of Macwanpur, the army of Górc'hà returned to Népál to direct their operations against the city of Cat'hmándú, where Gainprejas was, who had applied for succour to the English. During the siege of Cat'hmândú the Bráhmens of Górc'hà came almost every night into the city, to engage the chiefs of the people on the part of their king: and the more effectually to impose upon poor Gainprejas, many of the principal Bráhmens went to his house, and told him to persevere with confidence, that the chiefs of the Górc'hà army were attached to his cause, and that even they themselves would deliver up their king Prit'hwínáráyan into his hands. Having by these artifices procured an opportunity of detaching from his party all his principal subjects, tempting them with liberal promises according to their custom, one night the men of Górc'hà entered the city without opposition; and the wretched Gainprejas perceiving he was betrayed, had scarce time to escape with about three hundred of his best and most faithful Hindustáni troops towards Lelit Pattan; which place, however, he reached the same night.

The king of Górc'hà having made himself master of Cat'hmândú in the year 1768, persisted in the attempt of possessing himself also of the city of Lelit Pattan, promising all the nobles that he would suffer them to remain in the possession of their property, that he would even augment it; and, because the nobles of Lelit Pattan placed no reliance on the faith of his promises, he sent his domestic priest to make this protestation; that, if he failed to acquit himself of his promise, he should draw curses upon himself and his family even to the fifth past and succeeding generation; so that the unhappy Gainprejas and the king of Lelit Pattan, seeing that the nobility were disposed to render themselves subject to the king of Gorc'hà, withdrew themselves with their people to the king of B'hatgàn. When the city of Lelit Pettan became subject to the king of Górc'hà, he continued for some time to treat the nobility with great attention, and proposed to appoint a viceroy of the city from among them. Two or three months afterwards, having appointed the day for making his formal entrance into the city of Lelit Pattan, he made use of innumerable stratagems to get into his possession the persons of the nobility, and in the end succeeded; he had prevailed upon them to permit their sons to remain at court as companions of his son; he had dispatched a noble of each house to Navacút, or New Fort, pretending that the apprehensions he entertained of them had prevented his making a public entrance into the city; and the remaining nobles were seized at the river without the town, where they went to meet him, agreeably to a prior engagement. Afterwards he entered the city, made a visit to the temple of Baghero, adjoining to our habitation, and passing in triumph through the city amidst immense numbers of soldiers, who composed his train, entered the royal palace, which had been prepared for his reception: in the mean time parties of his soldiers broke open the houses of the nobility, seized all their effects, and threw the inhabitants of the city into the utmost consternation. After having caused all the nobles who were in his power to be put to death, or rather their bodies to be mangled in a horrid manner, he departed with a design of besieging B'hatgán: and we obtained permission, through the interest of his son, to retire with all the Christians into the possessions of the English.

At the commencement of the year 1769, the king of Górc'hà acquired possession of the city of B'hatgán by the same expedients to which he owed his former successes; and on his entrance with his troops into the city, Gainprejas, seeing he had no resource left to save himself, ran courageously with his attendants towards the king of Górc'hà, and, at a small distance from his palanquin, received a wound in his foot, which a few days afterwards occasioned his death. The king of Lelit Pattan was confined in irons till his death; and the king of B'hatgán, being very far advanced in years, obtained leave to go and die at Banares. A short time afterwards, the mother of Gainprejas also procured the same indulgence, having from old age already lost her eye-sight; but before her departure, they took from her a necklace of jewels, as she herself told me, when she arrived at Patna, with the widow of her grandson: and I could not refrain from tears, when I beheld the misery and disgrace of this blind and unhappy queen.

The king of Górc'hà having thus, in the space of four years, effected the conquest of Népál, made himself master also of the country of the Cirátas, to the east of it, and of other kingdoms, as far as the borders of Cóch Bihár. After his decease, his eldest son Pratáp Sinh,* held the government of the whole country; but scarcely two years after, on Pratáp Sinh's death, a younger brother, by name Bahádar Sáh, who resided then at Bettia with his uncle Delmerden Sáh, was invited to accept of the government; and the beginning of his government was marked with many massacres. The royal family is in the greatest confusion, because the queen lays claim to the government in the name of her son, whom she had by Pratáp Sinh; and perhaps the oath violated by Prit'hwínáráyan will, in the progress of time, have its effect. Such have been the successors of the kingdoms of Népál, of which Prit'hwínáráyan had thus acquired possession.

* Pertaub Singh.

INDEX

Of the Names of the Principal Towns, Rivers, Mountains, &c. mentioned.

☞ Those names printed in Italics between parentheses are so spelt in the course of the Work, but must be read as in the Roman characters.

A

CATALOGUE

OF

THE PRINCIPAL BOOKS

PUBLISHED BY

WILLIAM MILLER, ALBEMARLE-STREET,

UP TO THE SPRING OF 1811.

N. B. The Books are sold in Boards at the Prices here affixed.

	£.	s.	d.
ARABIAN NIGHTS (Forster's), *a new edition, with twenty-five plates*, 5 vols. *demy* 8vo.	3	0	0
———, 4 vols. *royal* 18mo. (*no plates*) *a new edition*	1	4	0
Amsinck's Tunbridge Wells, 48 *plates and vignettes, by Letitia Byrne, imperial* 4to.	4	14	6
Ancient British Drama, 3 vols. *royal* 8vo. *double columns, and vignette title-pages*	3	9	0
Art of Tormenting, *foolscap* 8vo.	0	6	0
Affection, a poem, by Smithers, 5 *vignettes, imperial* 8vo.	1	1	0
Anacreon (Greek), *Forster's edition*, 15 *vignettes, post* 8vo.	0	15	0
———, *on French plate paper*	1	1	0
Atkinson's Costume of Great Britain, *imperial folio*, Vol. I.	5	5	0
Babylon and other Poems, by the Honble. Annabella Hawke, *foolscap*, 8vo.	0	6	0
Blomefield's History of Norfolk, *complete in* 11 vols. *royal* 8vo. *all the plates re-engraved*	9	18	0
———, *royal* 4to.	23	2	0
——— History of Norwich, 2 vols. *royal* 8vo.	1	16	0
Baxter's Egyptian, Grecian, and Roman Costume, *imperial* 8vo.	0	16	0
———, *royal* 4to.	1	11	6
Bibliosophia; or Book Wisdom, *foolscap*	0	5	0
Beattie's Minstrel, *with portrait*	0	5	0
British Gallery of Engravings, No. 1, 2, 3, 4, 5, 6, and 7, *small paper*	14	14	0
———, *large paper*	25	14	6
British Drama (Modern), *a new Edition, considerably enlarged, and handsomely printed in Five thick volumes, royal octavo*	5	10	0
Balfour's Music, a poem, 2 *plates, royal* 8vo.	1	1	0
Butterflies (Coloured Specimens of), *imperial* 4to. *half-bound, morocco*	6	6	0
Bath, *illustrated by Nattes, super royal folio*	7	7	0
Carlisle's Topographical Dictionary of Ireland, *demy* 4to. *just published*	2	12	6
Chalmers's British Poets, 21 vols. *royal* 8vo.	25	0	0
——— Translations, *separate*, 3 vols. *royal* 8vo.	2	12	6
Chronological Abridgment of the History of Great Britain, from the first Invasion of the Romans to the present Reign. By Ant. Fr. Bertrand de Moleville, vol. 1 and 2	1	4	0
———, *large paper*	2	2	0

N. B. This work will be completed in four vols. The last published in 1812.

	£.	s.	d.
Costume of China, by Alexander, 50 *coloured plates*, 4to.	6	6	0
———, by Mason, 60 *plates imperial* 4to.	6	6	0
——— Turkey, 60 *plates imperial* 4to.	8	8	0
——— Russia, 72 *plates, imperial* 4to.	8	8	0
——— Austria, 50 *plates, imperial* 4to.	6	6	0
——— England, 60 *plates, imperial* 4to.	9	0	0
Punishments of China, 22 *plates, imperial* 4to.	3	13	6
Cottagers of Glenburnie, *foolscap*	0	3	6
Ciceronis Opera Omnia, Ernesti, 8 vols. 8vo.	6	0	0
Clavis Ciceroniana, *demy* 8vo.	0	15	0
Claims of Literature, 8vo.	0	7	6
Cambrian Pictures, a Novel, by Anne of Swansea, three vols. *just published*	0	18	0
DANIELL'S Oriental Scenery, in Four Series.—Excavations of Ellora, one Series.—Indian Antiquities, one Series. *Each plate mounted, and the whole done up in six portfolios complete, with the octavo letter-press*	210	0	0
N. B. Any single series may be had, price	35	0	0
Dryden's Works, by Walter Scott, Esq. 18 vols. *demy* 8vo.	9	9	0
——— Life, *printed separately, royal*, 4to.	2	12	6
Debrett's Baronetage, 2 vols.	0	18	0
——— Peerage, 2 vols.	0	18	0
Description of the Ancient Terracottas in the British Museum, *with Forty-one Engravings*, 4to.	1	11	6
———, *large elephant*, 4to.	2	12	6

N. B. The descriptive part is by T. Combe, Esq. and the Engravings from Drawings by W. Alexander, Esq. Published by order of the Trustees of the Museum.

	£.	s.	d.
Dibdin's Typographical Antiquities, including Ames and Herbert, *with numerous plates, demy* 4to. Vol. I.	3	8	0
Don Quixote (Jarvis's), 4 vols. *demy* 8vo. *a new edition*	2	8	0
ECCLESIASTICAL TOPOGRAPHY. A Collection of One Hundred Views of Churches, in the Environs of London, from Drawings expressly taken for this Work, with Descriptions from the best sources, in one volume, 4to.	4	4	0
——, *large paper, with first impressions*	6	6	0
N. B. This Collection is intended as an Illustration to Lysons's Environs of London.			
EXPOSE of Napoleon Buonaparte, *crown* 8vo.	0	6	0
Elegant Extracts, prose	1	0	0
——, verse	1	0	0
—— Epistles	0	18	0
English Brothers, a Novel, 4 vols.	1	1	0
Fox's James the Second, *demy* 4to.	1	16	0
——, *royal* 4to.	2	12	6
—— Appendix to ditto, translated, *demy* 4to.	0	5	0
GOLDSMITH's England, 4 vols. 8vo.	1	16	0
Grammont's Memoirs, *a new Edition, with a Life of the Author A. Hamilton, and embellished with Sixty-four Fine Portraits from well authenticated Pictures*, 2 vols. *royal octavo*	3	13	6
——, in 2 vols. *royal quarto with proof plates*	6	6	0
——, in French, 2 vols. *royal octavo*	3	13	6
HOARE's (Sir Richard) Ancient Wiltshire, *royal folio*, Part I.	4	4	0
——, *large paper*	6	6	0
—— Giraldus Cambrensis, *plates by Byrne, &c.* 2 vols. *royal* 4to.	8	8	0
——, *the Latin Edition, royal* 4to.	2	2	0
HAMILTON's (Sir William) Vases, by Kirk, *royal* 4to.	2	2	0
——, *duplicate plates (one set coloured)*	5	5	0
Howlett's Select Views in Lincolnshire, 63 *plates and vignettes, fine impressions, imperial* 4to.	5	15	6
Harleian Miscellany, vol. 1 to 7, *new edition*	22	1	0
Hopkins's Persian Vocabulary, *royal* 8vo.	1	16	0
Illustrations of Virgil's fourth Eclogue, *octavo*	0	15	0
Journal of a Tour in Ireland, by Sir Richard Hoare, *demy* 8vo.	0	10	
Johnson's Works, 12 vols. 8vo. *new edition*	4	16	0
—— Lives, 3 vols. *demy* 8vo.	1	4	0
KIRKPATRICK's Embassy to the Kingdom of Nepaul, *by order of the East India Company, with a Map and numerous Engravings*, 4to.	2	12	6
Lady of the Lake, by Walter Scott, Esq. *eighth edition, demy* 8vo.	0	12	0
—— ——, *royal* 8vo.	1	1	0

	£.	s.	d.
Lee's Pindar, a complete translation, including Mr. West's, *demy* 4to.	1	8	0
—— Hesiod, *royal* 8vo.	0	6	0
Marmion, by Walter Scott, Esq. 2 vols. *crown* 8vo. *with twelve engravings*	1	1	0
——, *demy* 8vo.	0	12	0
Miseries of Human Life, 2 vols. *foolscap*	0	16	0
——, the Plates only to *ditto*, by Atkinson, *coloured*	0	12	0
Montaigne's Essays, *a new and improved edition, with a Portrait, in* 3 vols. *royal* 8vo.	1	16	0
More's Utopia, by Dibdin, 2 vols. *crown* 8vo.	0	16	0
——, *in one volume* 4to. *with an additional plate*	1	11	6
Microcosm; or Picturesque Delineations of the Arts, &c. by Pyne, 2 vols. *oblong folio*	10	10	0
Master Passion, a Novel, 4 vols.	0	16	0
Mason on Self-knowledge, *foolscap*	0	5	0
Moral Legacy, *foolscap*	0	6	0
NATTES' Geometry, 40 *vignettes, royal* 8vo.	0	12	0
OSSIAN's Poems, 3 vols. *with* 12 *engravings* by Fittler, *post* 8vo.	1	16	0
PEARSON's Antiquities of Shropshire, 40 *plates oblong* 4to.	2	12	6
Psalms (Drummond's Select Portions), 12mo. *18th edition*	0	2	0
Pilkington's Dictionary of Painters, 4to.	2	2	0
RAYMOND's Life of Dermody, *portrait*, 2 vols. *crown* 8vo.	0	16	0
Rasselas, 5 *plates, after Smirke, finely printed, medium* 4to.	1	11	6
——, *large paper, proofs*	2	2	0
Richardson's Persian Dictionary, *new edition* by Wilkins, 2 vols. 4to.	12	12	0
——, *imperial* 4to.	21	0	0
Richardson's Works, *containing Pamela, Clarissa, and Grandison, with some preliminary matter, and a Fine Portrait, from an original Picture in the possession of* Earl Onslow, *handsomely printed in* nineteen vols. *crown octavo*	7	12	0
Sketch of the Political History of India, from the Introduction of Mr. Pitt's Bill, A. D. 1784, to the present date, by John Malcolm Lieut. Col. in the Madras Army, resident at Mysore and late Envoy at the Court of Persia, *royal octavo*	0	16	0
SALT's Twenty-four Large Views, to Lord Valentia's Travels, *mounted, and in a portfolio*	27	6	0
Sully's Memoirs, *with portraits, a new edition*, 5 vols. *royal* 8vo.	3	13	6
Schiller's Thirty Years' War, 2 vols. 8vo.	0	12	0
—— Don Carlos, 8vo.	0	5	0
Shee's Elements of Art, 8vo.	0	13	0
—— Rhymes on Art, *foolscap*	0	7	0

	£.	s.	d.
Swift's Works, 19 vols. 8vo.	9	0	0
Stoddart's Tour in Scotland, 35 *plates*, 2 vols. *royal* 8vo.	2	2	0
Ship of Fools, *foolscap*	0	8	0
Shipwreck by Falconer, *a new and most beautiful Edition, Embellished with Ten Engravings by* Fittler, *from new Drawings, by* N. Pocock, Esq. *finely printed, royal octavo*	1	5	0
Sadler's State Papers, 2 vols. 4to.	5	5	0
———————, *large paper*, 3 vols.	8	8	0
Somers' Tracts, by W. Scott, Esq. *new edit.* vol. 1 to 5	15	15	0
Sarratt on Chess, 2 vols. 8vo.	0	18	0
Shakspeare, 2 vols. *double columns, royal* 8vo.	1	10	0
———, *with* 38 *highly finished engravings*, 12 vols. *crown* 8vo.	6	6	0
———, *royal* 8vo.	10	16	0
Skurray's Bidcombe Hill, *crown* 8vo. *plates*	0	10	6
———————, 4to.	1	1	0
Scotia Depicta, in 50 *finished etchings*, by Fittler, *imperial long* 4to.	6	6	0
TURNOR's History of Grantham, *plates, imperial* 4to.	1	8	0
Tocquot's French and English Dictionary, 18mo.	0	7	0
VALENTIA's Travels, 3 vols *royal* 4to.	9	9	0
———————, *large paper*	13	13	6
WHITE on Billiards, *crown* 8vo.	0	10	0
Wilkinson's Epitome of Malta, *with a map, foolscap* 8vo.	0	6	0

LATELY WAS PUBLISHED,

TWENTY-FOUR LARGE VIEWS IN ARABIA, ABYSSINIA, EGYPT, &c. executed from Drawings by HENRY SALT, Esq. in the same size and manner as Mr. DANIELL's *Oriental Scenery*, being 24 by 18 inches. The whole are mounted and delivered in a Portfolio at the price of Twenty-Six Guineas the Set.

N. B. This Volume may be considered as a continuation to Mr. Daniell's Collection—being uniform in style and execution.

BRITISH GALLERY OF ENGRAVINGS,

In Super Royal Folio, Price Two Guineas each Number, and a limited number of copies on large Imperial Paper, and a different Type, with *Proof Impressions of the Plates*, price Three Guineas and a Half each Number. The FIRST SEVEN NUMBERS of this Splendid Work are already published, and contain the following Subjects:

NUMBER FIRST.

1st. *A Magdalen*, by Ludovico Carracci—Engraved by Anker Smith.
2d. *A View of Rome*, by Wilson—Engraved by Middiman.
3d. *Vandyk, as Paris*, by Vandyk—Engraved by Shiavonetti.
4th. *Christ in the Storm*, by Rembrandt—Engraved by Fittler.

NUMBER SECOND.

1st. *A Flemish Cottage*, by Ostade—Engraved by Fittler.
2d. *Salvator Rosa*, by Salvator—Engraved by Neagle.
3d. *Samuel and Eli*, by Rembrandt—Engraved by Fittler.
4th. *Holy Family*, by Murillo—Engraved by Heath.

NUMBER THIRD.

1st. *Canal of Dort*, by Cuyp—Engraved by Fittler.
2d. *Holy Family*, by L. Carracci—Engraved by Raimbach.
3d. *Flemish Pastime*, by Brawer—Engraved by Noble.
4th. *Joseph's Garment*, by Guercino—Engraved by Schiavonetti.

NUMBER FOURTH.

1st. *Sea View*, by Vandervelde—Engraved by Fittler.
2d. *Portrait of Berghem*, by Rembrant—Engraved by Schiavonetti.
3d. *Dutch Boors*, by A. Ostade—Engraved by Taylor.
4th. *Cartoon of Pisa*, by Michael Angelo—Engraved by Schiavonetti.

NUMBER FIFTH.

1st. *Magdalen*, by Dominichino—Engraved by Schiavonetti.
2d. *Landscape*, by G. Poussin—Engraved by Middiman.
3d. *The Good Shepherd*, by Murillo—Engraved by J. Heath.
4th. *Bears and Dogs*, by Snyders—Engraved by Fittler.

NUMBER SIXTH.

1st. *Sybil's Temple*, by Berghem—Engraved by Fittler.
2d. *Abel*, by Rubens—Engraved by Heath.
3d. *Archbishop of Spalatro*, by Tintoret—Engraved by Skelton.
4th. *Venus*, by Reynolds—Engraved by Raimbach.

NUMBER SEVENTH.

1st. *Flemish Family*, by Ostade—Engraved by Fittler
2d. *Infant Hercules*, by Reynolds—Engraved by C. Heath
3d. *Landscape*, by Claude—Engraved by Middiman.
4th. *Hippolytus*, by Rubens—Engraved by A. Smith.

N. B. All the Plates in this National Work will be engraved by the first Artists in the Country, in the *Line* or *Stroke* manner, being the only mode held in estimation by all true admirers of the Fine Arts.

The Work will consist of Twenty-five Numbers, and form a splendid Collection of ONE HUNDRED ENGRAVINGS, from the finest Pictures in this Country, and will contain (besides an Account of each Picture, and a Life of the Artist) a short History of the Arts of Painting and Engraving, including the Rise and Progress of those Arts in Great Britain.

By EDWARD FORSTER, A.M., F.R.S.

The Eighth Number is in great forwardness: and not less than three, nor more than five, Numbers will appear yearly.

A detailed Prospectus of the Work may be had of W. MILLER, where subscriptions are received, and the copies carefully delivered in the order they are subscribed for.

DANIELL'S ORIENTAL SCENERY.

WILLIAM MILLER begs leave to inform the Public, that by a recent agreement with MR. DANIELL, the sale of that Artist's magnificent Engravings on ORIENTAL SCENERY is in his hands, and are to be had at the following prices:

The Four Series of Oriental Scenery, each Series containing Twenty-four Views, placed in Portfolios.............	£.140
The Excavations of Ellora, in Twenty-four Views......	35
Indian Antiquities, in Twenty-four Views..............	35

This splendid Set of One Hundred and Forty-four Engravings, representing the most celebrated Buildings and Picturesque Scenery on the Continent of India, are executed from Drawings made on the spot, and are coloured so as to imitate Nature. They are all of one dimension (24 by 18); each Plate is mounted, and the whole placed in Six Large Portfolios, with a short printed Description attached to each

N. B. As these Plates were published at different periods, Gentlemen who have incomplete Sets, are respectfully informed that they can now be made perfect by the purchase of any one particular Part.